DAILY PRAYER
IN THE EARLY CHURCH

DAILY PRAYER IN THE EARLY CHURCH

*A Study of the Origin and Early
Development of the Divine Office*

PAUL F. BRADSHAW

New York
OXFORD UNIVERSITY PRESS
1982

Library of Congress Cataloging in Publication Data

Bradshaw, Paul F.
    Daily prayer in the early church.

    Bibliography: p.
    Includes indexes.
    1. Prayer—History—Early church, ca. 30-600.
I. Title.
BV207.B68   1982   264′.1′09015   82-8116
ISBN 0-19-520394-1   AACR2
ISBN 0-19-520395-X (pbk.)

First published in Great Britain 1981
for the Alcuin Club by SPCK

First published in the United States 1982
by Oxford University Press, Inc.

Copyright © Paul F. Bradshaw 1981

Printing (last digit): 9 8 7 6 5 4 3 2 1

Printed in the United States of America

To my father
and
in memory of my mother

Contents

Abbreviations

ALW	*Archiv für Liturgiewissenschaft*
EL	*Ephemerides Liturgicae*
JJS	*Journal of Jewish Studies*
JQR	*Jewish Quarterly Review*
JTS	*Journal of Theological Studies*
LMD	*La Maison-Dieu*
NTS	*New Testament Studies*
OC	*Oriens Christianus*
OCP	*Orientalia Christiana Periodica*
PL	J. P. Migne (ed.), *Patrologia Latina*, Paris 1844–64
S.–B.	H. Strack & P. Billerbeck, *Kommentar zum Neuen Testament aus Talmud und Midrasch*, Munich 1922–8
SE	*Studia Evangelica*
SL	*Studia Liturgica*
SP	*Studia Patristica*
TDNT	*Theological Dictionary of the New Testament*, Grand Rapids, Michigan 1964f.
TZ	*Theologische Zeitschrift*
de Vogüé, *RB* 5	Adalbert de Vogüé, *La Règle de Saint Benoît*, vol. 5, *Sources Chrétiennes* 185, Paris 1971

The Hebrew numbering of the Psalms is followed throughout: where the Septuagint/Vulgate numbering is used in a quotation, the Hebrew numbering is supplied in square brackets.

Place of publication is not given for books published in the United Kingdom.

Preface

In liturgical study, and especially in English liturgical study, the subject of the daily office has always been something of the poor relation. The attention of scholars has been concentrated to such an extent upon the Eucharist and upon the rites of Christian Initiation in recent years that many other fields have not received their due consideration, and thus the time seems more than ripe for a new study of the origins and early history of the office. Almost the only textbook on the subject which is available to English students of liturgy is *The Influence of the Synagogue upon the Divine Office* by Professor C. W. Dugmore, first published by the Oxford University Press in 1944 and reissued by the Alcuin Club in 1964 (Alcuin Club Collections No. 45). While in its day this made a major contribution to the subject, it is now not only out of print but also seriously out of date in the light of the enormous strides in scholarship which have taken place in subsequent years. It is therefore extremely misleading for students to continue to use this work as though it were unquestionably accurate. However, since the majority of more recent research has been undertaken by continental scholars and their findings nearly all buried in the pages of learned journals in foreign languages, they have up to now been effectively inaccessible to most English-speaking students.

Moreover, not only translation but also bridge-building is called for, since such work as has been done has on the whole been pursued in separate, seemingly watertight, compartments: Jewish scholars have worked largely in isolation from New Testament scholars, New Testament scholars largely in isolation from liturgical scholars, and so on, with the result that hardly at all have the findings in one area been related to those in another. Even among liturgical scholars study has tended to be restricted to small areas of the subject, and the effects of new perspectives and discoveries in one historical period or geographical area upon the understanding of the office at other times and in other places have rarely been considered or worked out in full. Even more importantly, there has been a need for some cherished assumptions to be exposed to further scrutiny, assumptions which have been repeated by successive generations of scholars but have not thereby become any more assured of veracity than when they were first made. A fresh look at the evidence, freed from the blinkers of traditional presuppositions, often yields surprising results.

This book is therefore offered as a contribution to a much neglected field of study, and I am grateful to Gabriele Winkler who many years ago encouraged me to begin my labours on it. I would also like to express my gratitude to the Reverend Dr. Geoffrey Cuming for his constant help and interest in my studies, and for his kindness in allowing me to quote extensively from his translation of the *Apostolic Tradition* of Hippolytus, and also to my colleagues on the Alcuin Club committee for accepting my work for publication.

1. Daily Prayer in First-Century Judaism

Contrary to the assumptions made by many scholars of previous generations, and regrettably still made by some of this generation, the Jewish worship to which Jesus and his followers were accustomed was not necessarily identical with that which is found in the second century and later. Judaism in the New Testament era had not reached the stable and fixed form which it was to have at a subsequent period, but was still in the process of development and change: orthodoxy had not yet become crystallized, variant traditions existed side by side, and new elements were constantly being added. It is therefore extremely dangerous to read back the practices of later Rabbinic Judaism into the New Testament period as though they were unquestionably the universal customs of the time, and we must proceed with great caution in attempting to reconstruct the pattern of daily prayer current among Jews in the first century.

Although it is not strictly a prayer but rather a creed, the recitation of the *Shemaʿ* (Deut. 6.4–9; 11.13–21; Num. 15.37–41) is well attested as the fundamental daily devotion of Jews in the first century, both in Palestine and in the Diaspora.[1] The custom of reciting it twice a day, 'when you lie down and when you rise' (Deut. 6.7; 11.19), according to the Mishnah in the morning between dawn and sunrise and in the evening after sunset,[2] is first mentioned in the *Letter of Aristeas* (145–100 B.C.),[3] it is referred to by Philo and by Josephus,[4] and it was also apparently observed at Qumran.[5] The obligation to recite it came to be laid upon all free males from their twelfth birthday onwards, whereas women, children, and slaves were free from this and from all other acts which had to be performed at specific times because their time was not considered to be at their own disposal.[6] According to the Mishnah the *Shemaʿ* was to be accompanied by a series of fixed benedictions: 'In the morning two benedictions are said before and one after; and in the evening two benedictions are said before and two after, the

1

one long and the other short'.[7] Whether or not these were in use in the first century is not certain, and it is possible that only the benediction *Yozer 'Or*, which blesses God for the gift of light and darkness, dates from this period.[8] For some time the Decalogue was recited together with the *Shema*ʿ, both in the synagogue liturgy and at Qumran, but it was dropped, according to the Talmud, 'because of the fault-finding of the heretics (*minim*)', who said that only the Decalogue and not the *Shema*ʿ had been given to Moses at Sinai.[9] It is not clear whether these *minim* are to be identified with the early Christians or with some earlier heretical group.[10]

Alongside the twofold recitation of the *Shema*ʿ we find in Rabbinic Judaism the quite different custom of praying three times a day—morning, afternoon, and evening, the first and last being in practice combined with the saying of the *Shema*ʿ.[11] The observance of the afternoon time of prayer is mentioned in the New Testament: Peter and John go up to the Temple 'at the hour of prayer, the ninth hour' (Acts 3.1), and Cornelius the centurion keeps the ninth hour of prayer in his house (Acts 10.3, 30). The ninth hour, 3 p.m., appears to have been chosen for the afternoon prayer in order that it might coincide with the time of the offering of the evening sacrifice in the Herodian Temple.[12] The origin of this custom of threefold prayer has usually been attributed to the institution of the *ma'amadoth* or 'standing-posts'.[13] After the Exile the priests and Levites had been organized into twenty-four courses, each of which went up to Jerusalem to fulfil a week of service in turn, and attached to each course was a lay group called a *ma'amad*, part of which accompanied the priests and Levites to Jerusalem and was present at the daily sacrifices to represent the people and part of which remained at home and came together at the times of the morning and evening sacrifices in order to read the account of creation in Genesis and to pray, thus participating in the offering from a distance.[14]

There are, however, problems in ascribing the origin of the practice of threefold daily prayer to these assemblies, in that there are significant differences between them which are not easy to explain. Firstly, the *ma'amadoth* services were gatherings of specific groups of men in specific weeks of the year, whereas the times of prayer were observed throughout the year and were a general obligation upon all members of a household, including—unlike the recitation of the *Shema*ʿ—women, children, and slaves.[15] Professor Joachim Jeremias would attribute to the Pharisees the responsibility for bringing about this somewhat radical change, but he has no real evidence to support this conjecture: the book of Judith and the Psalms of Solomon which he cites are evidence only that the Pharisees kept times of prayer, not that these times were derived from the *ma'amadoth* services.[16] Secondly, the times of prayer could be observed individually as well as corporately in the synagogues, and contained no trace of the reading of the account of creation. Thirdly, except on Sabbaths, new moons, and festivals, when an additional sacrifice was appointed, there were normally only two daily sacrifices in the Temple, morning and evening: how then did they give rise to a threefold pattern of daily prayer? Dugmore appears to believe that this development came about as a result of the transfer of the evening sacrifice from its original time of twilight[17] to the afternoon, the evening time of prayer being moved to the afternoon to correspond with the new time of the sacrifice while the practice of praying again after sunset along with the recitation of the *Shema'* tended to continue, although this third time of prayer only became obligatory in the second century.[18] Jeremias, on the other hand, believes that the evening sacrifice already took place in the afternoon in the time of the *ma'amadoth* and that they assembled three times a day—at the morning and afternoon sacrifices, and again at the closing of the Temple gates—a view already expressed in the Mishnah, *Ta'an.* 4.1.[19] This passage, however, looks very like an early attempt to find a link between the *ma'amadoth* and the times of prayer, as it does not harmonize with the description of the *ma'amadoth* which follows: instructions are given for the reading of the account of creation only at the times of the two daily sacrifices, and the additional sacrifice when prescribed, and it is explicitly stated that, even when there was an additional sacrifice, the *ma'amadoth* assembled no more than three times a day.[20]

In any case it has been suggested that the *ma'amadoth* may have been a much later institution than the establishment of the synagogue,[21] and so the only firm link between them is that two of the times of prayer do correspond with the times of the daily sacrifices, and hence with the assembly of the *ma'amadoth*. Moreover, even the link between the times of prayer and the daily sacrifices is not as strong as might appear at first sight. In contrast to the more precise rules governing the recitation of the *Shema'*, no attempt was made to regulate the times of prayer so that they should always coincide exactly with the times of the sacrifices: the Mishnah records that the morning prayer might be said at any time until midday, the afternoon prayer until sunset, and the evening prayer had no set time.[22] Thus although no doubt in Jerusalem, where at the moment of the sacrifice loud trumpets were sounded from the Temple over the city,[23] and perhaps also in other places where these prayers were said corporately in the synagogues, they would tend to be at the hours of the sacrifices, elsewhere when they were said privately by individuals there might well have been considerable variation in their times.[24] Furthermore, there was no universally accepted Rabbinic tradition which linked the times of prayer with the sacrifices but, while some thought that they were derived from the Temple cult, others believed that they originated with the patriarchs, and others linked them with the threefold prayer mentioned in Dan. 6.10 and Ps. 55.17.[25] Finally, if the times of prayer had been instituted as the counterpart of the daily sacrifices, then one might have expected this to have been strongly reflected in the content of the prayers used at those times. This, however, does not appear to have been the case: in the earliest written form of the prayers preserved in Rabbinic Judaism there are only two very brief references to the Temple cult.[26] These considerations at least suggest the possibility that the association of the daily prayers with the times of sacrifice was a secondary development, and encourage consideration of an alternative hypothesis to account for their primary origin.

Moreover, there is some evidence to suggest that at least one other pattern of daily prayer was also current in Judaism in the first century, alongside that which ultimately became normative. The evidence for this comes principally, though not exclusively, from Qumran. Two parallel passages in the Dead Sea Scrolls appear to describe the daily cycle of prayer followed by members of the community:

1 QS 10.1–3a	1 QH 12.4–7
at the times which he has ordained,	at all times and seasons,
(a) at the beginning of the rule of light,	at the coming of light from [its dwelling],

4

(b) at its turning-point,	at its turning-point in its ordered course, in accordance with the laws of the great luminary,
(c) at its being gathered to the dwelling decreed for it,	at the turn of the evening and the departure of the light,
(d) at the beginning of the watches of darkness when he opens his treasury and sets him above,	at the beginning of the rule of darkness,
(e) at its turning-point,	in the season of the night, at its turning-point,
(f) at its being gathered from before the light,	at the turn of the morning and the time when it is gathered to its dwelling before the light,
(g) at the appearance of the luminaries from their holy realm,	at the departure of the night,
(h) and at their being gathered to the abode of glory;	and at the coming of the day;

The translation and interpretation of these passages is not without its difficulties. S. Holm-Nielsen would prefer to take the 1 QH text as not referring to definite times of prayer at all but describing 'the continual relationship between the righteous and God', but admits that it is not possible to ignore the idea of fixed times because of the similarity of the 1 QS passage, and therefore concludes:

> The real solution could be that there is indeed reference to set times, but that the text is not designed to present an argument for the practice of set times for prayer, but is intended for those to whom such practice was a matter of course; this would make it understandable that it is expressed in more fluid terms, giving most nearly the impression of wanting to show the eternally valid nature of the state of prayer.[27]

A. R. C. Leaney believes that the 1 QS passage enjoins only two times of prayer each day, morning and evening, but describes them in three ways, although this does involve, as he admits, treating it as poetical repetition.[28] He would thus take (a) and (b) above together, as both referring to the morning prayer, and (c) as referring to the evening, (d) as the evening again, and (e) and (f) together as the morning, and finally (g) as the evening and (h) as the morning for the third time. He further claims that 1 QS 10.10, 1 QM 14.12–14, and 1 QH 12.4–7 support this interpretation. We have already suggested that 1 QS 10.10 refers to the recitation of the *Shema'* and not the daily times of prayer,[29] and the same may also be true of 1 QM 14.12–14, since there is some slight similarity between the two passages.[30] Moreover, 1 QH 12.4–7 will not provide an exact parallel to his interpretation of 1 QS 10.1–3a, since (g) and (h) in that document must refer to the same time of day, and not the evening and the morning. However, the view that only two times of daily prayer are intended in these passages is also shared by Geza Vermes in his translation and by M. Delcor in his commentary on 1 QH,[31] and it does accord with the practice of the Therapeutae near Lake Mareotis in Egypt, as described by Philo, who have some affinities with the community at Qumran and who prayed only twice each day, in the morning and the evening.[32] C.-H. Hunzinger claims that a manuscript from Cave 4 at Qumran contains the text of the morning and evening prayers for each day of the month,[33] but this has not so far been published and in any case appears to be so fragmentary that it is impossible to be certain that it may not also have included prayers for other times of the day.

On the other hand, S. Talmon would find in these two passages no less than six times of prayer assigned to every period of twenty-four hours, one to each of the six parts into which the day was divided in Jewish tradition, three for the period of daylight, morning (a), noon (b), and evening (c), and three for the three night watches (d, e, and f–h).[34] A similar position was adopted by Josef Jungmann, who saw a link between them and the Christian observance of the third, sixth, and ninth hours, evening, midnight, and morning.[35] However, it is difficult to see that a clear distinction in time is intended between the departure of light (c) and the coming of darkness (d), especially when the end of night and the beginning of day (g & h) are regarded as referring to the same time, or that this latter occasion is to be distinguished from a subsequent 'coming of light' mentioned in (a). A modified version of Talmon's interpretation may therefore be preferred, that prayer morning, noon, and evening are intended in (a), (b), and (c), as he claims, but that (d) is a continuation of the reference to the evening prayer, (e) refers, as he says, to midnight prayer, and (f), (g), and (h) complete the cycle by returning to the morning prayer with which the description began. That the community did observe a regular time of prayer at night is confirmed by 1 QS 6.7–8a ('and the many shall keep vigil in community for a third of all the nights of the year, to read the Book and to study its decree and to bless God in community'), and as Leaney himself admits, the description by Josephus of the daily routine of the Essenes—if, as is generally accepted, the community at Qumran is to be identified with the Essenes—is as consistent with a practice of threefold daily prayer as with prayer twice a day: the assembly in the middle of the day for ablution and food may or may not have included a time of prayer, and the absence of any explicit mention of it is not conclusive, as Josephus similarly makes no explicit reference to evening prayer.[36] T. H. Gaster also interprets the two passages in this manner in his translation of them, but in his notes equates the three times of prayer during the day with those prescribed in Rabbinic Judaism.[37] It is, however, unlikely that the community at Qumran would have described 3 p.m. as the 'turning-point' of the day, or would have adhered to a timetable of prayer regulated by a sanctuary which they regarded as corrupt. Nor does the fact that at Qumran praise and prayer, 'the offering of the lips', and a life of obedience to the Law were seen as temporary substitutes for the Temple sacrifices[38] necessarily imply that their prayers were offered only at the times of the morning and evening sacrifices.

Clearly much depends upon the precise sense of the word *tequphah*, literally 'circuit' or 'revolution', translated as 'turning-point' in the above passages. Holm-Nielsen would prefer to take it as meaning 'course' or 'duration' here, but allows that 'zenith' is a possible alternative rendering.[39] Others would translate it as the 'completion of the course' or 'end of the circuit',[40] as in Ps. 19.6. It can be translated as 'turning-point' in the other three Old Testament instances of the word, in Exod. 34.22; 1 Sam. 1.20; 2 Chron. 24.23,[41] though again others would prefer 'end' here.[42] The possibility of the rendering 'turning-point' in the Qumran texts is perhaps strengthened by the fact of the Rabbinic use of *tequphah* for solstice and equinox.

Apart from a few references to prayer at night in the Psalter (Pss. 63.6; 88.1; 92.2; 119.55, 62, 148; 134.1; cf. also Neh. 1.6), the significance of which is difficult to determine, evidence for a regular practice of night prayer in Judaism outside Qumran is lacking. However, the possibility of the existence of a cycle of daily prayer morning, noon, and evening does receive some support from other sources:

(i) Daniel 6.10: 'When Daniel knew that the document had been signed, he went to his house where he had windows in his upper chamber open towards Jerusalem; and he got down upon his knees three times a day and prayed and gave thanks before his God, as he had done previously.' Some have supposed that these three times of prayer were morning, afternoon, and evening as in later Judaism,[43] but this theory can only be upheld if the time of the evening sacrifice had already been changed to the afternoon before the book of Daniel was composed (c. 165 B.C.). Although the date of this change is unknown, there is no indication anywhere in the Old Testament that the sacrifice was offered at any other time than the evening,[44] and the book of Judith (c. 160 B.C.) which Jeremias cites as evidencing morning prayer (12.5f.), prayer at the time of the 'afternoon' sacrifice (9.1), and evening prayer (13.3f.)[45] does not in fact do so, since the first and the last references are to the same time of prayer—made at night 'towards the morning watch'—and the sacrifice is said to be offered in the evening. Moreover, there is a significant difference between Daniel's prayer and that of later Rabbinic Judaism: it was made kneeling and not standing. If therefore the sacrifice was still offered in the evening at this period, what was the middle time of prayer observed by Daniel? Ludwig Blau suggested that it corresponded 'perhaps with the sacrifices offered by individuals between the official morning and evening sacrifices',[46] Dugmore that it 'may have been at noon, though we are not told that it was, and was probably purely private custom, for we have no other reference to a regular daily prayer either at noon or in the afternoon at that period'.[47] It is unlikely, however, that the author of the book of Daniel would have referred to the custom if it had not been widely observed at that time: if the regular practice had been to pray twice a day, would he not have spoken of Daniel praying twice and not three times a day?

(ii) Ps. 55.17: 'Evening and morning and at noon I utter my complaint and moan, and he will hear my voice'. This verse may be thought to be no more than a poetic way of expressing the fact that the psalmist prays continually, just as in Ps. 119.164 the psalmist says 'seven times a day I praise thee for thy righteous ordinances', but it is at least possible that it is a reference to a regular pattern of threefold prayer.

(iii) 2 Enoch 51.4: 'It is good to go morning, midday, and evening into the Lord's dwelling for the glory of your creator'. The common assumption that this book originated some time in the first century before the fall of Jerusalem and was the work of a Hellenistic Jew of Alexandria has been challenged in respect of both date and provenance.[48] If however the traditional origin can still be accepted, then this verse would seem to indicate the observance of a custom of praying morning, noon, and evening in Hellenistic Judaism, or at least at Alexandria, in the first century. If, on the other hand, as some scholars have suggested, the book is a Jewish Christian work originating from Syria towards the end of the first century,[49] then it constitutes valuable evidence for the adoption of these times of prayer by the Church at an early date, and so again points indirectly towards a Jewish origin for them.

(iv) Epiphanius, *Adv. Haer.* 29.9: 'rising up in the morning and in the middle of the day and in the evening, three times a day, when they say their prayers in the synagogues . . .'. If this is an accurate account of Jewish worship, then prayer morning, noon, and evening persisted, at least in some places, up to the fourth century. The expression 'middle of the day' (*meses hemeras*) may, however, only be a loose way of speaking of 3 p.m.

(v) The final piece of evidence is the pattern of Christian prayer which, as we shall show, existed by the end of the second century, or earlier if 2 Enoch is indeed a Jewish Christian composition, consisting of prayer morning, noon, evening, and midnight.[50] Although Christian practice can hardly be used as a decisive argument to establish Jewish practice, the Church must have had some reason for adopting this particular arrangement of daily prayer, and therefore it does lend some weight to the possibility that such a custom already existed in Judaism in the first century.

Clearly none of these offers conclusive proof for the existence in Judaism of the practice of prayer morning, noon, and evening, but cumulatively they may be thought to add some strength to the theory. What, however, might have given rise to such a pattern? It has been established that sun-worship was prevalent in Israel and even associated with the Temple, no doubt in a syncretistic manner, at least until the time of the

Exile, and quite probably after the return.[51] Although successive attempts were made to purify the worship of Yahweh, there is no reason to suppose that every trace of the old religion was eliminated, and we find what appear to be elements of it incorporated into the life and teaching of the Essenes: in the Qumran material the light/darkness antithesis features prominently; God is identified with the heavenly light and the community designate themselves as 'sons of light'; and in contrast to orthodox Judaism they follow a solar and not a lunar calendar.[52] As the passages quoted earlier reveal, their times of prayer too seem to have been regulated by the coming of light and darkness and by 'the laws of the great luminary', i.e. the sun (cf. Gen. 1.16), and this is confirmed by Josephus: 'their piety towards the deity takes a peculiar form, for before the sun has risen they utter no profane word, but certain traditional prayers towards him, as though beseeching him to rise'.[53] With this may be compared Philo's description of the Therapeutae: 'twice each day they are accustomed to pray, at dawn and in the evening, at sunrise asking for a fine day, fine in the sense that their minds may be filled with heavenly light . . . . They stand with their faces and whole body turned to the east, and when they see the sun rise, stretching their hands towards heaven, they pray for a fine day and truth and clarity of thought.'[54] We need not accuse either of these communities of importing an idolatrous sun cult: they no doubt considered that they were preserving an ancient and essential element in the worship of Yahweh, which they regarded as being wrongly suppressed by the adherents of what came to be orthodox Judaism; and we may note Josephus' designation of the Essene prayers as *patrious*, 'traditional'.

The attribution of the ultimate origin of their times of prayer to the veneration of the sun does not of course require the conclusion that the community at Qumran necessarily followed a pattern of threefold daily prayer—morning, noon, and evening—(and in the case of the Therapeutae this certainly was not so) but it does at least make such an arrangement a natural one, the sun being honoured at the cardinal points of its course. It is even possible that the Rabbinic custom of prayer in the morning, afternoon, and evening may have been a later adaptation of this pattern, an attempt to eradicate what was seen as a corrupt practice by associating two of the times of prayer instead with the Temple sacrifices, but something which was not followed universally in Judaism until after the close of the New Testament era. Thus the *ma'amadoth* services may not have constituted the origin of the daily prayers but rather a step towards their association with the times of sacrifice. The fact that at the end of the first century A.D. the rabbis were still disputing whether the evening time of prayer was obligatory does not count against this conjecture, as the debate was an entirely academic matter, concerned with whether a Scriptural warrant could be adduced for the custom, and the time was generally observed in practice.[55]

If this hypothesis is correct, then the Rabbinic custom of facing in the direction of the Temple at Jerusalem while praying[56] was also an adaptation of an earlier orientation towards the east,[57] which was continued by the Therapeutae and the Essenes, and quite possibly by others as well. It would seem from the passages quoted from Josephus and Philo that in these communities the eastward prayer had acquired an eschatological dimension, the 'fine bright day' for which the Therapeutae prayed being apparently the messianic age and the Essene prayer towards the sun 'as though beseeching him to rise' being a petition for the coming of the priestly Messiah, this interpretation being confirmed by passages in the Qumran literature which speak of the Messiah as the 'great luminary'.[58] Similar ideas are found in the Old Testament,[59] in the Testaments of the Twelve Patriarchs,[60] and also in the benediction *Yozer 'Or* accompanying the recitation of the *Shema',*[61] which indicate that it did not originate with the Essenes, nor was it confined to them. Once again we may refer to Josephus' designation of the Essene prayers as 'traditional' and observe that the orthodox prayer towards Jerusalem also came to have eschatological significance, in expectation of a messianic coming to the city.[62]

Just as there was some variation in the times and orientation of the daily prayers in the first century A.D., so also was there variation in their form and content. Three main types of formal prayer may be identified in early Judaism,[63] or rather three variants which, though identical in purpose, are quite distinct in form, and all of these can be found in the Old Testament. A major weakness of nearly all earlier studies of Jewish prayers has been the failure to distinguish different forms and the tendency instead to reduce them all to a single classification.[64]

1. The classical form of prayer in Judaism, and the one which ultimately became normative in the synagogue, was the *berakah*, 'benediction', in which God was blessed for what he had done for his people. In its most ancient form found in the Old Testament it occurs principally not in a cultic setting but as a response to some event which has befallen the speaker, and it consists of the following elements:

(a) the opening blessing, always the stereotyped formula, 'Blessed be the Lord', using the passive participle of the verb *barak*;

(b) further appellatives of God, although this element is sometimes omitted;

(c) a relative clause, using the third person singular of an active verb in the perfect tense and expressing the particular grounds for the blessing.

Although it is impossible for man to bestow blessing on God in the sense in which human beings may be blessed, yet by this proclamation the speaker acknowledges that what has befallen him is not mere chance but the result of the activity of God and so ascribes to him the praise and glory for it. Thus, for example, when Abraham's servant is successful in finding a wife for Isaac, he praises God and acknowledges this event as his work: 'Blessed be the Lord, the God of my master Abraham, who has not forsaken his steadfast love and his faithfulness towards my master'.[65] This simple type of *berakah* might be extended, especially when used in a liturgical setting, by the addition of other elements:

(d) The *anamnesis* of God's activity might be expanded into a more detailed description by the enlargement of the relative clause and by the addition of a further sentence or sentences, as in 1 Sam. 25.39 where David, on hearing of the death of Nabal, says: 'Blessed be the Lord, who has avenged the insult I received at the hand of Nabal, and has kept back his servant from evil. The Lord has returned the evil-doing of Nabal upon his own head.'[66] Frequently the relative clause itself constitutes an initial summary of the detailed narrative which is to follow in the subsequent sentences, as in 1 Kgs. 8.15–21, part of Solomon's prayer at the dedication of the Temple. It is true that in these examples, as J. M. Robinson has pointed out, 'one has to do with rather wooden insertion of the material from the surrounding narrative into the formulae'.[67] In other words, the form is literary rather than liturgical. Yet it would seem improbable that the Biblical authors would have expanded the prayers in this way had it not been customary to do so in their culture, and certainly when one finds *berakoth* in their original settings and not at secondhand in literary works, the longer narrative form with the relative clause acting as an initial summary is not unknown.

(e) Petition and intercession might follow on from the *anamnesis* and in subordination to it, the recalling of God's past goodness constituting the ground on which he might be asked to continue his activity among his prople, as in 1 Kgs. 8.56–61, another extract from Solomon's prayer. This element generally ends with some statement indicating that the purpose of what is being asked is not just for the benefit of the suppliants but for the advancement of God's praise and glory, in order that the whole world may see his works and thus be led to worship him and acknowledge his greatness, as his people do now in the *berakah*. Thus Solomon's prayer ends (1 Kgs. 8.60): 'that all the peoples of the earth may know that the Lord is God; there is no other'.

(f) When used in a liturgical setting it became customary to conclude the developed form with a short *berakah*, thus reiterating the opening of the prayer and inviting the congregation to associate themselves with it in the response 'Amen'. Characteristic of the early form of these short *berakoth* is the extension of the praise into infinity. Formulae of this type are found at the end of the five books into which the Psalter is divided, except for the last where Ps. 150 itself forms the doxology, and they well illustrate the development and elaboration of this element. Ps. 89.52 is cast in the simplest form of all: 'Blessed be the Lord for ever. Amen, Amen'. In Ps. 41.13 and Ps. 106.48//1 Chron. 16.36 the form is slightly elaborated: 'Blessed be the Lord, the God of Israel, from everlasting to everlasting'. According to the Mishnah (*Ber.* 9.5), the development of the concluding phrase in this way was a reaction against heretics who taught that there was only one world. Ps. 72.18–19 is the most fully elaborated version: 'Blessed be the Lord, the God of Israel, who alone does wondrous things. Blessed be his glorious name for ever; may his glory fill the whole earth! Amen and Amen'. Here we can see the first example extant of a new version of the *berakah* which was to become well-established in the intertestamental period and in which the relative clause was replaced by a participial phrase, although translated here as 'who alone does wondrous things'. This version was used not only as the standard conclusion of a prayer in place of the other forms but also frequently as an alternative to the traditional opening.[68]

2. The *hodayah* is parallel in its construction to the *berakah*, with the verb *yadah*, or sometimes some other verb, used in place of *barak*, but in an active and not passive form, and with God addressed directly in the second person. It is usually translated into English as 'I will give thanks to you, O Lord . . .' but 'praise' might be a better rendering, since its primary significance is not the expression of gratitude but, just as in the *berakah*, the confession or acknowledgement that it is God who has acted,[69] and the same verb is also used for the confession of sin.[70] In the Old Testament the verb *yadah* is restricted mainly to Chronicles, Ezra, and Nehemiah, and to the Psalter, where it is evidenced more in brief responsory forms than in the fully developed *hodayah*, as for example, 'O give thanks to the Lord, for he is good, for his steadfast love endures for ever' (e.g. Pss. 106.1; 107.1; 118.1; 138.1). The *hodayah* may conceivably have its origins in the cult, as a liturgical form to accompany the *todah*, a noun from the same *yadah* root denoting the sacrifice offered in response to an act of divine goodness and mercy. The reason for the praise is expressed in a subordinate clause, usually introduced by *ki* (LXX: *hoti*) and using the second person singular of an active verb in the perfect tense, as in Is. 12.1: 'I will give thanks to you, O Lord, for though you were angry with me, your anger turned away, and you comforted me'. As with the *berakah*, the basic form might be extended into a more detailed *anamnesis* of God's works, or lead into petition and intercession,[71] and the doxological conclusion, where it was appended, reiterated the opening of the prayer, as in Ps. 30.12: 'O Lord my God, I will give thanks to you for ever'. In the Septuagint both meanings of *yadah*, praise and the confession of sin, are generally translated by the compound verbs *exomologoumai* (noun *exomologesis*) and *anthomologoumai* (noun *anthomologesis*) rather than the simple *homologeo* (noun *homologia*) more common in secular Greek, perhaps because the legal and commercial sense of the latter made it seem too profane for this purpose.[72] *Homologeo* does, however, occur in the sense of 'praise' in 1 Esd. 4.60; 5.58A. On the other hand, the verb *eucharisteo*, 'give thanks', begins to be used to express

praise towards God in those books of the Septuagint which do not form part of the Hebrew canon, and seems to have become established as a variant for *exomologoumai* in the *hodayah* in Hellenistic Judaism.[73] The way in which it is used by Josephus in his paraphrase of Solomon's prayer in 1 Kgs. 8.15f. suggests not only that Hellenistic Judaism found the *hodayah* a much more natural and familiar form than the *berakah* but also that the preference for *eucharisteo* was the result of an attempt to accommodate Hebrew thought to Greek ideas—the rejection of the belief in material sacrifice in favour of the sacrifice of thanksgiving,[74] and it is interesting that the noun *todah*, though translated in the Septuagint as *thusia tes aineseos*, 'sacrifice of praise', is rendered as *eucharistia* in the version of Aquila.[75]

3. What might be called the direct *anamnesis* type of prayer is again a variant of the *berakah* which dispenses entirely with any introductory formula of praise and begins immediately to recount God's mighty works, usually addressing him in the second person, although hymnic forms in the third person are also found, and it may, like the other two types, pass on to petition or intercession. Examples in the Old Testament include the central section of Solomon's prayer at the dedication of the Temple (1 Kgs. 8.23–53) and Hezekiah's prayer when Jerusalem was besieged by Sennacherib (2 Kgs. 19.15–19//Is. 37.16–20).[76] Neither of these has a concluding doxological formula, but the Prayer of Manasses in the Apocrypha, which also adopts this form, has as its conclusion 'yours is the glory for ever. Amen', and 4 Maccabees ends similarly, and so it is probable that this was the normal ending for this type of prayer.[77]

In the course of time various changes and developments took place in these three forms of prayer. Firstly, 'where religious experience became more cultic and less historic, as in "normative" Judaism, the formulae tended to undergo alterations which avoided the need of a specific event; for example, the second line of the *berakah* ("who has . . .") could be replaced by a *berakah* upon God's name, or the "occurrence" could be vague, general, or unhistoric, such as the provision of food through nature'.[78] Secondly, not only were the variant forms used as alternatives to one another, but elements of each type came to be combined in the same prayer.

Thus the prayer in Dan. 2.20–3 begins as a *berakah*, but continues (v. 23) in the *hodayah* form. The same construction can be seen in the blessing at the meal in *Jubilees* 22.6–9, and indeed in the standard Jewish grace after meals, the *Birkat ha-Mazon*.[79] The reverse is the case in 2 Macc. 1.11–17, which is a *hodayah* but ends with the concluding formula of a *berakah*. Thirdly, quite possibly as a result of this tendency to combine the different types of prayer, there is a marked change in the form of the *berakah* towards the end of the Old Testament period—the abandonment of the unvarying use of the third person and a growing preference for the second person, as in the other forms. Only three instances of this found their way into the Old Testament itself (1 Chron. 29.10f.; Neh. 9.5; Ps. 119.12), but it is well evidenced in the intertestamental literature,[80] and eventually became normative in the synagogue in the stereotyped form: 'Blessed are you, O Lord our God, King of the universe . . .'. The relative clause, however, tended to remain in the third person as before. The distinction between the different types of prayer became even more blurred by the fact that the Greek verb *eulogeo*, which was normally used to translate the Hebrew verb *barak* in the *berakah*, was also occasionally used in an active form as the opening of the *hodayah* (e.g. LXX: Is. 12.1), and sometimes the *berakah* might include a subordinate clause introduced by *ki* (LXX: *hoti*) and the *hodayah* a relative clause instead.[81] Finally, the Rabbinic insistence on the *berakah* as the normative type of prayer eventually led not only to each prayer having to begin and end with this form, and all variants being suppressed, but to each section within a prayer also being assimilated to this form by the addition of a short concluding *berakah*, the content of which recalled and summarized the theme of the foregoing unit of prayer, usually employing the present participle and often being an Old Testament quotation. This concluding *berakah*, generally termed by Jewish liturgiologists today the *chatimah* or 'seal', was in the course of time even added to the opening paragraph of a prayer, which already began with a *berakah*.[82]

It has often been assumed that not only were these Rabbinic rules already in force in the first century but the precise form and content of the prayer to be said at the daily times of prayer had already been fixed.[83] This prayer, called in the oldest sources simply *Tefillah*, 'The Prayer', came to be termed *Shemoneh 'Esreh*, 'Eighteen', because its content was fixed at eighteen (later nineteen) paragraphs or *berakoth*.[84] It is known, however, that in reality not all of these date back to the early part of the first century: at least some were composed after the fall of Jerusalem in A.D. 70, while the Talmud attributes the present arrangement of the prayer to Simeon ha-Pakoli (*c.* A.D. 110).[85] Moreover, even to this prayer the individual was still free to add his own petitions, and different religious groups within Judaism were characterized by the particular prayers which they used.[86] When the *Tefillah* was said in the synagogues, where unlike the *Shema'* it was not recited corporately but prayed by one on behalf of all, often by the *hazzan* ('the attendant' in Lk. 4.20), the congregation responding with *Amen* after each benediction, a period of silence was included for such individual prayers.[87] Nevertheless even scholars who have recognized this degree of variation have tended to suppose that beneath it all there was still an ancient stratum of fixed prayer to which other elements were later added,[88] but more recent research suggests that one ought to be much more cautious about asserting the extent to which there was any common form of prayer at this period or to which the Rabbinic rules about the structure of prayers had already become established.

> The Jewish prayers were originally the creations of the common people. The characteristic idioms and forms of prayer, and indeed the statutory prayers of the synagogue themselves, were not in the first place products of the deliberations of the Rabbis in their academies, but were rather the spontaneous, on-the-spot improvizations of the people who gathered on various occasions to pray in the synagogue. Since the occasions and places of worship were numerous, it was only natural that they should give rise to an abundance of prayers, displaying a wide variety of forms, styles and patterns. Thus the first stage in the development of the liturgy was characterized by diversity and variety—and the task of the Rabbis was to systematize and to impose order on this multiplicity of forms, patterns and structures. This task they undertook after the fact; only after the numerous prayers had come into being and were familiar to the masses did the Sages decide that the time had come to establish some measure of uniformity and standardization.[89]

This process took place gradually: first came the obligation to mention certain things in the prayer, then from the third century onwards the opening and concluding formulas of the prayer began to be fixed while the rest remained relatively free and different versions continued to exist side by side, and much later still a definitive text was prescribed.[90]

Thus there are good grounds for believing that in the New Testament period a number of different orders of prayers were in use, having some features and subjects in common with one another, but not as yet restricted to any definitive wording, structure, or liturgical form. There was also some variation in language—both the *Shema'* and the *Tefillah* might be said in any language, although Hebrew and not ·Aramaic seems to have been used in Palestine[91]—and very possibly in the posture adopted for prayer: the posture to be adopted for the recitation of the *Shema'* was still a matter for debate between the Rabbinic schools of Hillel and Shammai in the first century A.D.,[92] and although no such debate is recorded in the Mishnah in the case of the daily prayers but it is accepted that they are to be said standing, nevertheless the practice of kneeling for prayer may also have existed in the first century, especially as the Old Testament references to kneeling for prayer suggest that the custom was later than that of standing and arose only in the post-exilic period.[93] Whether kneeling or standing, however, the suppliant's hands were lifted up and spread out towards heaven.[94]

Were the times of daily prayer observed corporately in the synagogues or privately by individuals wherever they happened to be? Dugmore argues that the former was the general rule: 'Although it may be true that not every tiny village community was able to go *en bloc* daily to the synagogue, at least in the larger towns, where it would be easier to obtain the requisite minimum of ten males and where the homes of the people were grouped more closely around the synagogue, daily attendance at the public worship of the community would be the practice of every devout Jew'.[95] The number of places, however, where it was possible to find the Rabbinic quorum of ten males with both the leisure and the piety to attend the synagogue for the daily times of prayer was probably more limited than this sentence would seem to suggest, and while it is no doubt true, as Dugmore goes on to say, that daily services would have been found in such places as Jerusalem, Caesarea, Antioch, and Rome, nevertheless it is almost certain that for the great majority of Jews the times of prayer were of necessity private devotions. It would appear that even members of the Pharasaic party were not above deliberately absenting themselves from the daily worship of the synagogue in order to be seen at their prayers in the streets (Mt. 6.5), and the fact that there were people to see them shows how limited was attendance at the synagogues for the times of prayer. The Essenes, on the other hand, did meet together for their daily prayers,[96] whereas the Therapeutae lived in recluse and assembled together for worship only on the Sabbath.[97]

On certain days of the week, however,—the Sabbath, Monday, and Thursday—there would undoubtedly have been public services in the synagogues, and on these days the liturgy included not merely the *Shema‘* and the *Tefillah* but also a reading from the Law, which was on the basis of *lectio continua*, possibly on an annual or triennial cycle.[98] In addition, there was a reading from the Prophets at the Sabbath morning service, but little is known about this: there may have been an independent cycle of readings, or they may have been arranged to complement the readings from the Law,[99] or they may simply have been chosen by the reader, the ruler of the synagogue, or the *hazzan*. The readings were accompanied in Palestine by a translation into Aramaic (in the Diaspora they were read in Greek), and might be followed by an exposition, delivered by the speaker seated, and any male member of the congregation could be invited to read, translate, or give this address.[100] St. Luke describes in detail one visit of Jesus to the synagogue on the Sabbath when he read the lesson from the Prophets and gave the exposition (Lk. 4.16–30).

Several points should be noted about this ministry of the word. Firstly, there was originally only one reading from the Law prescribed for each week, that for the Sabbath morning service: the readings at the other services—the Sabbath afternoon, and Monday and Thursday mornings—were merely repetitions of the portion prescribed for the following Sabbath morning.[101] Secondly, the repetition on these occasions appears to have been introduced not because of any intrinsic religious significance in the days themselves but simply because they were the times when people might be expected to be able to attend the synagogue in some numbers, Monday and Thursday being the market days in Palestine when the country folk would congregate in the villages and towns. The adoption of these two days as fast-days seems to have been a consequence and not the cause of the liturgical observance, since such regular fasting was an entirely voluntary act undertaken by the Pharisees and others.[102] Thirdly, the ministry of the word appears not to have been incorporated into the service proper, but rather tacked on to the end as a quasi-independent unit, since the Aaronic blessing,[103] which formed the conclusion of the service on other days, preceded the reading on these occasions. Louis Bouyer has tried to argue that the ministry of the word was originally at the beginning of the service, as it was in Christian practice, and was transferred to this point at a later date when the Christians placed the Eucharist in this position as the climax of their service,[104] but he has no evidence for this theory and it seems at least as probable that the change in the order was made by the Christians for reasons of their own[105] as that it was made by the Jews in reaction to Christian practice.

These three considerations, together with the fact that the reading of the Law was done on the basis of *lectio continua*, except for such times as the major festivals of the year when passages of the Scriptures appropriate to the occasion were prescribed, point to the conclusion that the ministry of the word was not seen as an integral element in the act of worship but rather as an occasional appendix to it, made simply for the sake of convenience, because the congregation happened to be gathered together already for that purpose, and not because any intrinsic connection was envisaged between the prayer and the reading—rather like the way in which a sermon came to be appended to the Sunday services of Morning and Evening Prayer in the Church of England. It may be termed a 'didactic' liturgy of the word, as distinct from a 'kerygmatic' type in which a relationship does exist between the reading(s) and the act of worship and about which more will be said later,[106] and was nothing more or less than the orderly and continuous study of the Scriptures, a part of the regular reading and ceaseless meditation upon the Word of God which constituted an ideal of Jewish spirituality and formed a third element, along with the *Shema'* and the *Tefillah*, in the daily devotion of every pious Jew. Within the community at Qumran an attempt was made to put this ideal into practice in a more formal way. Here the Monday and Thursday liturgies of the word appear to have been unknown, and instead arrangements were made for a continuous exposition of the Law to take place within the community day and night, presumably on some sort of rota basis, and for the corporate vigil lasting a third of every night during which the Law was read and studied.[107]

Whether or not the Psalter was in use in the synagogue services during the first century is far from clear. In the Temple liturgy some psalms were used, on a selective basis, each day of the week having its proper psalm sung at the morning and evening sacrifice by the Levites,[108] and appropriate psalms were also prescribed for the festivals. All these were eventually taken over into the synagogue services, but at what date is unknown, and gradually other psalms were added to them. It has been suggested that there was a triennial cycle for the Psalter at the Sabbath afternoon service, corresponding to that for the Law, in which the psalms were read through in order, but if that is true it is strange that it has left no trace on the later synagogue liturgy, since even in the modern Jewish services only about half of the psalms are ever used.[109] Claims have also been made that at an early date certain pious individuals were in the habit of reciting some or all of the psalms, in particular Pss. 145–50, before the daily morning prayer,[110] and even that Pss. 148–50 were already incorporated into the morning synagogue service in the first century.[111] However, the only foundation upon which these extravagant claims rest is very late: the Talmud speaks of some who recite Ps. 145 three times a day (*b. Ber.* 4b) and some who recite the 'verses of song' every day (*b. Shab.* 118b), but it is several centuries later still before these 'verses of song' are identified with Pss. 145–50 by Jewish sources.[112] We thus have no way of knowing how old this practice was, or how widespread. What was certainly happening in the first century, however, was that new psalms and hymns were being composed for use in worship, to which the large collection of *hodayoth* from the community at Qumran bears witness.[113] Philo speaks of chants, hymns, and songs being employed in Jewish worship,[114] and when describing the customs of the Therapeutae says that in their solitude 'they do not only contemplate but also compose songs and hymns to God in all sorts of metres and melodies'.[115] He also tells how at their festal meals,

> the president rises and sings a hymn addressed to God, either a new one which he has composed or an ancient one by poets of old. . . . After him the others take their turn in the order in which they are arranged, while all the rest listen in complete silence, except

when they have to chant the closing lines and refrains, for then they all, men and women, sing. . . . After the supper they keep the sacred vigil. The vigil is kept in this way. They rise up all together, and in the middle of the refectory two choirs are formed first, one of men and one of women. . . . Then they sing hymns to God composed of many measures and many melodies, sometimes chanting together, sometimes in antiphonal harmonies. . . .[116]

Finally, mention should be made of another element in the daily piety of the devout Jew, the blessings pronounced before everything that was eaten, said both by individuals when eating alone and by one on behalf of all when eating together. The evening meal on Fridays and Saturdays in every Jewish home was also accompanied by the further ceremony of the lighting of a lamp with the benediction, 'Blessed are you, O Lord our God, King of the Universe, who creates the light of fire', which marked the beginning and end of the Sabbath.[117] All these elements formed the devotional background of the first converts to Christianity and were to leave their mark, as we shall see, upon the daily worship of the Church.

2. *Daily Prayer in First-Century Christianity*

According to Acts 1.14, after the ascension of Jesus the disciples 'with the women and Mary the mother of Jesus and with his brothers were persevering with one accord in the prayer' (*proskarterountes homothumadon te proseuche*). The phrase also appears in the summary of the main features of the life of the earliest Christian community in Jerusalem in Acts 2.42, though this time with the noun in the plural: 'they were persevering in the apostles' teaching and fellowship, in the breaking of bread and the prayers' (*proskarterountes ... tais proseuchais*), and it is repeated, with the noun in the singular, in Acts 6.4, Rom. 12.12, and Col. 4.2. The suggestion that this activity in a Christian context 'involves a different attitude and manner of prayer from those customary in contemporary Judaism, which had fixed hours and patterns of prayer'[1] has no real evidence to substantiate it, and Jeremias' translation of the verb as meaning 'faithfully to observe a rite' in relation to regular times of prayer[2] is to be preferred, especially in the light of Acts 2.42 where the plural *tais proseuchais* most naturally suggests the observance of a fixed pattern of prayers and where the 'breaking of bread' can hardly have been a continuous activity unrelated to set times. Jeremias himself, however, improbably and somewhat inconsistently, would exclude the occurrence of the expression in Acts 2.42 from his definition and interprets it there as denoting merely the final component of a daily eucharistic rite.[3] Equally improbable in the light of the other passages is the translation of the phrase in Acts 1.14 as 'attending the synagogue'.[4]

What then were the times and content of this regular pattern of prayer which the early Church observed and which it is implied was inherited from Jesus himself? Because all four evangelists record his frequent attendance at the synagogue services on the Sabbath and his participation in them by preaching and teaching,[5] and because his followers are said to have continued to attend the Temple and the synagogues, very many scholars have supposed that at first the Christians simply joined with other Jews in their daily worship and only began to hold their own services, except for the Eucharist, when they were eventually expelled from the synagogues and the *Birkath ha-Minim*, a malediction against Christians and other heretics, was incorporated within the *Shemoneh 'Esreh* in order to exclude them from participation in the services.[6] Thus they are described as 'continually in the Temple blessing God' (Lk. 24.35) and as 'persevering with one accord (*proskarterountes homothumadon*) daily in the Temple' (Acts 2.46), and on his missionary journeys Paul regularly goes to the synagogue on his arrival in a town (Acts 13.5,14; 14.1; 16.13; 17.1f.,10,17; 18.4,19; 19.8). Other passages, however, suggest that from the first the Christians tended to form a distinct group within Judaism, like the Essenes and others, and to worship apart: the reference to prayer in Acts 1.14 is linked with the upper room; the assembly in the morning before 9 a.m. on the day of Pentecost (Acts 2.1; cf. 2.15) was probably for worship and appears to have been held in a private house; this may also be true of the assembly mentioned in Acts 4.23–31; many of the Jerusalem church gather to pray at night in the house of the mother of John Mark (Acts 12.5,12); even in the Temple the Christians are said to congregate together (*homothumadon*) in Solomon's Portico and thus mark themselves off from 'the rest',[7] certainly in order to teach and very likely also for their prayers; and Paul's visits to synagogues may have been more for the purpose of evangelism than in order to participate in the worship. Such an early separation of the Christian community would be hardly surprising. As Willy Rordorf rightly remarks,

> Christians could no longer feel at home in the synagogues precisely because there was lacking in Jewish worship that which was for them of decisive importance—the reference to Jesus Christ, on whom was centred all the worshipping activity of the new people of God.... It was, therefore, imperative that the Christian community should form itself as a clearly defined entity distinct from the Jewish community. It had become the Church perhaps even before it had realized that this had happened.[8]

On the other hand, we cannot be certain whether the author of Acts is really presenting an accurate historical picture of the life of early Christianity in Jerusalem or is instead projecting back upon it the practices of his own time. If the injunction in Mt. 6.5–6 not to pray in the synagogues but to 'go into your room and shut the door' can be considered a genuine saying of Jesus, then the tradition of worshipping apart from other Jews may go back into his lifetime, and in any case both this saying and the frequent use of the phrase 'their synagogues' in Matthew[9] seem to point to the existence of separate Christian synagogues by the time of the composition of this gospel, which it has been argued was prior to the final break with Judaism.[10]

The impression given by the passages in Acts, and especially by the frequent use of the adverb *homothumadon*, 'together, with one accord' (Acts 1.14; 2.46; 4.24; 5.12), is of a corporate observance of daily prayer in the early Christian community, but once again whether these statements present an accurate picture of the life of the church in Jerusalem or are a retrospective idealization of it, and if accurate, how long this practice survived, or how true it was of Christians as a whole in the New Testament era and not just of the community in which the book of Acts was composed, are questions to which it is impossible to give any sure answers. G. J. Cuming concludes: 'we cannot claim that daily common prayer can be certainly proved from the New Testament. The most that can be said is that it was the rule in the synagogue, that the first Christians continued to attend the synagogue, and that it is likely, therefore, to have been the rule in the Church'.[11] Doubts have already been expressed above as to how far this 'rule in the synagogue' was a reality for the majority of Jews from whom the first Christian converts came,[12] and how far the early Christians really did continue to attend the synagogue, and if therefore they were accustomed as Jews to offer their daily prayers individually, it is likely that this would in general have tended to continue to have been the practice after their conversion to Christianity, in spite of the fact that the Rabbinic quorum of ten males seems to have been dispensed with: 'where two or three are gathered in my name, there am I in the midst of them'.[13]

Even if Christians did cease to pray in common with other Jews at an early date, the pattern of their worship was undoubtedly very strongly influenced by the Jewish worship from which it sprang, and therefore we might expect *a priori* the first converts to have continued to adhere to the pattern of daily prayer which was observed by Jews of the time, and which we may suppose with some assurance had been followed by Jesus himself, and to have enriched and adapted this in the light of their new experience. As we have seen, however, that pattern was itself subject to some considerable variation. The injunction in *Didache* 8.3 to say the Lord's Prayer three times a day might be thought to suggest that the early Church kept to the three times of prayer observed in Rabbinic Judaism, provided that this document can be treated as evidence for the practices of first-century Jewish Christianity,[14] since the absence of any specific directions as to when these three prayers were to be offered does not mean, as some have supposed, that no particular hours were intended but rather that the times were traditional and unchanged, and so needed no explicit mention, while the innovation was the inclusion of the Lord's Prayer. There is, however, a reference in Acts 10.9 to Peter praying at the sixth hour, which may indicate that the Christians observed noon and not 3 p.m. as the middle of the three times of prayer. On the other hand, this may not have constituted one of the regular hours of prayer at all but merely be a further example of Luke's tendency to associate important moments in the life of Jesus and of the early Church with prayer.[15] Similar uncertainty exists about the references to prayer at night: the Jerusalem church prays at night for the imprisoned Paul (Acts 12.5,12), and Paul and Silas pray and sing hymns to God at midnight while in prison (Acts 16.25); but whether these are examples of a regular practice or are simply occasioned by the particular circumstances is difficult to decide. The *Didache* has no mention of night prayer but, on the other hand, New Testament references to prayer 'night and day' (Lk. 18.7; 1 Thess. 3.10; 1 Tim. 5.5) would seem to imply its existence, and since both these hours—noon and midnight—together with the morning and the evening were being observed as the accepted times of Christian daily prayer before the end of the second century,[16] it is not impossssible that the custom existed from the earliest days of the Church, especially in the light of our earlier claim that this pattern may already have been followed at Qumran and elsewhere in Judaism at this time.[17]

We may also note another contrast to Rabbinic Judaism in the New Testament: both kneeling and standing are evidenced as commonly adopted postures for Christian prayer.[18] Indeed there is only one explicit reference to standing (Mk. 11.25),[19] although other passages seem to imply this posture—but in relation to meals and healings and not the daily prayers (Mt. 14.19//Mk. 6.41//Lk. 9.16; Mk. 7.34; Jn. 11.41; 17.1), while Luke consistently indicates that kneeling is the norm for him (Acts 7.60; 9.40; 20.36; 21.5; cf. also Eph. 3.14; Phil. 2.10), and he even amends the account of Jesus' prayer in the Garden of Gethsemane so that it mentions kneeling (Mt. 26.39//Mk. 14.35//Lk. 22.41).[20] This may lend a little weight to our hypothesis about the times of prayer, since kneeling was also the posture described in Dan. 6.10, which it has been suggested above may refer to prayer at morning, noon, and evening.[21]

It is highly improbable that the Lord's Prayer constituted the sum total of the Christian daily prayer in the New Testament period or indeed that the *Didache* intended it to be so, as some scholars have concluded,[22] but much more likely that it was to be incorporated within the normal Jewish forms. This accounts for the abrupt ending of the prayer without a doxology in the gospel texts: it would never have been prayed in this bald form but as part of a longer act of prayer.[23] The giving of this prayer to his disciples by Jesus—if indeed it can still be considered as having originated from Jesus and not from the evangelists[24]— to be used as the group's prayer in the daily *Tefillah* is in accordance with the established practice of the time,[25] and the context in which it is set in Luke's gospel suggests that the disciples of John the Baptist had a similar group prayer. It stands more in the tradition of private Jewish prayers, which are usually brief, simple, often in Aramaic, and on the whole address God directly in the second person, than of formal synagogue prayer. The claim that the direct source of the first part of it is the *Kaddish*, an Aramaic prayer from the synagogue service,[26] rightly recognizes the similarity of content between the two, but overlooks the difference of form and function: prayers of the *Beth-Midrash* type, of which the *Kaddish* is one, are always in the third person, not the second, and their *Sitz im Leben* is in conjunction with the public exposition of Scripture, not the daily prayers as such.[27] In any case the content of the prayer embodies the heart of Jesus' own mission and teaching.

Jeremias has argued that Jesus' familiarity with the *Shema'* is indicated by his quotation of part of it (Mk. 12.29–30//Mt. 22.37//Lk. 10.26–7) but that its recitation had been abandoned by the Christian community by the time that the synoptic gospels were composed, because Deut. 6.5 is quoted by the three evangelists in versions which differ both from one another and from the Hebrew and Septuagint texts of the Old Testament, something which would not have been the case had it formed part of a liturgical form in current use.[28] This, however, is scarcely conclusive evidence: Jewish liturgical texts were much less rigidly fixed in the first century than Jeremias supposes,[29] and even the Lord's Prayer itself has been transmitted in divergent forms! On the other hand, there is certainly no trace of the use of the *Shema'* by Christians at a later date, and this is not surprising since it would hardly have served as an adequate creed for a community moving towards a Trinitarian belief. It has been suggested that Christians did continue to recite the Decalogue for some time after this in view of the prominence which it is given in the writings of the early Fathers,[30] but it should be noted that (a) there are doubts whether it was in any case still being used in Jewish worship at the time of the birth of the Church;[31] (b) there is no reference anywhere in early Christian literature to its liturgical, as distinct from catechetical, use, except for one possible allusion in Pliny's letter to Trajan (*c.* A.D. 110);[32] and (c) if it ever was used it has disappeared inexplicably leaving no trace at all upon later Christian worship.

No examples of a Christian *Tefillah* have survived from the first century, and this is not surprising since both Jewish and Christian liturgical forms were transmitted orally at this period. The collection of prayers in Book 7 of the *Apostolic Constitutions* is so Jewish in character that it is difficult to escape the conclusion that what we have here is a Christianized order of prayer derived from Hellenistic Judaism and committed to written form at an early stage with the result that it retains many primitive elements,[33] but it is impossible to determine to what extent it has been subsequently expanded and worked over from its original version. Incidentally, this series of prayers seems to confirm our earlier claim[34] that different forms of the daily prayers were still in circulation and the Rabbinic rules concerning the *berakah* were not yet universally accepted in the first century or whenever this particular text was taken over by the Christians. Nevertheless, although recovery of the precise forms of prayer used by the first-century Church may be out of the question, the New Testament does contain an abundance of liturgical fragments and allusions which enable us to glimpse something of their themes, content, style, and language. Some care, however, is required in handling this material. One must beware of what has been called 'a certain panliturgism', the tendency to find liturgical texts everywhere in the New Testament, often on the strength of no more than the use of the same phrase in a much later liturgy. On the other hand, one must not automatically draw the conclusion that the first time a phrase is found in a liturgical text is the first time that it was so used. Jeremias shows his awareness of this important canon of liturgical study in his comments on the use of the address 'Father' to God in prayer: 'in investigating a form of address used in prayer we must not limit ourselves to dating the prayers in which it occurs; we must also take into consideration the fact that forms of address in prayer stand in a liturgical tradition and can therefore be older than the particular prayer in which they appear'.[35] Unfortunately he neglects to apply this consideration more widely and so, for example, believes that the occurrence of the phrase 'Lord of heaven and earth' in a prayer attributed to Jesus (Mt. 11.25//Lk. 10.21) indicates Jesus' familiarity with at least the first of the Eighteen Benedictions because he can find no other extant example of this particular invocation of God from Palestinian Judaism apart from the one in that prayer.[36] The phrase is, however, simply a variant of a common liturgical form of the period.[37] Similarly, even the phrases in 1 Cor. 15.51 and 1 Clement 59 noted by Dugmore as resembling parts of the *Shemoneh 'Esreh* may not be derived from it but may well have constituted part of the stock vocabulary of prayer in the first century.[38]

Indeed, one ought not to expect to find close verbal similarity between New Testament passages and Jewish liturgical texts, as earlier generations of scholars tended to try to do:[39] nearly all these texts belong in the form in which we have them to a period after the composition of the New Testament, and in view of the fluidity of the form of the *Tefillah* in Judaism in the first century, it is not surprising that the Christian version developed in independence of the emerging *Shemoneh 'Esreh*. It is even misleading to think of the relationship between the two as that of parent and child, as some have done, and to explain differences between them as the deliberate rejection by the child of the stance and outlook of the parent. They should rather be envisaged as two children of the same family who grew up in increasing estangement from one another, and so exhibit a mixture of similarity and difference in their characters. Moreover, one must avoid making a rigid and artificial distinction between 'corporate liturgical worship' and 'individual private prayer' when considering the New Testament material. Even if the common practice was for the early Christians to say their daily prayers alone, that does not necessarily mean that they were regarded in theory as 'individual private prayers', or that they were not subject to any common form or liturgical pattern. Although no doubt there was considerable variation in content from individual to individual, there is no reason to suppose, for example, that what was said by St. Paul in his prayers bore no resemblance to the way in which other Christians were praying, or that such prayers were totally uninfluenced by the style of prayer adopted in communal worship, with the result that passages in the New Testament identified as 'liturgical' can give no clue at all to the forms of prayer used by Christians when praying alone. A considerable degree of interplay between the two areas, the corporate and the individual, must surely be expected, especially when one considers the close relationship which existed between the times of prayer and the synagogue services in Judaism, and also the strongly corporate character of early Christianity in which even 'private prayer' would be offered as part of the whole Body of Christ.

A survey of the prayer material in the New Testament reveals that petition and intercession feature prominently,[40] and that they are frequently found in conjunction with praise and the proclamation of the acts of God, which suggests, as we might expect, that the *berakah* style of prayer was continued by the early Christians. However, the passive opening formula, 'blessed be ...', is rare in the New Testament, occurring only four times, in the Benedictus (Lk. 1.68), where it is followed by a subordinate clause introduced by *hoti*, and at the beginning of three epistles (2 Cor. 1.3; Eph. 1.3; 1 Pet. 1.3), where it is followed by participles in each case. It is perhaps significant that on none of the four occasions is the blessing linked with petition or intercession but it leads only into extended praise, and so suggests a liturgical setting other than that of the daily prayers.[41] Furthermore, any use of the verb *eulogeo* to express a blessing directed towards God is rare in the New Testament: apart from blessings at meals, it occurs only three times, twice in Luke, in the infancy narrative (2.28) and in the final verse of the gospel (24.53), which together with the Benedictus may either be deliberate archaisms or reflect the terminology of an early Palestinian source,[42] and once in the very strongly Jewish Epistle of James (3.9). In addition to the four instances of the passive prayer form mentioned above, the adjective *eulogetos* occurs only four more times in the New Testament, in pious interjections or as a reverential circumlocution for God (Mk. 14.61; Rom. 1.25; 9.5; 2 Cor. 11.31), and the noun *eulogia* in the sense of a blessing directed towards God appears only in doxological formularies in the Book of Revelation (5.12–13; 7.12). In the Apostolic Fathers, except for Old Testament quotations, the *berakah* form occurs only twice (Ignatius, *Eph.* 1.3; *Barnabas* 6.10). Thus it would seem that as the Christian community developed this form tended to drop out of use.

In its place the Christians, like the Hellenistic Jews, seem to have preferred the active *hodayah* opening formula of prayer.[43] The more ancient rendering of this into Greek by means of the verb *homologeo* and its compounds is found only once in the New Testament, in one of the few prayers attributed to Jesus (Mt. 11.25–6//Lk. 10.21):

> I thank (*exomologoumai*) thee, Father, Lord of heaven and earth, that thou hast hidden these things from the wise and understanding and revealed them to babes; yea, Father, for such was thy gracious will.

On the other hand, there are references to it in Lk. 2.38 (*anthomologeito*, 'she gave thanks to God') and in Heb. 13.15: 'through him let us continually offer up a sacrifice of praise to God, that is, the fruit of lips that acknowledge (*homologounton*) his name'. We may notice a parallel with Qumran here in the idea of prayer as a sacrifice and the allusion to Hos. 14.2.[44] The *hodayah* form of prayer may also lie behind the references to the *homologia*, 'confession', in Hebrews (3.1; 4.14; 10.23) and at least some of the New Testament passages which speak of confessing Jesus as Lord, since the confession may originally have been not a credal statement as is generally believed but a form of prayer which attributed Christological titles to Jesus. The verb *exomologoumetha* also occurs in a concluding doxological formulary in 1 Clement 61.3. In accordance with the practice of Hellenistic Judaism, however, the normal verb used in the New Testament is *eucharisteo*, and prayers of this type are put into the mouth of Jesus in Jn. 11.41, into the mouths of the twenty-four elders in Rev. 11.17–18, and even into the mouth of a Pharisee in his daily prayer in the Temple in Lk. 18.11–12, all three instances no doubt reflecting the common liturgical forms of early Christianity. This type of prayer is found linked with petition and intercession in the Pauline epistles, nearly all of which open with a thanksgiving for some particular gift bestowed by God on the recipients of the letter and then move on to refer to the author's continuous prayer for them, this movement of thought almost certainly corresponding with the structure and content of his regular prayers themselves, as for example in Rom. 1.8–9:

> First, I thank (*eucharisteo*) my God through Jesus Christ for all of you, because your faith is proclaimed in all the world. For God is my witness, whom I serve with my spirit in the gospel of his Son, that without ceasing I mention you always in my prayers, asking that somehow by God's will I may now at least succeed in coming to you.[45]

The same combination of thanksgiving and petition is also mentioned in the body of his letters: 'in everything by prayer and supplication with thanksgiving let your requests be made known to God' (Phil. 4.6; see also Col. 4.2; 1 Thess. 5.16–18).

It is frequently suggested that the verbs *eucharisteo* and *eulogeo* are used as synonyms in the New Testament,[46] but this is not the case, and it ignores the quite distinct liturgical forms to which each of them refers. Not only, as we have seen, is the use of *eulogeo* and *eulogia* for a blessing directed towards God very rare in the New Testament and the preference of the authors is to employ *eucharisteo* and *eucharistia* instead,[47] but there is even a strong tendency to do this in the case of blessings at meals also. Thus, although *eulogeo* is used in the feeding of the five thousand in the synoptic gospels (Mk. 6.41//Mt. 14.19//Lk. 9.16), we may notice the substitution of *eucharisteo* both in the Johannine version (Jn. 6.11,23) and in the feeding of the four thousand (Mk. 8.6//Mt. 15.36). Similarly in the accounts of the Last Supper, although *eulogeo* is used for the bread and *eucharisteo* for the cup in Matthew and Mark, Luke and Paul use *eucharisteo* for both (Mk. 14.22–5//Mt. 26.26–7//Lk. 22.17–19; 1 Cor. 11.24). The retention of *eulogeo* in all these instances, as well as in Lk. 24.30, is most probably to be explained as fidelity to the language of the sources used rather than as representing the current terminology of the authors, for all other references to meal blessings in the New Testament use *eucharisteo* and *eucharistia* (Acts 27.35; Rom. 14.6; 1 Cor. 10.30; 1 Tim. 4.3–4), with only three exceptions, and these are unusual in form: (a) Mk. 8.7, where *eulogeo* is added to *eucharisteo* in the feeding of the four thousand, not absolutely as elsewhere but with what is eaten as the direct object of the verb, as is also the case in the Lucan version of the feeding of the five thousand mentioned above (9.16), which might seem to betray the evangelists' ignorance of the *berakah*;[48] (b) 1 Cor. 10.16, where Paul uses the traditional Jewish expression 'the cup of blessing' but follows it with the unusual construction 'which we bless', which in this case can hardly be attributed to ignorance of the liturgical form but suggests that a rather different sense of 'bless' with a material thing as the object was uppermost in his mind, a usage not found in Rabbinic Judaism but attested twice at Qumran (1 QS 6.5–6; 1 QSa 2.19), where too the use of the *hodayah* form seems to have been common, and once in the Old Testament (1 Sam. 9.13); (c) 1 Cor. 14.16f., where Paul begins with *eulogeo* but immediately goes on to employ *eucharisteo* and *eucharistia* as though these were more familiar to him. Furthermore, the prayers in *Didache* 9–10, whether belonging to a Eucharist or an *agape* or both, are all cast in the *hodayah* form, and this has had the result that the prayer in ch. 10, although obviously derived from the standard Jewish grace after meals, the *Birkat ha-Mazon*, deviates from it in order to conform to the *hodayah* model: the second paragraph of the grace, which was already in the *hodayah* form, has been moved to become the opening of the prayer, and the original opening, dropping the *berakah* introduction, now comes after it.[49] All of this points to the conclusion that as the Christian community developed it tended to adopt the *hodayah* form as its standard liturgical pattern not only for the daily prayers but also for the eucharistic prayer proper and to cease to use the *berakah* form as such. In so doing, it contrasts with Rabbinic Judaism which did precisely the reverse as it developed, selecting the *berakah* form as normative for synagogue prayer and suppressing all other variants.[50]

Alongside this, however, one other liturgical form can be found in first-century Christianity, also inherited from early Judaism,[51] prayer which begins directly with an *anamnesis* of God's mighty works, without any introductory formula, and may then proceed to petition and intercession. The clearest example of this in the New Testament is in Acts 4.24–30. Although this is obviously an artificial composition by the author, since the psalm quotation with its Christian interpretation (vv. 25–8) fits awkwardly into the prayer and is probably an adaptation of pre-existing exegetical material around which the rest has been woven,[52] there can be little doubt that the general style and language of the remainder of the prayer reflect the liturgical forms with which he was familiar. It has sometimes been supposed that he has drawn on the Septuagint version of Is. 37.16–20 as the model for this prayer, and so it owes more to that than to any contemporary Christian liturgical form, but in reality the verbal resemblance is very slight and any similarity can be better explained as conformity to a common tradition than as a specific borrowing.[53] The same basic liturgical structure is found in Acts 1.24–5, the prayer which Luke includes at the election of Matthias, though in this case the *anamnesis* section has been reduced to a mere adjectival phrase, and may possibly underlie 2 Tim. 4.17–18 and Eph. 3.14–21, unless the latter should be regarded as the continuation of the original opening *berakah* of the epistle,[54] and also the long liturgical passage in 1 Clement 59–61, where praise and petition alternate in what is in effect a series of such prayers and one which undoubtedly gives an accurate picture of the type of regular intercessory prayer used in the Roman church at this period and not, as is often supposed, of its eucharistic prayer proper, though J. M. Robinson has argued strongly that this would in actual use have been introduced by the *hodayah* formulary, mainly on the strength of a comparison with the *hodayah* prayer found in the later *Martyrdom of Polycarp* (14).[55]

Further information can be gleaned from our sources about the contents of the prayers. Although Jesus seems to have instructed his disciples to speak to God with the new and intimate address *abba*, and this word seems to have been retained at least for a little while in the prayer language of the early Greek-speaking churches alongside its Greek equivalent,[56] nevertheless the Christian invocation of God was apparently not restricted to the term 'Father' and we also find other, more formal, titles and appellatives, generally *kyrios*, 'Lord', the normal Greek rendering of the Hebrew circumlocution for the divine name, often accompanied or even replaced by some expression of his omnipotence and/or his creative activity. God's omnipotence had usually been expressed by the title *despotes*, 'Master', in the Septuagint, especially in those books which did not form part of the Hebrew canon, in Philo, and in Josephus (where it was the most common form of address in prayer), either on its own or as part of a phrase such as 'Master of all' (Job 5.8; Wisd. 6.7; 8.3), 'Master of heaven and earth' (Judith 9.12), 'Master of every age' (Josephus, *Ant.* 1.272),[57] while his creative activity was expressed in a relative clause, 'who made heaven and earth' (Gen. 14.19; 2 Chron. 2.12), or more commonly, 'who made heaven and earth and the sea and everything in them' (e.g. Exod. 20.11; Neh. 9.6; Ps. 146.6). The latter is continued in first-century Christianity (Acts 4.24; 14.15; Rev.. 10.6; 14.7), while the word *despotes*, though rare in the New Testament,[58] occurs frequently in 1 Clement, once in the *Didache* (10.3), and occasionally in other early writings, but is short-lived and appears much less often after the middle of the second century. Other terms are, however, used to express God's omnipotence, as for example, 'Lord (*kyrie*) of heaven and earth' (Mt. 11.25//Lk. 10.21), 'The God . . . being Lord (*kyrios hyparchon*) of heaven and earth' (Acts 17.24), and the very common Septuagint designation *pantokrator*, 'almighty' (Rev. 1.8; 4.8; 11.17; 15.3; 16.7,14; 19.15; 21.22; *Didache* 10.3; *Martyrdom of Polycarp* 14.1). There are also abundant examples of concluding doxological formulas, nearly all of which can be paralleled in early Judaism, together with the continued use of the synagogue response 'Amen', even in Greek-speaking communities.[59] The objects of intercession in the prayers are not just fellow-Christians, but the scope extends beyond the Church to its enemies and persecutors (Mt. 5.44//Lk. 6.26; see also Rom. 12.14), and indeed to all mankind, including 'kings and all who are in high positions' (1 Tim. 2.1–7).[60] The same is true of the Apostolic Fathers: 1 Clement 59–61 lists in detail those for whom intercession is made and includes an extensive prayer for earthly rulers; Ignatius of Antioch bids his readers to pray unceasingly for the rest of mankind 'for we can always hope that repentance may enable them to find their way to God' (*Ephes.* 10); and Polycarp makes petition for 'all those under heaven who shall one day come to believe', and instructs: 'pray for all God's people; pray too for our sovereign lords, and for all governors and rulers; for any who ill-use you or dislike you; and for the enemies of the Cross' (*Phil.* 12).

The most distinctive feature of Christian prayer, however,

was that it was made 'in the name of Jesus' (Jn. 14.13–14; 15.16; 16.23f.). This does not necessarily mean that this particular phrase was an invariable element in every Christian prayer—indeed there is no strong evidence that it was ever used as an actual liturgical formula in this way[61]—but only that some reference to Jesus would be included either in the opening address or in the *anamnesis* section of the prayer, as constituting the ground upon which petition might now be made, or in both, and it would be this which would fundamentally distinguish Christian prayer from that of other Jews. It has already been suggested above that this may well have been what was originally meant by 'confessing Jesus as Lord'. To judge from the examples which remain in the literature of the period, the early Christian *berakah* form seems to have adopted the stereotyped address, 'Blessed be the God and Father of our Lord Jesus Christ. . . .' (2 Cor. 1.3; Eph. 1.3; 1 Pet. 1.3; cf. 2 Cor. 11.31), while the *hodayah* form apparently had a corresponding opening ('We thank you, O God, the Father of our Lord Jesus Christ': see Col. 1.3, and also Eph. 1.17), or alternatively the thanks were offered 'through Jesus Christ' (see Rom. 1.8; 7.25; Col. 3.17; 1 Pet. 2.5), and the same expression was sometimes added to the praise in concluding doxologies also (see Rom. 16.27; 2 Cor. 1.20; 1 Pet. 4.11; Jude 25; *Didache* 9.4; 1 Clement 61.3). A variant ending is found in Eph. 3.21: 'to him be glory in the Church and in Christ Jesus . . .'. Thus praise and thanksgiving to God *through* Christ and *for* his mighty works in Christ are normal in the New Testament era, but direct praise and prayer addressed *to* Christ are exceptional, the only clear examples being the cry of Stephen at the moment of his martyrdom (Acts 7.59–60), the dialogues represented as taking place between Paul and Jesus in visions (Acts 22.8f., 19f.; and possibly 2 Cor. 12.8), the invocation *Maranatha*, 'Our Lord, come!' (1 Cor. 16.22; *Didache* 10.6; and in Greek in Rev. 22.20), the hymn to Christ in Rev. 5.9–13, and two other doxological ascriptions addressed to Christ instead of God the Father (2 Pet. 3.18; Rev. 1.6).[62] The common New Testament expression 'call upon (*epikaleisthai*) the name of Jesus' (Acts 2.21; 9.14,21; 22.16; Rom. 10.12f.; 1 Cor. 1.2) does not mean prayer addressed directly to him but rather the confession of his name in baptism and in prayer.[63] On the other hand, even if he was not normally addressed directly, blessings could be described as proceeding from both him and

God the Father, as in the liturgical salutation which stands at the head of nearly every Pauline letter: 'Grace to you and peace from God the Father and the Lord Jesus Christ'.[64]

A final characteristic of prayer in the New Testament which must be mentioned is its eschatological dimension: prayer is regarded as the proper mode of eschatological vigilance. Thus the verbs *gregoreo* and *agrypneo*, which are used of watching in relation to the *parousia*, are also found linked with prayer: 'watch and pray that you may not enter into trial (*peirasmon*)', says Jesus to his disciples in the Garden of Gethsemane (Mk. 14.38//Mt. 26.41; see also Mk. 13.33; Lk. 21.36), and the same advice is repeated in the epistles: 'persevere in the prayer, being watchful (*gregorountes*) in it with thanksgiving . . .' (Col. 4.2); 'praying at all times in the Spirit, and to that end being watchful (*agrypnountes*) in all perseverance and supplication for all the saints . . .' (Eph. 6.18); and in a slightly different way in Phil. 4.5–6 (see also 1 Pet. 4.7): 'the Lord is at hand. Have no anxiety about anything, but in everything by prayer and supplication with thanksgiving let your requests be made known to God'. Not only is the instruction to pray set in an eschatological context (see also the parable on prayer in Lk. 18.1–8), but the content of the prayers themselves, as we might expect, seems to have been of an eschatological nature: the reference to thanksgiving in two of the above quotations suggests that the prayers were to offer praise to God for what he had already done in inaugurating the new age, and certain other allusions to prayer in the New Testament imply that the object of the petition often had an eschatological purpose,[65] as indeed is the case in the Lord's Prayer, the model of all Christian prayer.[66]

It is frequently supposed that such 'watchful prayer' was intended to be habitual and entirely 'private', and had nothing to do with regular, fixed times of prayer, but we have already indicated that some caution is required in speaking of a definable class of private prayer at this period, and we may also note the occurrence in one of the above quotations of the phrase 'persevere in the prayer' (*te proseuche proskartereite*), which it has earlier been suggested referred to a fixed pattern of prayer,[67] and in another of the corresponding noun 'perseverance' (*proskarteresis*). To this may be added a number of other considerations. Firstly, as we have seen, the fixed times of prayer in Judaism, and especially among the Essenes, had eschatological significance.[68] Secondly, not only are there possible similarities between New Testament Christianity and Qumran, as we have already seen, in the times adopted for prayer, and perhaps a preference for the *hodayah* form of prayer, but evidence from the end of the second century indicates that, like the Essenes, Christians adopted an eastward orientation when praying, and that their times of prayer were linked to the expectation of the *parousia*, and there is no reason to suppose that these features were late additions to the tradition and do not date from the first century.[69] Indeed, it is even possible that the saying 'as the lightning comes from the east and shines as far as the west, so will be the coming of the Son of man' (Mt. 24.27) refers not just to the sudden, spectacular, and universal nature of the *parousia*, but also to the direction from which it was expected.[70] Thirdly, there are also strong resemblances in their eschatological thought, and especially in the use of the light/darkness motif and of the 'great light' and 'morning star' as messianic titles[71]—ideas which receive their most natural liturgical expression, as at Qumran, in regular prayer towards the east. Fourthly, it is the Lord's Prayer, the model of eschatological prayer, which Jesus gave to his disciples to use at the fixed hours of prayer and which *Didache* 8.3 orders to be recited three times a day.

Moreover is it too fanciful to suggest that the precise form in which the account of Jesus praying in the Garden of Gethsemane is cast in Mark, followed by Matthew, where Jesus comes three times and finds his disciples sleeping, having failed to obey his command to 'watch and pray', in contrast to his coming only once in Luke (Mk. 14.32–42//Mt. 26.36–46; cf. Lk. 22.40–6), reflects the same tradition of eschatologically orientated Christian prayer offered three times a day—and probably the Lord's Prayer in view of the occurrence of the word *abba* and of the expression of submission to God's will in Jesus' prayer, and also of the clause 'that you may not enter into *peirasmon*' in his advice to the disciples[72]—and was intended to encourage perseverance in this practice lest, like the disciples, Christians should be unaware when 'the hour has come' (Mk. 14.41) and unprepared to face the trial?[73] What is more certain is that the stress on the advent of the *parousia* 'as a thief in the night' (Mt. 24.43–4//Lk. 12.35–40; 1 Thess. 5.2f.; 2 Pet. 3.10; Rev. 3.3; 16.15) would have encouraged, if not initiated, the practice of regular prayer in the middle of the night. Indeed, D. G. Delling would understand the verb *agrypneo* in the New Testament as intended literally and not figuratively, as an injunction to stay awake and pray throughout the night,[74] and although that seems unlikely, the vigils, *agrypniai*, mentioned in 2 Cor. 6.5 & 11.27 do certainly appear to be definite periods of voluntary staying awake at night corresponding to the daytime fasts, but how frequently they were observed, and whether they involved any liturgical activity, or are to be distinguished from the practice of rising at night for prayer cannot be established. It is conceivable that an original practice of occasionally staying awake throughout the night in expectation of the *parousia*, or for a section of the night as at Qumran, eventually developed into the regular custom of rising briefly in the middle of each night for prayer found in the second century.

There are, therefore, good grounds for concluding that the primary purpose of the observance of fixed times of daily prayer in the early Christian community was none other than the liturgical expression of constant readiness for, and expectation of, the *parousia*. This supplies the answer to one possible objection to the existence of a 'liturgy of time' in the earliest days of the Church, that the Christians were so concerned with their eschatological hope that they could have no possible interest in this world and its time which was about to pass away. There is no need to resort to the idea of a 'liturgical dualism', as Alexander Schmemann does,[75] to explain the retention of the old liturgy of time alongside the new eschatological worship. For the observance of fixed times of prayer, far from being opposed to the expectation of an imminent *parousia*, was on the contrary the very expression of it: the realization that the new age had already begun was embodied in *eucharistia* for what God had done, constant readiness for the Kingdom of God was embodied in regular petition for its final consummation, and participation in the apostolic mission to the world was embodied in intercession for the salvation of all mankind: 'this is good, and it is acceptable in the sight of God our Saviour, who desires all men to be saved and to come to the knowledge of the truth' (1 Tim. 2.3–4).[76]

Although it has been suggested so far that as a general rule the daily prayers would tend to have been said individually, this is not to deny that there were very probably occasional assemblies not only for the community meals but also for the ministry of the word. As we have seen, the synagogue services on Monday, Thursday, and the Sabbath included a ministry of the word as well as the prayers, and since there is abundant evidence that the early Christians used these occasions for proclaiming the gospel, as Jesus himself had done, it is reasonable to suppose that they also held similar assemblies of their own. If the evidence of Acts can be granted any historical reliability, just such an assembly was held regularly in the Temple—and may even have been initiated by Jesus himself, who is said by the evangelists to have taught in the Temple (see Mk. 14.49; Lk. 19.47; 21.37–8; Jn. 10.23f.)—and also in the homes of the believers: 'and every day in the temple and at home they did not cease teaching and preaching Jesus as the Christ' (Acts 5.42). It is most unlikely, however, that these assemblies were everywhere the daily occurrence that Acts claims them to have been in Jerusalem, just as it is unlikely that the Eucharist was celebrated daily,[77] and more probable that they tended to be restricted to certain days of the week. Since evidence from a later period indicates that a service of the word was held on Wednesdays and Fridays and that these days were also designated for regular fasting,[78] we might suppose that at some stage the Christians transferred both their services of the word and also their practice of fasting to these days from the Mondays and Thursdays observed by Rabbinic Judaism for both these purposes, and indeed *Didache* 8.1 is usually interpreted as a prescription to do just that: 'your fasts should not coincide with those of the hypocrites. They fast on Mondays and Thursdays; you should fast on Wednesdays and Fridays'. On the other hand, Rordorf has claimed that this passage 'does not read like the introduction of a new fasting custom, but rather as the defence of a traditional Christian fasting custom against Judaistic tendencies. In *Didache* 8.1, therefore, we are not dealing with the birth certificate of the Christian practice of fasting'.[79]

Whether this is true or not, we still need to ask the question why the early Christians chose these particular days and not, for example, Tuesdays and Fridays. As A. Jaubert has remarked, it is not sufficient to say that they wanted to change and picked these days at random: 'ces vues superficielles ne tiennent aucun compte de la profondeur d'enracinement des usages liturgiques'.[80] We have already noted above that the community at Qumran followed a solar calendar in contrast to the lunar calendar of Rabbinic Judaism. One of the most striking features of this calendar is that, being composed of exactly 52 weeks (364 days), each date always fell on exactly the same day of the week in each year, and furthermore nearly all important dates fell on Sunday, Wednesday, and Friday.[81] Although there is no evidence that these days were marked each week at Qumran or elsewhere by special assemblies for worship,[82] it is not improbable that this calendar had some influence on the primitive Church,[83] especially in view of the other similarities we have observed between Qumran and early Christian liturgical practice. Since second-century evidence reveals the existence of a service of the word on Sundays, as well as Wednesdays and Fridays, though this time combined with the celebration of the Eucharist,[84] we may reasonably conjecture that in the first century, because Sunday already had importance for the early Christians as a result of the Easter event,[85] and probably Friday also because of the crucifixion, the prominence of all three days in the solar calendar with which they were familiar led them to choose those days of the week for services of the word, as their equivalent of the synagogue assemblies on Monday, Thursday, and the Sabbath. It would then be natural for fasting also to be transferred to the Wednesday and Friday.[86] Quite probably at least some Jewish Christian communities would in addition have continued to observe the Sabbath, but it seems unlikely that this day would have been given any special liturgical significance in predominantly Gentile churches.[87]

Oscar Cullmann has maintained that any such assemblies for the ministry of the word would invariably have been linked with the celebration of the Eucharist in New Testament times,[88] but this theory does not offer a satisfactory explanation as to why the Eucharist, held in the evening in the first century,[89] was transferred to the morning in the second century onwards, nor does it account for the existence of services of the word without a Eucharist in later centuries. An alternative hypothesis may therefore be advanced, that in the first century the service of the word was held in the early morning on the customary days, like its Jewish counterpart,[90] and when at the end of the century the Eucharist was detached from the meal, this brief ritual was transferred to become the climax of the Sunday morning service,[91] while the Wednesday and Friday assemblies continued as pure services of the word. This view is not affected by the fact that at the Eucharist at Troas (Acts 20.7f.) Paul addressed the gathering, since it is not being suggested that the eucharistic meal in the first century never included readings, hymns, or sermons—indeed we shall argue below that it regularly did so—but only that there existed alongside this relatively informal arrangement a more formal service of the word which was independent of the Eucharist. This service would have included not merely the reading of the Old Testament and its interpretation in the light of the gospel, but also in the course of time the reading of the New Testament writings as they were composed, and indeed attempts have been made to show that various New Testament books may have been composed for public reading against the background of the supposed Jewish lectionaries of the period, though none of these theories has so far won widespread acceptance.[92]

It is possible that the situation underlying Pliny's letter to Trajan, to which reference has already been made,[93] is of a Sunday morning assembly for the ministry of the word and prayer and an evening assembly for a eucharistic meal, before Eucharist and *agape* became separated. The relevant passage of the letter reads:

> They maintained, however, that this had been the whole of their fault or error, that they were accustomed on a fixed day (*stato die*) to assemble before daylight and recite by turns a hymn to Christ as god (*carmen Christo quasi deo dicere secum invicem*); and that they bound themselves by an oath (*sacramento obstringere*) not for any crime but not to commit theft, robbery, or adultery, not to break faith, and not to refuse a deposit when demanded. After this was done, their custom was to depart and to meet again to take food, but ordinary and harmless food; and even this they had ceased to do after my edict, by which in accordance with your commands I had forbidden the existence of clubs.[94]

Unfortunately alternative explanations of this passage have also been advanced—that the morning assembly was a celebration of the Eucharist and the evening meal simply an *agape*, that the morning assembly was for the purpose of baptism, or that the second gathering was not in the evening but was a Eucharist held later in the morning—and the meaning of various expressions within it has been disputed: it has been generally accepted that *stato die* refers to Sunday, but at least four different interpretations have been given to the phrase *carmen Christo quasi deo dicere secum invicem*—that it refers to an Old Testament psalm, to the baptismal interrogation, to antiphonal responses, or to a hymn addressed to Christ—and similarly the term *sacramentum* has been variously understood as alluding to the Eucharist, to the recitation of the Decalogue in the morning prayers, or to the baptismal vow.[95] We must also remember that the information is second-hand, and may therefore not be accurate. Thus it would seem unwise to base any hypothesis upon the evidence of this letter. In any case there is nothing in the text to indicate that the morning assembly included a ministry of the word and was not just a meeting for prayer.

Just as there is uncertainty whether or not the Psalter was used in synagogue worship in the first century, so also there is uncertainty what part it played in early Christianity. Although the New Testament indicates that the Book of Psalms was the best known and best loved of all the Old Testament Scriptures among the first Christians—it is cited more often than any other book[96]—that is not to say that it featured prominently in their daily prayers. The evidence suggests that the primary use of the Psalter was for preaching and apologetic: it was seen as a prophetic book, fulfilled in Christ (see for example Lk. 24.44: '... everything written about me in the law of Moses and the prophets and the psalms must be fulfilled'), each psalm being understood as speaking of Christ, or to Christ, or as Christ speaking, and this Christological interpretation was continued in the second and third centuries.[97] If the psalms had any liturgical use, therefore, it was probably as readings, a part of the ministry of the word rather than as an act of prayer or praise, and there are possibly vestigial traces of this in the practice of later centuries: in the third-century *Didascalia* the paschal vigil appears to include readings from 'the prophets, the gospel, and the psalms' (5.19.1), though this interpretation of the text has been challenged,[98] and at Jerusalem on Good Friday in the fourth century the readings are said to have been 'all about the things Jesus suffered: first the psalms on this subject ...'.[99] Following Anton Baumstark's rule that the solemn seasons tend to preserve ancient elements in the liturgy, these references may point to the original place of the Psalter in Christian worship. The heading of one of Augustine's sermons also describes the epistle, psalm, and gospel at the Eucharist as 'three readings' (*Serm.* 176).

There are also examples of this sort of use in the New Testament itself, but it is not at all clear whether the references here are to the canonical psalms or to the hymns and psalms which the early Christians, like their Jewish contemporaries, were composing. Thus with regard to 1 Cor. 14.26, 'when you come together, each one has a hymn (*psalmon*), a lesson, a revelation, a tongue or an interpretation', Cuming has suggested that what was intended 'was probably one of the Old Testament psalms, for it is hardly to be thought that every member of the Corinthian *ecclesia* produced a new piece of religious poetry every week',[100] but the passage does not necessarily mean that every single person produced one, and C. K. Barrett's interpretation, 'a fresh, perhaps spontaneous, composition',[101] is at least equally probable. 'Psalms, hymns, and spiritual songs' are mentioned in parallel passages in Colossians and Ephesians, but since it is improbable that any clear distinction was drawn between these three terms, reference to the canonical psalms may not have been intended:

Eph. 5.18–19	Col. 3.16
Do not get drunk with wine, for that is debauchery; but be filled with the Spirit, addressing one another in psalms and hymns and spiritual songs, singing and making melody to the Lord with all your heart. . . .	Let the word of Christ dwell in you richly, as you teach and admonish one another in all wisdom, and as you sing psalms and hymns and spiritual songs with thankfulness in your hearts to God.[102]

In any case, it is clear that what was envisaged in all three passages was not a formal service of the word as such, but a more informal communal context in which the compositions, together with other forms of inspired teaching according to 1 Cor. 14.26, were addressed by individuals to others for their encouragement and stimulation, what we might call a 'paracletic' in contrast to a 'didactic' or 'kerygmatic' ministry of the word. This may very likely be the occasion of the Christian community meals, especially as this practice continued to be a feature of the *agape* in the second and third centuries: Barrett argues that the service in 1 Cor. 14 is a Eucharist as in 1 Cor. 11, and Rordorf suggests that the warning in Eph. 5.18, 'do not get drunk with wine', implies that what follows is associated with a meal.[103] Jewish precedent for surrounding a meal with hymns and sermons is provided by the *haggadah* and *hallel*, the discourses at the *haburah* meals, and the customs of Therapeutae mentioned earlier.[104]

Thus the original use of the Psalter may possibly have been in the formal services of the word and alongside non-canonical compositions at the *agape*, but there is nothing to suggest that it found a place in the daily hours of prayer themselves, and in view of the extremely small number of psalms which are found in the cathedral office in the fourth century, we may conjecture that at the most individual verses from psalms were incorporated into Christian hymns and prayers and given a Christian interpretation, especially in the light of the way in which passages from the Psalter are quoted and alluded to in the New Testament, and in particular the use of Ps. 1.1–2 in Acts 4.25–6. For although this particular prayer is an artificial composition, as has already been said, it is very probable that the inclusion of psalm verses within it reflects customary practice.

On the other hand, we cannot even be certain that Christian hymns were themselves included in the daily prayers as well as in the community meals. The phrase in Pliny's letter, *carmen Christo quasi deo*, is again in a communal context, though not this time that of a meal, but in any case, as we have seen, it is obscure and its meaning much disputed. Jas. 5.13 ('Is anyone cheerful? Let him sing praise, *psalleto*') is too vague to be of any assistance, as is the description of Paul and Silas 'praying and singing hymns (*hymnoun*)' at midnight (Acts 16.25). If one could be certain that this referred to the regular practice of night prayer, then at least it would be clear that some form of psalm or hymn was generally used on such occasions. However, it seems unlikely that there were any fixed forms which were used for long periods and more probable that if any hymns were included in the daily prayers they were of a relatively ephemeral nature. One possible exception is the Sanctus which may originally have been a feature not of the eucharistic prayer itself, where it is, in the words of Gregory Dix, 'a sort of liturgical cuckoo',[105] but rather of the morning prayers, at least on occasions if not daily, and from there was eventually moved into the Eucharist after the two services were combined, as seems also to have been the case with the Lord's Prayer.[106] In addition to the Lucan canticles and the songs in the Book of

Revelation, which though perhaps not actual forms used in worship are no doubt very similar to the type of composition current at the time, various other passages in the New Testament have been claimed as Christian hymns, but it is extremely difficult to establish objective criteria to distinguish hymns proper from mere poetic passages, or even hymns from prayers, since both might use the *hodayah* structure and involve petition, and the latter might be characterized by an extensive narrative of praise and thanksgiving like the former.[107]

3. *The Second and Third Centuries*

The theory advanced by Professor Dugmore,[1] that the primary stratum of the Christian daily office was morning and evening prayer taken over from the Jewish synagogue, to which the custom of prayer at the third, sixth, and ninth hours was eventually added, has been accepted almost without challenge. Yet not only does it not explain why the early Christians, so conservative in their observance of Jewish liturgical practice in almost every other respect, should have been so selective in this case as to have retained only two of the three hours of prayer observed by the Jews, but it also does not even do justice to the evidence for the practice of Christian prayer in the second and third centuries. Those who have espoused this view have tended to pass rapidly over the writings of Clement of Alexandria and Origen, seeing in them only confirmation of their hypothesis, and have concentrated on the rather fuller information provided by writers in the West at this period. The evidence of the East, however, is crucial for the recovery of the earliest pattern of Christian daily prayer, and so it is to there that we must first of all turn.

The devout Christian of the second and third centuries was expected to take seriously the apostolic injunction to 'pray without ceasing' (1 Thess. 5.17), which is quoted by many authors from Ignatius of Antioch onwards, and this idea is extensively developed by Clement of Alexandria (*c.* 150–*c.* 215), who paints a picture of the true Christian ('the Gnostic') constantly engaged in singing the praise of God at every moment of his life:

> we are commanded to reverence and to honour the same one, being persuaded that he is Word, Saviour, and Leader, and through him the Father, not on special days, as some others, but doing this continually in our whole life, and in every way. . . . Whence not in a specified place, or selected temple, nor on certain festivals and appointed days, but during his whole life, the Gnostic

in every place, even if he happens to be alone by himself, and wherever he has any of those who share the same faith, honours God, that is, acknowledges his gratitude for the knowledge of the way to live. . . . Holding festival, then, in our whole life, persuaded that God is altogether on every side present, we cultivate our fields, praising; we sail the sea, hymning. . . .[2]

At the same time, however, Clement speaks of specific moments in the day which are set aside for prayer, not just morning and evening to which scholars have drawn attention,[3] but others as well: 'He all day and night, speaking and doing the Lord's commands, rejoices exceedingly, not only on rising in the morning and at noon, but also when walking about, when asleep, when dressing and undressing . . .'.[4] Here obviously Clement is expecting the 'perfect Christian' to go beyond the accepted norms for prayer, but in so doing he indicates that both morning and noon were usual times of prayer for all Christians. Elsewhere he mentions mealtimes and during the night, along with the evening: 'His whole life is a holy festival. His sacrifices are prayers and praises and reading of the Scriptures before meals, and psalms and hymns during meals and before bed, and prayers also again during the night. Through these he unites himself to the divine choir, engaged by continual recollection in everlasting contemplation'.[5] Thus the pattern of Christian prayer at Alexandria appears to have been prayer at meals, prayer three times a day—morning, noon, and evening—and prayer again during the night, a pattern which we have already seen to have possible parallels in first-century Judaism and which may therefore have been practised continually from the earliest days of the Church.[6]

Confirmation of the existence of this pattern of prayer is provided by Origen (c. 185–c. 254). Like Clement, he insists that a Christian should make the whole of his life one long prayer, but he also counsels the observance of certain definite times:

The man who links together his prayer with deeds of duty and fitting actions with his prayer is the man who prays without ceasing, for the deeds of virtue or the commandments he has fulfilled are taken up as a part of his prayer. For only thus can we accept the saying 'Pray without ceasing' as being possible, if we can say that the whole life of the saint is one great integrated prayer. Of such prayer, part is what is usually called 'prayer', and ought not to be performed less than three times each day. This is clear from the practice of Daniel who, when great danger threatened him, prayed three times a day. And Peter, going up to the housetop to pray about the sixth hour, when also he saw the vessel let down from heaven, let down by four corners, gives an example of the middle of the three times of prayer spoken of by David before him: 'In the morning you shall hear my prayer; in the morning I will stand beside you, and will look to you'. The last of the three is indicated in the words, 'the lifting up of my hands as an evening sacrifice'. But not even the time of night shall we rightly pass without such prayer, for David says, 'At midnight I rose to give thanks to you because of your righteous judgements', and Paul, as related in the Acts of the Apostles, at midnight together with Silas at Philippi prayed and sang hymns unto God, so that the prisoners also heard them.[7]

Dugmore has suggested that, because the middle of these three times is explicitly said to be the sixth hour, the other two are probably the third and the ninth,[8] and this assumption has also been made more recently by I.-H. Dalmais,[9] followed by J. H. Walker,[10] both of whom assert that it was the Lord's Prayer which was to be said at these three times, without any real evidence other than the belief that the three times of prayer mentioned in *Didache* 8.3 were also intended to be at the third, sixth, and ninth hours. E. G. Jay has challenged this view and claimed that the three times of prayer advocated by Origen are night, noon, and evening.[11] However, although he would seem to be correct in identifying the third time as the evening and not 3 p.m., because of Origen's quotation of the psalm verse 'the lifting up of my hands as an evening sacrifice' as indicating this third time of prayer, the subsequent reference to night prayer is almost certainly not to be taken as one of the three times already mentioned but as an addition to them, especially in the light of the evidence provided by Clement, so that Origen is here commending a pattern of prayer three times during the day—morning, noon, and evening—together with a further occasion of prayer during the night. This night prayer enjoyed equal status with the times of prayer during the day, for Origen elsewhere speaks of Christians using 'the appointed prayers continually and in the proper way night and day'.[12]

Clement is also aware of the existence of other fixed times of prayer, the third and the ninth hours, which some apparently had added to the daily cycle, but he seems to imply that they were not widely observed in his region, which the silence of

Origen about them would appear to confirm:

> if some assign fixed hours for prayer—as, for example, the third
> and sixth and ninth—yet the Gnostic prays throughout his whole
> life, endeavouring by prayer to have fellowship with God.
> And, briefly, having arrived there, he leaves behind him all that is
> of no service, as having now received the perfection of one who acts
> by love. But the distribution of the hours into a threefold division,
> honoured with as many prayers, those are acquainted with who
> know the blessed triad of the holy abodes.[13]

Even at the end of the fourth century in Jerusalem these two
hours did not have the same status as the others in the daily
cycle. As we shall see,[14] the ninth hour was omitted on
Wednesdays and Fridays, when it gave way to a service of the
word, and probably also on Sundays, while the third hour was
publicly celebrated only during Lent, which suggests that it had
been adopted here at a later date than the ninth hour.

In the West, on the other hand, all these times of prayer—
morning, third, sixth, and ninth hours, evening, and night—
were being observed by the end of the second century. In Africa
Tertullian (c. 160–c. 220) stated that, 'concerning times of
prayer nothing at all has been prescribed, except of course to
pray at every time and place', but went on to counsel:

> the observance from extraneous sources of certain hours also will
> not be superfluous. I speak of those common ones which mark the
> intervals of the day, the third, sixth, and ninth, which can be found
> in the Scriptures in established use. The Holy Spirit was first
> poured out upon the assembled disciples at the third hour. On the
> day on which Peter experienced the vision of everything common
> in that vessel, it was at the sixth hour that he had gone to the
> housetop to pray. He also, along with John, was going up to the
> Temple at the ninth hour when he restored the paralytic man to
> wholeness. Although these are simple statements, without the
> precept of any observance, yet let it be good enough to establish
> some presumption which may both enforce a command to pray
> and as if by a law drag us from business for a while for such duty,
> so that (as we read also was observed by Daniel, evidently from
> Israel's discipline) we may worship not less than at least three times
> a day, being the debtors of three, the Father, the Son, and the Holy
> Spirit, in addition of course to our obligatory prayers which
> without any command are due at the coming in of daylight and
> night.[15]

The expression 'obligatory prayers' (*legitimis orationibus*) has led many scholars to the conclusion that morning and evening were the only obligatory times of prayer and the other hours were merely 'recommended'.[16] It must, however, be seen in the context of the whole passage. Tertullian has begun by saying that he can find no specific times of prayer prescribed in the New Testament, but the third, sixth, and ninth hours are at least mentioned there, and he believes that this is sufficient to justify the obligation (*quasi lege*, 'as if by a law') to keep those. Since he can bring forward no such examples for the morning and evening times, he has to resort to calling them 'obligatory prayers which are due without any command'. Thus he clearly expects all devout Christians to pray at least five times in the day—norning, evening, and at the three hours—and he also refers elsewhere to prayer at night, raising objection to mixed marriages on the grounds that a Christian wife will not be able to escape her pagan husband's notice when she rises by night to pray.[17]

Tertullian also indicates that mealtimes were accompanied by prayer: 'it is fitting for the faithful not to take food or go to the bath without first interposing a prayer: for the refreshment and food of the spirit ought to have priority over that of the flesh, because heavenly things have priority over earthly'.[18] He refers to the custom of making the sign of the cross before meals,[19] and also describes the *agape*:

> They do not recline before prayer to God is first tasted. Only as much is eaten as satisfies the hungry; only as much is drunk as is fitting for the chaste. They are satisfied as those who remember that even during the night they have to worship God; they talk as those who know that the Lord hears. After washing the hands, and the lighting of lamps, each is invited to stand in the middle and sing a hymn to God, from the holy Scriptures or of his own composition as he is able. This proves how little is drunk. Similarly prayer ends the feast.[20]

As might be expected, this meal seems to bear the marks of Jewish influence. The ablutions and the bringing in of the lamps resemble Jewish customs[21] (and indeed Tertullian himself says that the lamp ceremony is derived from Judaism[22]), although the order is different: they would have preceded the meal in Jewish practice. The description of the singing is also reminiscent of 1 Cor. 14.26 and of Philo's account of the festal meals of the Therapeutae.[23]

The same pattern of prayer is attested by Cyprian (d. 258):

in the offering of prayer we find that the three children with Daniel, being strong in faith and victors even in captivity, observed the third, sixth, and ninth hours, in as it were a symbol of the Trinity which in these last times should be revealed. For the progress of the first hour to the third shows the perfected number of the Trinity; likewise from the fourth to the sixth declares another Trinity; and when the period from the seventh to the ninth is completed, the perfect Trinity is numbered through a triad of hours each. These spaces of hours were long ago fixed upon by the worshippers of God, who observed them as the appointed and lawful times for prayer. Afterevents have made it manifest that of old these were types, inasmuch as righteous men thus formerly prayed. For at the third hour the Holy Spirit descended upon the disciples and fulfilled the gracious promise of the Lord. Likewise at the sixth hour Peter, going up to the housetop, was instructed as well by the sign as by the voice of God bidding him admit all to the grace of salvation, when he was doubtful previously whether Gentiles ought to be cleansed. And from the sixth to the ninth hour the Lord, being crucified, washed away our sins in his own blood; and that he might redeem and quicken us he then perfected his victory by his passion. But for us, dearly beloved brethren, in addition to the hours anciently observed, both the times and the rules of prayer have now increased in number. For we must pray also in the morning, in order that the resurrection of the Lord may be celebrated by morning prayer. . . . Likewise at sunset and the decline of day we must needs pray again. For since Christ is the true Sun and true Day, when we pray at the decline of the world's sun and day and entreat that the light may again come upon us, we are asking for the advent of Christ, which will bestow upon us the grace of eternal light. . . . But if in the Holy Scriptures Christ is the true Sun and true Day, there is no hour excepted when Christians ought not constantly and continually to worship God; so that we who are in Christ—that is, in the true Sun and Day—may all day long be instant in entreaties and prayers; and when by the world's law the revolving night, recurring in its alternate changes, succeeds, there can be no loss to us from its nocturnal shades, because to the sons of light it is day even in the night. For when can he be without light who has the Light in his heart? Or when is the sun and the day not his to whom Christ is both Sun and Day? Let us then who are ever in Christ—that is, in the Light—cease not from prayer even by night. Thus the widow Anna without ceasing persevered with constant prayer and watching in being well-pleasing to God; as it is written in the gospel: she departed not from the temple, serving with fasting and prayers night and day.[24]

His claim that the observance of the third, sixth, and ninth hours as times of prayer is older than that of the morning and evening is clearly not historically reliable,[25] as it is obviously based entirely upon his mistaken identification of the times of prayer observed by Daniel with the third, sixth, and ninth hours. Cyprian also refers briefly to the *agape*, mentioning the common cup[26] and the singing of psalms: 'nor let even mealtimes be without heavenly grace. Let the temperate meal resound with psalms; and as your memory is tenacious and your voice musical, undertake this duty, as is your custom'.[27]

The evidence of the *Apostolic Tradition* of Hippolytus (*c.* 215) is rather more problematic. It is generally agreed that at one time there were two versions of this document in circulation, the shorter lacking chs. 39–41,[28] and so having only a brief reference to morning prayer and daily instruction in 35, which is duplicated and expanded in 41 in the longer version, together with reference to prayer at other times of the day. Unless both versions are held to have stemmed from the pen of Hippolytus—and it is hard to conceive of him writing two such very different endings[29]—one is forced to ask which of them is the original. As a general rule one would expect a shorter liturgical text to be the earlier and a longer version to be an expansion. If this is true in this case, then we learn very little about the times of daily prayer in the period of Hippolytus from it. On the other hand, most of the practices mentioned in the longer text are otherwise attested as having existed in the second and third centuries, so that it is possible that this could have been written in Hippolytus' day, though that is not to say that it has not undergone some degree of subsequent expansion and elaboration. Attempts to reconstruct the original text here are made more difficult by the fact that there is a gap in the manuscript of the Latin version at this point and so part of this section is missing from it.

After referring to morning prayer and daily instruction (for which see below, p. 69), ch. 41 in the longer version continues as follows:

And if you are at home, pray at the third hour and bless God. But if you are somewhere else at that moment, pray to God in your heart. For at that hour Christ was nailed to the tree. For this reason also in the Old (Testament) the Law prescribed that the shewbread should be offered continually as a type of the body and blood of

Christ; and the slaughter of the lamb without reason is this type of the perfect lamb. For Christ is the shepherd, and also the bread which came down from heaven.

Pray likewise at the time of the sixth hour. For when Christ was nailed to the wood of the cross, the day was divided, and darkness fell. And so at that hour let them pray a powerful prayer, imitating the voice of him who prayed and made all creation dark for the unbelieving Jews.

And at the ninth hour let them pray also a great prayer and a great blessing, to know the way in which the soul of the righteous blesses God who does not lie, who remembered his saints and sent his word to give them light. For at that hour Christ was pierced in his side and poured out water and blood; giving light to the rest of the time of the day, he brought it to evening. Then, in beginning to sleep and making the beginning of another day, he fulfilled the type of the resurrection.

Pray before your body rests on the bed. Rise about midnight, wash your hands with water, and pray. If your wife is present also, pray both together; if she is not yet among the faithful, go apart into another room and pray, and go back to bed again. Do not be lazy about praying. He who is bound in the marriage-bond is not defiled.

Those who have washed have no need to wash again, for they are clean. By signing yourself with moist breath and catching your spittle in your hand, your body is sanctified down to your feet. For when (prayer) is offered with a believing heart as though from the font, the gift of the Spirit and the sprinkling of baptism sanctify him who believes. Therefore it is necessary to pray at this hour.

For the elders who gave us the tradition taught us that at that hour all creation is still for a moment, to praise the Lord; stars, trees, waters stop for an instant, and all the host of angels (which) ministers to him praises God with the souls of the righteous in this hour. That is why believers should take good care to pray at this hour.

Bearing witness to this, the Lord says thus, 'Lo, about midnight a shout was made of men saying, Lo, the bridegroom comes; rise to meet him'. And he goes on, saying, 'Watch therefore, for you know not at what hour he comes'.

And likewise rise about cockcrow, and pray. For at that hour, as the cock crew, the children of Israel denied Christ, whom we know by faith, our eyes looking towards that day in the hope of eternal light at the resurrection of the dead.

Although all the other hours of prayer are spoken of by other authors at this period (as we have seen), prayer at cockcrow is unknown elsewhere at such an early date, and when it does make its first appearance in some fourth-century monastic rules, it is usually as an alternative to midnight prayer and not as an additional time as it is here.[30] Therefore at least this element is very probably a later addition to the document, for it seems unlikely that this hour of prayer constituted a part of the regular daily pattern at Rome at the beginning of the third century but failed to be adopted elsewhere for such a long time. Similarly the explanations which are given here for the adoption of the third and sixth hours as times of prayer are not the ones usually advanced in the literature of this period: Tertullian and Cyprian both think of the giving of the Holy Spirit as the scriptural precedent for the practice of prayer at the third hour, and not of the Marcan timing of the crucifixion nor of the offering of the shewbread, and of the prayer of Peter on the housetop for the sixth hour, although Cyprian does mention the passion in relation to prayer at the ninth hour; and Tertullian associates it with the observance of the ninth hour on station days,[31] but not directly with the daily times of prayer, referring instead to Peter and John going up to the Temple at the ninth hour in Acts 3.1. On the other hand, the justification for prayer at midnight has been thought to contain certain primitive indications, although this is the only document of the period to specify 'midnight' and not just 'during the night' for prayer: Jean Daniélou has argued that the expression 'the elders who gave us the tradition' refers back to Jewish Christianity,[32] and Henry Chadwick has concluded from a comparison with the Testament of Adam that 'behind the tradition of the elders preserved by the Apostolic Tradition there probably lies an originally Jewish tradition'.[33]

The document also deals with the *agape*, although here again there are problems. Chs. 24 and 25 occur in full only in the Ethiopic version and are placed in that manuscript after ch. 29, an order which Gregory Dix accepted in his edition of the text,[34] but as there was no place for them in the Latin version at this point, he was forced to conclude that this section was an eastern interpolation into the text, though 'not necessarily much, if at all, later in date than Hippolytus' genuine work'.[35] Subsequently, however, it has been argued both by Botte[36] and by Chadwick[37] that the passage is genuine, but displaced by the Ethiopic version from an original position after ch. 23, where there is a lacuna in the Latin manuscript. The *agape* is described in chs. 25 and 26:

25. When the bishop is present, and evening has come, a deacon brings in a lamp; and standing in the midst of all the faithful who are present, (the bishop) shall give thanks. First he shall say this greeting:

> The Lord be with you.

And the people shall say:

> With your spirit.
>
> Let us give thanks to the Lord.

And they shall say:

> It is fitting and right: greatness and exaltation with glory are his due.

And he does not say 'Up with your hearts', because that is said (only) at the offering. And he shall pray thus, saying:

> We give you thanks, Lord, through your Son Jesus Christ our Lord, through whom you have shone upon us and revealed to us the inextinguishable light. So when we have completed the length of the day and have come to the beginning of the night, and have satisfied ourselves with the light of day which you created for our satisfying; and since now through your grace we do not lack the light of evening, we praise and glorify you through your Son Jesus Christ our Lord, through whom be glory and power and honour to you with the holy Spirit, both now and always and to the ages of ages. Amen.

And all shall say:

> Amen.

They shall rise, then, after supper and pray; and the boys and the virgins shall say psalms.

And then the deacon, when he receives the mixed cup of the offering, shall say a psalm from those in which 'Alleluia' is written, and then, if the priest so directs, again from the same psalms. And after the bishop has offered the cup, he shall say the whole of a psalm which applies to the cup, with 'Alleluia', all joining in. When they recite psalms, all shall say, 'Alleluia', which means, 'We praise him who is God; glory and praise to him who created every age through his word alone'. And when the psalm is finished, he shall give thanks over the cup and distribute the fragments to all the faithful.

26. And when they have supper, the faithful who are present shall take from the bishop's hand a little bit of bread before they break their own bread; because it is blessed bread and not the eucharist, that is, the body of the Lord. It is fitting that all, before they drink, should take a cup and give thanks over it, and so eat and drink in purity.

It is possible that the change in order was made by the tradition underlying the Ethiopic version so that the sequence of the *agape* might harmonize with that followed in the community through which the text was transmitted, for as we have seen from Tertullian[38] at least in North Africa if not elsewhere the lighting of the lamp and the singing of psalms came after the meal itself, and not before it, as may have been originally intended here. It is also possible that in this process the details of the description of the lighting of the lamp and the psalm-singing have been altered and expanded, the most obvious point of suspicion being the inclusion of the words, 'they shall rise then after supper and pray',[39] although the whole of what follows exhibits such confusion that it is difficult to be sure what the original said. However, the main point is fairly clear: the psalms were recited by one person while the rest joined in the Alleluia refrain, a custom also mentioned by Tertullian, as we shall see.[40] One may also suspect that the statement at the end, that each person gives thanks over his own cup, has been added to the text to harmonize with the current practice known to the redactor, since it contradicts the thanksgiving over the common cup described earlier, and this suspicion is encouraged by the clear difference in the grammatical construction of the Latin version, which reappears at this point: '. . . you who are present, and so feast. But to the catechumens shall be given exorcized bread, and each shall offer a cup'. The direction that the catechumens are each to offer a cup would have much greater point if the faithful shared in the common cup denied to them.

We have already suggested that the first pattern of daily prayer which is encountered at this period—that at morning, noon, evening, and night—probably goes back to the beginnings of the Church and may have its roots in an ancient Jewish tradition of praying at the cardinal points of the day which was especially preserved among the Essenes. We may also note that, as with the Essenes, these times of prayer appear to have had a strong eschatological dimension. Clement of Alexandria indicates that the practice of night prayer was linked with the expectation of the *parousia*:

We must therefore sleep so as to be easily awaked. For it is said, 'Let your loins be girt about, and your lamps burning; and ye yourselves like to men that watch for their lord, that when he returns from the marriage and comes and knocks, they may straightway open to him. Blessed are those servants whom the

Lord, when he cometh, shall find watching'. For there is no use of a sleeping man, as there is not of a dead man. Wherefore we ought often to rise by night and bless God. For blessed are they who watch for him, and so make themselves like the angels, whom we call 'watchers'.[41]

Since 'watchers' is one of the characteristic names for the angels in Jewish Christianity, and since the section of the *Apostolic Tradition* referring to midnight prayer, which similarly mentions angels and the return of the Bridegroom, is also thought to derived from the primitive Jewish Christian community, the eschatological note would appear to belong to the inception of the custom of night prayer rather than to be a *post factum* interpretation by later authors.[42] The passage from Cyprian quoted above indicates that this *parousia*-motif extended also to the daytime prayers: 'Likewise at sunset and the decline of day we must needs pray again. For since Christ is the true Sun and true Day, when we pray at the decline of the world's sun and day and entreat that light may again come upon us, we are asking for the advent of Christ, which will bestow upon us the grace of eternal light'.[43] The language used here shows close similarities not only with New Testament eschatology but also with that of the Therapeutae and of the Essenes in relation to their daily prayers.[44]

A further link with the Essenes appears in the eastward orientation for prayer practised by the early Christians. The custom is attested by Tertullian,[45] and by Clement of Alexandria,[46] and a passage in Origen's treatise on prayer shows that it applied to individual as well as communal prayer:

Now also we must say a few things about the region towards which we must look to pray. There being four regions, towards north and south, towards sunsetting and sunrising, who would not at once agree that the region towards the sunrising clearly indicates that we ought to make our prayers facing in that direction, in symbolic manner—as though the soul beheld the rising of the true light? But, since the door of the house may face in any direction, if someone wishes to offer his intercessions rather in the direction that the house opens, saying that the view of heaven has something more inviting about it than sight of the wall, if the doors of the house happen not to look towards the sunrising, we must say to him that since it is by arrangement that the buildings of men open towards this or that region, while it is by nature that the east is preferred before the other regions, we must put that which is by nature before that which is by arrangement. Moreover, according to this argument, why should a man who wishes to pray in an open space pray towards the east rather than towards the west? But if the east is reasonably to be preferred there, why is this not to be done everywhere?[47]

Origen also provides evidence of the existence of oratories in private houses at this period,[48] and other sources tell of the custom of marking the east wall of them with a cross in order to indicate the direction of prayer, following the similar Jewish custom of marking the direction of Jerusalem on the synagogue wall.[49] The cross too was an eschatological symbol in Jewish Christianity: the appearance of the glorious cross was to precede the *parousia*, and this idea may even have been a transformation of the messianic star of Essene thought.[50]

There are, therefore, good grounds for assigning an apostolic origin to this primary pattern of daily prayer. What, however, of the secondary times of prayer—the third and ninth hours? All authors, both ancient and modern, have been misled in grouping together the sixth hour with the third and ninth, and in seeking a common origin for all three. Nevertheless, since it is at least possible that their suggestions may still hold good for two of these times, they warrant some examination. Clement in the east, as we have seen, gives no clue as to their origin and merely offers an allegorical interpretation of them: 'the distribution of the hours into a threefold division, honoured with as many prayers, those are acquainted with who know the blessed triad of the holy abodes'.[51] This is not, as is sometimes supposed, a reference to the Trinity but, as Origen makes clear elsewhere, to the promised hundredfold, sixtyfold, and thirtyfold yield of Mt. 13.8.[52] On the other hand, the western authors have abundant reasons to offer for their adoption. Tertullian, in the passage quoted above,[53] first of all remarks that these hours are 'the common ones which mark the intervals of the day', and in his treatise on fasting he expands on this: they are 'more significant in human affairs—they divide the day, they mark out the times for business, they are publicly announced'.[54] From this Dugmore concluded that it was probably this secular division of the day which made it natural for the Christians to fix upon these particular times for prayer,[55] but J. H. Walker has asserted that the public announcement of these hours was not a widespread custom throughout the Roman empire at this time, and therefore this is unlikely to have constituted the reason for their adoption as Christian hours of prayer.[56] Tertullian secondly refers to what he supposes were Scriptural precedents for the practice: Daniel prayed three times a day; the Spirit was given to the disciples at the third hour; Peter went up to the housetop to pray at the sixth hour; and Peter and John went into the Temple to pray at the ninth hour. The same precedents, with the exception of the last, are also cited by Cyprian.[57] We have already established that these biblical passages, with the possible exception of Peter's prayer at the sixth hour, do not in reality furnish evidence for the practice of this pattern of prayer—Daniel's three times were quite different ones, the Spirit was given to the apostles assembled *before* the third hour, and Acts 3.1 does not say that Peter and John went regularly to the Temple to pray but only that they were going there 'at the hour of prayer'—but we cannot immediately rule out the possibility that it was the subsequent interpretation of these texts as indicating that such a pattern had existed in New Testament times which gave rise to it in the early Church. Both Cyprian and Tertullian then go on to associate these hours with the Trinity, but like Clement's allegorical interpretation this is unlikely to have constituted the real ground for their original adoption.

Walker's own solution to this question is that they were intended as a memorial of the passion.[58] As we have seen above, the *Apostolic Tradition* associates all three hours with the passion;[59] Cyprian links the period from the sixth to the ninth hour with the passion;[60] and Tertullian mentions the death of Christ in association with the ninth hour, but only with reference to the station days and not, as Walker supposes, directly in relation to the daily prayers.[61] Walker maintains that Hippolytus in the *Apostolic Tradition* 'clearly used St. Mark's account of the passion not only in the wording of the incidents but also because Mark is the sole evangelist to mention the third hour in the crucifixion narrative', and suggests that the original text of the document may have followed the Marcan narrative at the ninth hour and given as the reason for prayer 'because in this hour Jesus prayed and gave up his spirit into the hands of his Father', a reading preserved in the *Canons of Hippolytus*, and not the reference to the piercing of Christ's side. She concludes that these three hours of prayer were at first a local Roman custom, intended to recall the events of the passion, and were already being observed when Mark wrote his gospel in Rome about A.D. 65, and this accounts for the precise chronology of the Marcan passion, which Vincent Taylor had already suggested 'may reflect the catechetical and liturgical interests of the Church at Rome'.[62]

This hypothesis is not convincing. There is clearly a link between the times of prayer prescribed in the *Apostolic Tradition* and the chronology of the Marcan passion, but this does not establish that the Marcan chronology is the *result* of a liturgical practice which already existed when the gospel was written: it could equally well be the *cause* of a subsequent liturgical pattern, and is more likely so, since it seems inconceivable that such a complete cycle of daily prayer existing before A.D. 65 in Rome could have travelled so slowly that it was still virtually unknown in the East at the end of the second century, and was only exported in a piecemeal fashion, so that the ninth hour was apparently adopted before the third in Jerusalem.[63] Nor does the hypothesis of an anterior cycle of prayer really explain the precise chronology of the passion narrative: one would still have to ask why it was that the events of the passion were assigned to those particular times in the liturgical cycle. If, on the one hand, it was because there was a tradition that the events had actually happened at those times, then the chronology of the narrative is simply reflecting the historical tradition and the liturgical hypothesis is redundant. If, on the other hand, it was because those times constituted the natural divisions of the day, then again we may dispense with any cycle of prayer and suggest that the author of the gospel, rather than the worshipping community, attached the events to this natural timetable. For in spite of R. H. Lightfoot's claim that the marking out of the passion narrative in regular intervals is 'an exactness of temporal reckoning to which St. Mark is usually indeed a stranger',[64] the evangelist does appear to do this elsewhere in the gospel (cf. 6.47–8; 'when evening came . . . and about the fourth watch of the night. . . .'), and so it is not so remarkable that he should do it with the longest piece of continuous narrative which he has.

Nevertheless, Walker's theory does appear to point in the right direction, in suggesting that it is the link with the passion of Christ which is the real clue to the origin of the secondary times of prayer. As we shall see below, apparently from early in the Church's history a service of the word was held on

Wednesdays and Fridays at 3 p.m., and this constituted the end of the period of fasting commonly observed on those days, the time having been chosen to coincide with the hour of Christ's death.[65] It is known that many individuals fasted voluntarily on other days in addition to these,[66] and it is therefore likely that they would have concluded their fasts with an act of worship at 3 p.m. From this it is only a short step for prayer at the ninth hour to be included in the cycle on a regular daily basis, except on Wednesdays and Fridays when there was the service of the word, and on Sundays, and every day in Eastertide, when there was never any fasting, and this is precisely the situation which we find prevailing at Jerusalem in the fourth century,[67] but which seems to have originated in the West sometime in the second century. Once both sixth and ninth hours were observed with prayer in this way, it would have been natural for the remaining division of the day, the third hour, to be added, so that by the end of the second century this time was generally observed in the West, but spread more slowly to the East, with the result that even in the fourth century at Jerusalem it remained only an additional Lenten observance. If the *Apostolic Tradition* is to be trusted, this hour of prayer also came to be associated with the passion at Rome, where Mark's gospel is thought to have originated, but not apparently elsewhere, so that other justifications were advanced for its observance, and for the observance of the sixth hour, the origin of which had been forgotten.

Our sources provide further information about the content and manner of prayer in this period. Tertullian makes it clear that the Lord's Prayer still constituted the foundation of all prayer, terming it *legitima et ordinaria oratio*, 'the prescribed and regular prayer', but that to it was added a 'superstructure of petitions for additional desires'.[68] Elsewhere he indicates the scope of the intercession: it included prayer 'for the emperors, for their ministers and for all in authority, for the welfare of the world, for the prevalence of peace, for the delay of the final consummation'.[69] Cyprian confirms that such prayer for the salvation of all was not restricted to the Sunday assembly alone, but made by Christians unceasingly, day and night.[70] The *eucharistia* form seems to have become increasingly confined to the eucharistic prayer proper and, apart from a remnant of it in Polycarp's prayer before his death, we find no further trace of it in the normal daily prayers.[71] Origen, however, reveals that the structure of prayer inherited from Judaism was still preserved—praise and thanksgiving leading to petition and intercession and concluding with a doxology:

> according to our ability at the beginning and exordium of our prayer we must address praises to God through Christ, who is praised together with him in the Holy Spirit, who is likewise hymned; and after this each must place thanksgiving, both common—for those benefits to all—and for those things which each has received individually from God; and after thanksgiving it seems to me that one ought to become a bitter accuser of one's own sins before God, and to ask first for healing so as to be delivered from the state that leads to sin, and secondly for remission of what is past; and after confession, in the fourth place it seems to me we must add petition for the great and heavenly gifts for ourselves, and for people in general, and also for our families and friends; and in addition to all this, our prayer ought to end in praise to God through Christ in the Holy Spirit.[72]

Origen's reference to prayer at the third, sixth, and ninth hours quoted above,[73] suggests that these hours had acquired a fixed form consisting of three prayers at each, but whether this was universally true and what these three prayers were it is impossible to say. Since later evidence reveals three psalms as constituting the core of these hours of prayer, it is possible, though very far from certain, that the recitation of three psalms may also be meant here. The best attested liturgical use of the Psalter at this period is in relation to meals, and in particular the *agape*, and not in relation to the Eucharist, as is commonly supposed: there is in reality only one sure mention of psalms in connection with the Eucharist, and that is by Tertullian, and it concerns a Montanist service: 'whether it is in the reading of the Scriptures, or in the chanting of psalms, or in the preaching of sermons, or in the offering up of prayers . . .'.[74] This is a very uncertain foundation upon which to make any assertion about the catholic practice of the day. From the passages quoted above,[75] however, it is clear that the custom encountered in the New Testament[76]—of non-canonical compositions being sung at communal meals by individuals while the rest listened—continued, but that the canonical psalms were now certainly being included alongside them, even if they had not been before. According to the evidence of the *Apostolic Tradition* the gathering made the response 'Alleluia' to them, and as this was the way in which the *hallel* was sung in Judaism,[77] it appears probable that this represents an authentic tradition deriving from the earliest days of the Church.[78] It would seem, however, that this use of the psalms was also beginning to spread from these occasions to the regular times of prayer, at least when they were offered in a context where there were others present to listen and respond to the psalmody: Tertullian relates that 'those who are more diligent in praying are accustomed to include in their prayers Alleluia and this type of psalms, with the endings of which those who are present may respond',[79] and elsewhere speaks of married couples engaged in singing to one another psalms and hymns, 'and they mutually challenge each other which shall better chant to their God',[80] though in this latter case he may of course be referring to mealtimes, but certainly a domestic situation is intended, and the passage does not refer to two cantors at public worship, as has been erroneously concluded by several scholars.[81]

The thought of Hebrews 13.15, of prayer as a sacrifice offered to God, is picked up by authors of this period. Tertullian, in the first of the two passages quoted above, speaks of prayer as 'a spiritual oblation which has abolished the former sacrifices', and this we must 'bring to the altar of God to the accompaniment of psalms and hymns',[82] while Clement, as we have seen earlier,[83] talks of the whole life of a Christian as a holy festival in which the sacrifices are prayers and praises. Origen too sees the daily sacrifices of the Old Testament as being fulfilled in the ceaseless prayer of the Christians: 'it is therefore a festival of the Lord if we offer perpetually the sacrifice, if we pray without ceasing, if our prayer rises like incense before him in the morning and the lifting up of our hands is for him the evening sacrifice'.[84]

It is usually presumed that standing was the normal posture for prayer in the early Church and that the habit of kneeling only began to emerge in the second century as a gesture of penitence on fast days and from there spread to other weekdays as well.[85] On the other hand, in view of the evidence from the New Testament which suggests that prayer was then offered kneeling as well as standing,[86] it is possible that both customs are of equal antiquity and were both used on ordinary days, but that kneeling eventually came to be the rule on fast days and to be entirely forbidden on Sundays and during the fifty days of Easter, as being inappropriate to the celebration of the resurrection. That certainly seems to be what Tertullian implies: 'But on ordinary days who would hesitate to prostrate himself before God, at least at the first prayer with which we enter on daylight? On fasts moreover, and stations, no prayer is to be performed without kneeling and the rest of the attitudes of humility: for we do not only pray, but also make supplication and satisfaction to God our Lord'.[87] The reference to kneeling for the first prayer of the day is interesting, because it implies that this prayer was already relatively fixed and always had a penitential character, and in the fourth century we find that this place in the morning office was occupied by the penitential psalm 51, which may even be what is meant here.[88]

Prayer was normally made with upraised hands and head uncovered,[89] following Jewish custom, although Origen recognizes that circumstances may compel another posture to be adopted:

> Although there are innumerable dispositions of the body, that which involves the stretching out of the hands and the uplifting of the eyes is to be preferred before all. . . . And these things we say must be particularly observed, apart from any adverse circumstances; for when there is an adverse circumstance it is fittingly allowed sometimes to pray sitting because of some disease of the feet which cannot be regarded lightly, or even lying down because of fevers or such sicknesses; and in some circumstances, for example if we are on a voyage, or business does not allow us to return to fulfil our obligation of prayer, it is possible to pray without pretending to do this.[90]

Tertullian in one passage, however, suggests that humility dictates that the hands should not be raised too high and the eyes should not be lifted up,[91] and both authors indicate that the original lifting up of the hands in the *orant* position had given way to a stretching out of the hands in symbolic representation of the crucifixion.[92]

There is nothing in the evidence so far adduced which would lead to the conclusion that the times of daily prayer were celebrated corporately in the early Church, and much which would suggest the opposite, that daily prayer, at least as a general rule, was made by individuals in private. That is not to say, however, that the prayers were seen purely as an individual activity, and indeed Cyprian makes it clear that the individual's prayer is part of the prayer of the whole Church: 'Before all things the teacher of peace and master of unity would not have prayer to be made singly and individually, so that when one prays, he does not pray for himself alone. . . . Our prayer is public and common; and when we pray, we pray not for one, but for the whole people, because we the whole people are one . . .'.[93] Nor is it to deny that, at least for some people and on some occasions, the prayers would be offered by a family together or by a small group of friends: as we have seen, Tertullian speaks of 'those who are present' at the prayers, and mentions husband and wife praying together, as does the *Apostolic Tradition* with regard to prayer at midnight.[94]

Nevertheless, although firm evidence that the whole Christian community gathered together in any place on a daily basis to observe the times of prayer is lacking before the fourth century, the existence of certain regular assemblies for other acts of worship is attested. Firstly, there were services of the word on Sundays, Wednesdays, and Fridays. At least from the time of Justin Martyr in the middle of the second century, if not considerably earlier, the Sunday morning service of the word and the prayers was fused with the celebration of the Eucharist,[95] but we have suggested above that it originally existed independently, as a parallel to the synagogue service.[96] Its order was, however, different from that of the synagogue, where the prayers appear to have preceded the readings,[97] and this change is most probably to be explained as a result of the rule that the baptized might not pray with the unbaptized: thus the first part of the service could be open to all, and the unbaptized dismissed before the prayers began.[98]

With regard to Wednesday and Friday, we have seen that the *Didache* directed that they were to be regular days of fasting for Christians,[99] and both Clement of Alexandria and Origen confirm that this custom continued in the East in the second and third centuries.[100] In the West Hermas speaks of customary fasts which he calls 'stations',[101] and this term is explained by Tertullian: it was derived from military usage, where it meant the sentry's turn of duty, and was applied to Christians as being the soldiers of God.[102] In his treatise on fasting, Tertullian indicates that these stations were kept on Wednesdays and Fridays. It is incorrect to interpret his evidence to mean that such stations were introduced to the West by the Montanists and that fasting among the Catholics had previously been unrelated to specific days, as many scholars have done.[103] What was at dispute between the Catholics and the Montanists was not whether the regular stations should exist—both sides accepted that—but whether the fasting was obligatory, whether it should be prolonged beyond the ninth hour, and whether any additional fasting on other days was subject to rule or was entirely at the discretion of the individual. The conclusion of the station at the ninth hour among the Catholics clearly involved some form of service, since they apparently adduced as the Scriptural precedent for ending the fast at this hour Peter's visit to the Temple (Acts 3.1), and this service was also observed by the Montanists, even though it did not mark the conclusion of their fast, since Tertullian denies that, by rejecting Peter's visit as a precedent for concluding the station, they are slighting the ninth hour 'which on the fourth and sixth days of the week we most highly honour', and he goes on to give what he believes to be the worthier reason for their observance of the hour on those days:

> it comes from the death of the Lord, which although it ought always to be commemorated, without difference of hours, yet are we at that time more impressively commended to its commemoration, according to the actual name of Station. For even soldiers, though never unmindful of their military oath, yet pay a greater deference to Stations. And so the 'pressure' must be maintained up to that hour in which the world—involved from the sixth hour in darkness—performed for its dead Lord a sorrowful duty; so that we too may then return to enjoyment when the universe regained its light.[104]

This service at the ninth hour cannot have been a Eucharist. Tertullian elsewhere makes it clear that the normal time for the celebration of the Eucharist was the morning,[105] and although in his treatise on prayer he indicates that the Eucharist could be celebrated on station days, referring to the scruples felt by some that they would be breaking their fast if they were to make their communion, this only serves to confirm that the Eucharist must have been celebrated early in the day:[106] if it had been at the ninth hour, this problem would never have arisen, for by then the fast would have been over. On the other hand, it might be argued that it was later transferred to the ninth hour in order to solve this very problem, but in that case the Montanists would have put it even later, if they thought that it broke their fast, or kept it at the early hour, if they thought that it didn't, or at least been criticized by their enemies for breaking their fast by making their communion at the ninth hour. We may safely conclude, therefore, that it was a non-eucharistic service which was held at the ninth hour, and Tertullian himself indicates that such services existed in his day: 'You however have no cause for appearing in public except such as is serious: either some brother who is sick is to be visited or else the sacrifice is offered or else the word of God is dispensed' (aut sacrificium offertur, aut Dei verbum administratur).[107] Moreover, fourth-century evidence again confirms this conclusion, since services of the word at the ninth hour on Wednesdays and Fridays are still found then in various places.[108] As the synagogue equivalent of these services was held in the morning,[109] we may presume that the Christians transferred them to the ninth hour for the reason given by Tertullian—to commemorate the death of Christ—and this change must have been made at an early date for the Montanists at the beginning of the third century to have regarded it as an ancient custom which they would not set aside even though it no longer formed the conclusion of their station.

Whether or not there were also assemblies for worship on the Sabbath in the second and third centuries has been disputed: on the one hand Dugmore believes that Sabbath worship continued uninterrupted from the earliest days of the Church, while on the other hand Rordorf believes that regard for the Sabbath only began to emerge in the third century, as far as Gentile Christians were concerned.[110] What does seem to have continued uninterrupted was the tradition that the Sabbath was not a proper day on which to keep a voluntary fast, with the one exception of Holy Saturday when fasting was a universal rule, so that Tertullian can criticize as innovators those who in his time were adding a Saturday fast to their Friday station, probably in imitation of the pre-Paschal fast.[111] On the other hand, he also criticizes those who are moving in the other direction and have begun to refrain from kneeling on Saturday, thus treating it as equal to Sunday.[112] The only evidence for actual assemblies for worship on the Sabbath before the fourth century, however, is a passage in Origen's works, which is probably not meant to be taken literally at all,[113] and a reference to the celebration of the Eucharist on Saturdays in the Apostolic Tradition, which is quite likely a fourth-century interpolation, as Dix held.[114]

Even more uncertain is the existence of regular vigil services during the night. Many scholars would doubt whether at this period there was any more than one such service annually at Easter.[115] On the other hand, Tertullian has a phrase 'by day the station, by night the vigil' (*De Or.* 29), which sounds as if such vigils may have been a frequent occurrence and is reminiscent of 2 Cor. 6.5 & 11.27,[116] and elsewhere he speaks of 'night assemblies', *nocturnae convocationes* (*Ad. Uxor.* 2.4), as if they were distinct from the annual all-night Paschal vigil.

Finally, in the *Apostolic Tradition* we encounter assemblies for instruction and prayer, clearly something quite different from the services on station days, which are not mentioned in this document, though that does not prove that they did not exist at Rome at the time. Here the gatherings are explicitly said to be in the morning and not at the ninth hour, and they are apparently not restricted to specific days of the week:

35. The faithful, as soon as they have woken and got up, before they turn to their work, shall pray to God, and so hasten to their work. If there is any verbal instruction, one should give preference to this, and go and hear the word of God, to the comfort of his soul. Let him hasten to the church, where the Spirit flourishes. . . .

39. The deacons and priests shall assemble daily at the place which the bishop appoints for them. Let the deacons not fail to assemble at all times, unless illness hinders them. When all have assembled, let them teach those who are in the church, and in this way, when they have prayed, let each one go to the work which falls to him. . . .

41. Let every faithful man and woman, when they have risen from sleep in the morning, before they touch any work at all, wash their hands and pray to God, and so go to their work. But if instruction in the word of God is given, each one should choose to go to that place, reckoning in his heart that it is God whom he hears in the instructor. For he who prays in the church will be able to pass by the wickedness of the day. He who is pious should think it a great evil if he does not go to the place where instruction is given, and especially if he can read, or if a teacher comes. Let none of you be late in the church, the place where teaching is given. Then it shall be given to the speaker to say what is useful to each one; you will hear things which you do not think of, and profit from things which the holy Spirit will give you through the instructor. In this way your faith will be strengthened about the things you will have heard. You will also be told in that place what you ought to do at home. Therefore let each one be diligent in coming to the church, the place where the holy Spirit flourishes. If there is a

day when there is no instruction, let each one, when he is at home, take up a holy book and read in it sufficiently what seems to him to bring profit.

The last part is clearly a duplicate of the first and, because it is somewhat confused, may well be a later expansion.

With these should also be considered certain other sections of the document:

15. Those who come forward for the first time to hear the word shall first be brought to the teachers before all the people arrive, and shall be questioned. . . .

18. When the teacher has finished giving instruction, let the catechumens pray by themselves, separated from the faithful. . . .

19. After their prayer, when the teacher has laid hands on the catechumens, he shall pray and dismiss them. Whether the teacher is a cleric or a layman, let him act thus.

It is often assumed that the instruction of the catechumens was confined to their attendance at the first part of the Sunday Eucharist, where they would hear the readings and the sermon by the bishop, but that does not appear to be what is in mind here: the 'teachers' may be clerics or laymen, and it is they and not the bishop who lay hands on the candidates and dismiss them. Because the faithful are also said to be present on these occasions, it would seem probable that the gatherings should be identified with those for daily instruction quoted above, where again the bishop does not seem necessarily to have been involved, probably because these were assemblies occasioned by pastoral needs and not liturgical rites which had to be celebrated at a set time and over which he had to preside. Like the station day services, these too can be found surviving in the fourth century: Egeria tells of the presence of the faithful with the baptismal candidates at the bishop's daily morning *catechesis* in Jerusalem.[117] Nor were they restricted to Rome in the second and third centuries, as Origen's sermons provide evidence for the existence of a similar daily assembly for instruction in the East.[118] Catechumens were present at this,[119] but Origen criticizes those of the faithful who were reluctant to attend: 'Tell me, you who come together in church only on festivals, are not other days festal? Are they not days of the Lord? . . . Christians eat the flesh of the Lamb every day, that is they daily partake of the flesh of the word of God'.[120]

Dugmore uses Origen as his key witness to support his claim that the morning and evening offices were publicly celebrated every day in the second and third centuries,[121] but his error is to fail to distinguish the assemblies for instruction from the hours of prayer. Prayer and the study of the word of God were both essential elements in the life of the early Christian, but they were separate elements. Prayer was offered at set hours each day, while the study of the Bible was done (a) in an informal way through the contributions brought by participants at the *agape*, though psalms seem to have gradually assumed the dominant role here; (b) in a more formal way in the regular services of the word on Sundays, Wednesdays, and Fridays; (c) in the daily morning assemblies for instruction, when these were held; and (d) in private reading at home, unrelated to set times, at least for those who could read and possessed copies of the Scriptures.[122]

4. *The Cathedral Office in the East*

After the Peace of Constantine in the fourth century it became possible for local Christian communities to assemble together on a more regular basis for their daily prayers, and we find that in the ordinary non-monastic or secular practice, the 'cathedral office' as it is called by scholars,[1] the morning and evening times of prayer began to emerge as pre-eminent and to be celebrated daily as public services everywhere, while as a general rule the other pre-Nicene hours remained as purely individual observances, increasingly becoming the activity of the especially devout and ascetic alone.[2] Eusebius of Caesarea (*c.* 260–*c.* 340) is the first to attest this development:

> it is not a small sign of the goodness of God that throughout the whole world in the churches of God in the morning at sunrise and in the evening hymns and praises and truly divine pleasures are established to God. The pleasures of God are the hymns which everywhere in the world are offered in his Church at morning and evening time.[3]

It has been the general opinion of scholars that such evidence points to the conclusion that from the beginning these two hours had always been distinguished from the rest as the only obligatory times of prayer and were the only ones derived ultimately from Judaism. It has been our contention so far, however, that this was not the case, and we may now point out that at Jerusalem, as we shall see below,[4] and perhaps in other places other hours of prayer were also included in the cathedral cycle, apparently on an equal footing. Moreover it is possible to explain why elsewhere at this period the morning and evening offices should have begun to be singled out from the rest for communal celebration. Firstly, it was simply not practicable for the local congregation to assemble together to observe all the hours of prayer customary in the early Church: those which occurred during the working day would have had to remain in general as individual devotions, and similarly night prayer would normally be something to be observed privately in the home. On the other hand, the beginning and end of the day were ideally convenient times at which people might be free to come together for worship, and so practical considerations alone would have encouraged the choice of these hours for corporate celebration. Secondly, although earlier generations of Christians had regarded the offering of praise and prayer as a sacrifice, as we have seen, no attempt had been made to equate particular times of prayer with specific Old Testament sacrifices: instead it was *continual* prayer which was seen as the fulfilment of the morning and evening sacrifices of Israel.[5] Now, however, that was to change and, as part of a general movement linking Christian liturgical practices with those of the Old Testament cult, the morning and evening offices came to be regarded as the Christian fulfilment of the daily sacrifices, as John Chrysostom (c. 347–407) reveals: 'this was the command and law for the priests . . . to sacrifice and burn one morning and one evening lamb, the former being called the morning sacrifice and the latter the evening. God ordered this to happen, signifying by what happened that he ought always to be worshipped both at the beginning and at the ending of the day'.[6] This would also have helped to give a different status to the morning and evening offices from the other times of prayer in the day.

As the quotation from Eusebius at the beginning of the chapter indicated, praise and thanksgiving were dominant notes of these two offices, and this points to the preservation from early times of the *eucharistia* character of prayer, even though not its form. Alongside this, however, can be detected a strong penitential theme, as this extract from Chrysostom's baptismal instructions shows:

And I urge you to show great zeal by gathering here in the church at dawn to make your prayers and confessions to the God of all things, and to thank him for the gifts he has already given. Beseech him to deign to lend you from now on his powerful aid in guarding this treasure; strengthened with this aid, let each one leave the church to take up his daily tasks, one hastening to work with his hands, another hurrying to his military post, and still another to his post in the government. However, let each one approach his daily task with fear and anguish, and spend his working hours in the knowledge that at evening he should return here to the church, render an account to the Master of his whole day, and beg forgiveness for his faults. For even if we are on our guard ten thousand times a day, we cannot avoid making ourselves accountable for many different faults. Either we say something at the wrong time, or we listen to idle talk, or we think indecent thoughts, or we fail to control our eyes, or we spend time in vain and idle things that have no connection with what we should be doing. This is the reason why each evening we must beg pardon from the Master for all these faults. This is why we must flee to the loving-kindness of God and make our appeal to him. Then we must spend the hours of the night soberly, and in this way meet the confession of the dawn. . . .[7]

We have already observed above the existence of a penitential aspect at the beginning of the third century, at least in connection with the morning prayer,[8] but here Chrysostom seems to extend it equally to both offices.

Chrysostom's writings also show that the morning and evening offices at Antioch were composed of two main elements, psalmody and intercession. The regular morning and evening psalms, used each day, were Ps. 63 and Ps. 141 respectively. Other psalms and hymns may also have been included, and Chrysostom criticizes those who 'think that if they have joined in chanting two or three psalms and have shared in the usual prayers, they have done all that is required for their salvation',[9] which certainly suggests that at least one of the daily services involved more than the one psalm. He believes that the choice of these particular psalms was not motivated simply by the fact that 141 speaks of 'the lifting up of my hands as an evening sacrifice' and that 63 was then thought to refer to the morning—for many other psalms also referred to these times of day—but because of other aspects of their contents: 141 was 'a saving medicine and a purification of sins', while 63 'arouses the soul, sets it on fire, and fills it with great goodness and love'.[10] This may of course be no more than a subsequent rationalization of the choice. The intercessions, as in the pre-Nicene period, were not simply for the Church: Chrysostom, referring to 1 Tim. 2.1f. ('I urge that supplications, prayers, intercessions, and thanksgivings be made for all men . . .'), says, 'the initiated know how this happens every day both in the evening and in the morning, how we offer prayer for the whole world, for kings and all that are in authority'.[11]

The *Apostolic Constitutions*, which is thought to have originated in Syria in the second half of the fourth century, confirms and amplifies Chrysostom's evidence. Book II identifies the contents of the offices as psalmody and intercession, and prescribes the same daily psalms: 'assemble yourselves together every day, morning and evening, singing psalms and praying in the Lord's house, in the morning saying the 62nd [63rd] psalm and in the evening the 140th [141st]' (II.59.2). In Book VII the text of the Gloria in Excelsis is given as a 'morning hymn', and this is followed by an 'evening hymn', which includes *Te Decet Laus* and the Nunc Dimittis (VII.47–8). Finally, Book VIII gives details of the form of the daily intercessions: after the psalm the deacon is to pronounce biddings in turn for the catechumens, energumens, illuminandi, and penitents just as in the eucharistic rite, where the faithful, and especially the children, respond *Kyrie eleison*, and the group in question are then told by the deacon to bow their heads while the bishop says a prayer over them, after which the deacon dismisses them. At the morning and evening offices when these groups have been dismissed, there follows a litany for the faithful in the same manner, concluding with a benedictory prayer by the bishop and the deacon's dismissal, appropriate forms being provided for both times of day (VIII.35–9). It is interesting to observe that the Lord's Prayer no longer seems to have a regular place within the office.

Although the evening psalm is termed the 'lamplighting' psalm (*epilychnios psalmos*) in the *Apostolic Constitutions* (VIII.35.2), there is no evidence that anything more is intended by this than a reference to the time of day at which the psalm was sung. At least in Cappadocia, however, if not elsewhere, it was otherwise. Here apparently the evening office was designated as the 'thanksgiving at lamplighting' (*epilychnios eucharistia*), and included a ritual in connection with the lighting of the lamps. Gregory of Nyssa (*c.* 330–*c.* 395), in his account of the life of his sister Macrina, tells how at the end of a visit to her, 'the voice of the choir was calling me to the thanksgiving at lamplighting, and she sent me to church',[12] and later describes the ceremony—though in a domestic rather than an ecclesiastical setting—in his record of the last moments of her life:

> Meanwhile evening had come and a lamp had been brought in. All at once she opened her eyes and looked towards the light, clearly wanting to repeat the thanksgiving at lamplighting. But her voice

75

failed and she fulfilled her intention in the heart and by moving her hands, and her lips moved in sympathy with her inward desire. But when she had finished the thanksgiving, and her hand, brought to her face to make the sign, had indicated the end of the prayer, she drew a great deep breath and closed her life and her prayer together.[13]

Basil the Great (c. 330–79) reveals that the custom was already considered ancient in the fourth century, and implies that the hymn *Phos Hilaron* was used at it:

> it seemed good to our fathers not to receive in silence the gift of the evening light but as soon as it appeared to give thanks. Who was the author of those words of thanksgiving at lamplighting we cannot say, but the people pronounce the ancient formula and nobody ever thought them impious to say, 'we praise the Father, the Son, and the holy spirit of God.'[14]

Both F. J. Dölger and J. Mateos believe that this Christian practice arose out of the pagan light-cult which was widespread in the Eastern Mediterranean area,[15] but Gregory Dix and Gabriele Winkler seem to be more correct in seeing it as deriving ultimately from the lighting of the lamp in Judaism,[16] which was preserved in Christianity first of all in connection with the community meals, as we have seen above,[17] and would then have become attached to the evening office as a daily feature when those meals began to decline.

At a later stage the interpretation of the offices as the fulfilment of the daily sacrifices of the Old Testament led to a further development, the inclusion of a literal offering of incense in the morning and evening offices each day, in accordance with the prescription in Exod. 30.7–8: 'And Aaron shall burn fragrant incense on [the altar]; every morning when he dresses the lamps he shall burn it, and when Aaron sets up the lamps in the evening he shall burn it, a perpetual incense before the Lord throughout your generations'. The growth of this ceremony was also encouraged by the strongly penitential character of the offices, since the offering of incense was seen in the Old Testament as having expiatory power for the sins of the people (see Num. 16.46–7). The use of incense in this way in the Church seems to have originated in Syria and is first mentioned in the *Carmina Nisibena* of St. Ephraem, composed in A.D. 363, where Ephraem, addressing Abraham, the contemporary

Bishop of Nisibis, says:

> Thy fasts are a defence unto our land,
> Thy prayer a shield unto our city;
> Thy burning of incense is our propitiation;
> Praised be God, who has hallowed thine offering.[18]

There is no indication here whether this offering of incense took place in the office or in the Eucharist, but Theodoret, Bishop of Cyrrhus in Syria, writing sometime after A.D. 453 and comparing Christian worship with the Jewish rites inside the tabernacle, says: 'we celebrate the liturgy reserved to the interior. For we offer to God incense and the light of lamps, as well as the liturgy of the mysteries of the holy table'.[19] Mateos would interpret this as implying that the offering of incense and lights belongs to a different occasion from the 'mysteries of the holy table', and therefore to the daily offices,[20] and certainly in later centuries the offering of incense developed into a major element in the offices.[21]

We are fortunate in having a detailed picture of the practice at Jerusalem from the fourth-century pilgrim Egeria,[22] although this evidence must be treated with some care since the rite of such a pilgrimage centre was not necessarily typical of the daily offices elsewhere. Moreover, a large number of monks and nuns were also involved in the offices there, and this has obviously had some effect upon them. However, it is still possible to distinguish 'cathedral' and 'monastic' elements in the daily services, which as a general rule were held in what Egeria calls the *Anastasis*, 'Resurrection', a building surrounding the tomb in which Christ had been buried.[23] It is clear that the first service of the day which she describes, lasting from cockcrow to dawn, is principally monastic, with only some lay people attending:

> Every day before cockcrow all the doors of the *Anastasis* are opened, and the *monazontes* and *parthenae*, as they call them here, all enter, and not only these but also lay men and women besides who wish to keep an earlier vigil. From that time until dawn hymns are recited and psalms with their refrains, and antiphons too; and between each hymn there is a prayer, for two or three presbyters, and deacons also, are present by rota each day with the *monazontes* to say the prayers after each hymn and antiphon.[24]

This will be deferred for later consideration with other monastic offices,[25] and all we need note here is the presence of the deacons and priests: it was seemingly not thought proper for others to lead public prayer even in the monastic services. The fact that Egeria mentions both priests and deacons with regard to acts of prayer here and elsewhere is not coincidental: they were not alternatives, but the presence of both orders was required—the priest deputizing for the bishop and saying the prayer, and the deacon making the biddings, as he does in the evening office—and Egeria never speaks of a deacon saying a prayer himself.[26]

At the other four daily offices, in the morning, at midday, at 3 p.m., and in the evening, the whole Church was involved— the bishop, the clergy, the religious, the faithful, and the catechumens[27]—and this points to them all being considered as part of the cathedral cycle: there is no reason to suppose, from the evidence of Egeria, that the morning and evening offices should be singled out from the rest, as most scholars have tended to do, but rather it would appear that the Jerusalem church was keeping to what we have claimed to be the ancient tradition of treating all the hours on an equal basis. During Lent a further service at 9 a.m. was similarly included in the cycle, and this we have earlier suggested is an indication that it had been a more recent addition to the times of prayer: 'at the third hour they go into the *Anastasis* and do what they are accustomed to do at the sixth hour throughout the year, since this is also added in Lent, that they should go at the third hour'.[28] There were also variations on Sundays, Wednesdays, and Fridays, which we will consider later.[29]

With the exception of the evening office, which has certain peculiar features, the services all follow a common pattern, as this tabular arrangement of Egeria's description reveals:

Morning:	Noon, 3 p.m.:	Evening:
When it begins to get light, then	Likewise at the sixth hour all again enter the *Anastasis*, and	At the tenth hour (what they call here *Lychnicon* but we call *Lucernare*) all the people gather again in the *Anastasis*, and the lamps and candles are all lit, and the light is very bright. The light is not brought from outside, but is taken from inside the cave, that is from inside the screen, where a lamp is always burning night and day.

Morning:	Noon, 3 p.m.:	Evening:
they begin to recite the morning hymns. Then the bishop comes with his clergy and	psalms and antiphons are recited while the bishop is sent for; and again he enters, and does not sit, but	The *Lucernare* psalms and antiphons are recited for some time. Then the bishop is sent for, and he enters and takes his seat, and the presbyters also sit in their places. Hymns and antiphons are recited. When they have finished them according to their custom, the bishop rises and stands in front of the screen (that is the cave), and one of the deacons makes the commemoration of individuals according to the custom, and when the deacon says the names of individuals, a large group of boys always respond, *Kyrie eleison*, or as we say, 'Lord have mercy'. Their voices are very loud.[30] When the deacon has finished all that
immediately enters the cave, and from inside the screen	immediately goes inside the screen in the *Anastasis* (that is the cave where he went earlier), and from there	
he first recites the prayer for all, and he himself commemorates any names he wishes;	he again first recites a prayer;	he has to say, the bishop first recites a prayer and prays for all. So far the faithful and catechumens pray together. Now the deacon bids every catechumen to stand where he is and bow his head, and the bishop then recites the blessing over the catechumens from his place. There is another prayer, and again the deacon bids all the faithful to stand and bow their heads. The bishop
then he blesses the catechumens. He recites another prayer		
and blesses the faithful. After this, the bishop comes outside the screen, and all come to his	he then blesses the faithful, and comes outside the screen, and again they come to his	then blesses the faithful, and so the dismissal takes place at the *Anastasis*,

Morning:	Noon, 3 p.m.:	Evening:
hand, and he blesses them one by one as he comes out, and so the dismissal takes place when it is already light.	hand. The ninth hour is the same as the sixth hour.	and individuals come to his hand.[31]

As we can see, the evening office differs in two main respects from the others. Firstly, at the other services the bishop is not present for the psalms and hymns, but only for the inter-cessions, while in the evening he sits on arrival for the concluding part of the psalmody. Secondly, at the other services he conducts the intercessions alone and from inside the screen, while in the evening he remains in front of the screen, and the prayers have a fuller form, the deacon making biddings and the people responding, as in the rite in the *Apostolic Constitutions*. It may be thought that his late arrival was because he was only attending that part of the service which required his participation, but that does not explain why he should come earlier to the evening office or be present for the whole service on other occasions, as for example the Sunday vigil and the services of Holy Week.[32] We must therefore take a closer look at the evening office. We may notice that not only is it called *Lychnicon*, 'the Lamplighting', but that the lights ap-parently formed an important feature of it: Egeria tells us that a large number of lamps were lit, making it very bright, which implies that they were not merely functional but symbolic, and this is confirmed by the fact that they were lit not 'from outside' but from a lamp kept burning perpetually within the cave, very probably symbolizing the risen Christ as the light of the world and the source of all light.[33] We have suggested earlier that this ritual lamplighting at the evening office had been taken over from the *agape* and also that the inclusion of hymns and psalms in the hours of prayer had spread from their original use at such meals.[34] If the text of the *Apostolic Tradition* is a reliable guide to primitive practice at this point, the thanksgiving for light at the *agape* required the bishop to be present and preside over it: 'When the bishop is present, and evening has come, a deacon brings in a lamp . . .'.[35] It may therefore be that it is once again the Jerusalem liturgy's adherence to ancient custom which accounts for the bishop's involvement in the *Lucernare* 'hymns and antiphons', while the hymns and psalms at the other offices would be a secondary preamble which had been added to the original nucleus of those times of prayer and which the bishop, keeping to the more ancient tradition, did not attend. There is reason to believe that the first half of the psalmody at the evening office, from which the bishop was also absent, was a further addition from monastic practice, as we shall see later.[36] The transference to the evening hour of prayer of practices originally belonging to the *agape* may even account for the other difference between the services, the form of the intercessions, that in the evening in which all the members of the congregation played their part following the pattern of corporate prayer, that at the other offices in which the bishop prayed alone, naming any individuals for whom he wished intercession to be made, following the pattern of private prayer. It is clear from the *Apostolic Constitutions*, however, that elsewhere the morning office did not retain this form but was assimilated to the evening pattern.

The evening office at Jerusalem was also followed by a further act of worship, conducted around the site of the crucifixion:

> Afterwards, the bishop is led from the *Anastasis* to the Cross with hymns, and all the people go with him. When he has arrived, he first says a prayer, and then blesses the catechumens; then there is another prayer, and he blesses the faithful. After this the bishop and all the people go behind the Cross, and again do there what they did before the Cross. They come to the bishop's hand both before the Cross and behind the Cross, just as at the *Anastasis*. Great glass lanterns hang everywhere, and there are many candles, both in front of the *Anastasis* and also before and behind the Cross. It is dark when all this is finished.[37]

Since the evening office had already ended with blessings and dismissals, this would seem to be not the conclusion of that service but an entirely separate devotional act, not a part of the ancient tradition of daily prayer but an innovation peculiar to Jerusalem and arising from the existence of the holy places there, though it was subsequently to be imitated elsewhere.[38]

What, however, were the 'hymns', 'psalms', and 'antiphons' at the offices of which Egeria speaks? It would appear that she intended no particular distinction between these terms but employed them more or less interchangeably, as do other authors of the period, as for example Epiphanius (*c.* 315–403), Bishop of Salamis in Cyprus: 'in the holy Church there are always morning hymns and morning prayers, and similarly evening psalms and prayers'.[39] We cannot even be completely sure that any non-canonical compositions were included—though it is very likely that they were—as it was common in both East and West to use 'hymn' when speaking of one of the canonical psalms.[40] All we can say for certain is that each office included more than one of these hymns/psalms and that they were always appropriate to the occasion on which they were used: 'what is noticeable about all this is that the psalms and antiphons they recite are always appropriate, both those at night, those in the morning, and those during the day at the sixth and ninth hours and at *Lucernare*, always appropriate, suitable, and revelant to what is being celebrated'.[41] It is probable, therefore, that the hymn *Phos Hilaron* and Ps. 141 were used in the evening, as in our other sources. Since we have already encountered the tendency in early Christianity to group things in threes and will meet it again in various fourth-century rites,[42] it is not unreasonable to conjecture that there may have been, at least, a third hymn/psalm, and Mateos has concluded from a comparison of the common features of the various rites which are ultimately descended from the Jerusalem tradition that Ps. 142 may have been included in addition to Ps. 141.[43] Similarly we may suppose that the 'morning hymns' included Ps. 63 and perhaps also the Gloria in Excelsis. A third element here may have been Ps. 51, which, though mentioned as the beginning of the morning office in monastic rather than secular sources at this period,[44] may well have originated in the cathedral tradition, since it is a universal feature of later rites,[45] and as *the* penitential psalm would ideally have expressed the penitential aspect of this office evidenced by Chrysostom and implied by Tertullian more than a century earlier.[46] The canticle Benedicite is mentioned as coming between Ps. 63 and the Gloria in Excelsis in the morning office of one monastic source,[47] and as this again is an almost universal feature of later rites, it may well have formed a regular part of the early cathedral office: Rufinus (*c.* 345–410), who travelled extensively, said that it was sung by 'every church throughout the world'.[48] The universal belief among scholars that Pss. 148–150 constituted the nucleus of the morning office in the cathedral tradition has no firm evidence to support it and, as we shall see later, the truth would seem to be that these psalms belonged originally to the night prayer of the monastic tradition and only at a later period came to be included as part of the morning office.[49] There is insufficient evidence to enable identification of the psalms and hymns at the other hours of the day.

It has become accepted among recent continental scholars that a twofold tradition is to be discerned in the cathedral office, the Jerusalem, where several psalms were included each day in the evening office, and the Antiochene, where in contrast there was only one evening psalm.[50] This theory depends to a considerable extent upon the fact that both Chrysostom and the *Apostolic Constitutions*, our sole witnesses to the Antiochene tradition from this period, only identify one psalm in their description of the offices. Nevertheless, they do not explicitly deny that there were others, and scholars tend to assume that there were others unmentioned in the case of the morning office (i.e. Pss. 51, 148–150). Thus it would seem to be unwise to be too dogmatic about the difference of the contents of the evening office at Antioch from those elsewhere. The explicit mention of the particular morning and evening psalms may simply indicate that these were the only elements firmly fixed at this stage and that there was a certain amount of flexibility about the rest.

There appear to have been two main ways in which the psalms were used at this period. The more common is that attested in the third century and having its roots in New Testament times, where the Psalter was interpreted as a prophetic/Christological book on which one meditated, and thus the psalm was sung by an individual while the rest listened and responded with a refrain, what came to be known as the responsorial method.[51] Regular cantors have now replaced random contributions from individuals, however, and the refrain has developed from the simple 'Alleluia' to consist of a verse or part of a verse from the psalm itself,[52] which no doubt accounts for Egeria's use of the word 'antiphonae' to describe the psalms. Chrysostom underlines the significance and spiritual value of the refrain:

Do not then think that you have come here simply to say the words, but when you make the response, consider that response to be a covenant. For when you say, 'Like the hart desires the watersprings, my soul desires you, O God', you make a covenant with God. You have signed a contract without paper or ink; you have confessed with your voice that you love him more than all, that you prefer nothing to him and that you burn with love for him. . .[53]

The other, and apparently less ancient, use of the Psalter was to treat certain psalms as hymns or prayers addressed to God by the congregation and so sing them in unison. This is the way, for example, in which Ps. 51 was sung, according to Basil: 'all together, as with one voice and one heart, raise the psalm of confession to the Lord'.[54]

The Sunday services at Jerusalem differed considerably from those on weekdays. They began with a vigil, which was clearly part of the cathedral cycle, since it involved bishop, clergy, and laity:

> On the seventh day, that is the Lord's Day, before cockcrow there gather all the people, as many as can get in that place, as if it were Easter, in the basilica which is next to the *Anastasis*, but out of doors, where lamps are hung for this. For fear that they should not arrive in time for cockcrow, they come early and sit there. Hymns and antiphons are recited, and there are prayers after each hymn and antiphon. For presbyters and deacons are always there ready for the vigil because of the crowd which gathers there. For it is the custom not to open the holy places before cockcrow.
>
> But soon the first cock crows, and the bishop immediately enters and goes into the cave in the *Anastasis*. All the doors are opened, and all the people go into the *Anastasis*, where many lights are already burning. When the people are inside, one of the presbyters recites a psalm, and all respond; after this there is a prayer. Then one of the deacons recites a psalm, and again there is a prayer. A third psalm is recited by one of the clergy, there is a third prayer, and the commemoration of all. When these three psalms have been recited and the three prayers said, then censers are taken into the cave of the *Anastasis*, so that the whole *Anastasis* basilica is filled with the smell. Then the bishop stands inside the screen, takes the gospel book, and goes to the door and he himself reads the account of the resurrection of the Lord. When he begins to read, everyone groans and laments and weeps at what the Lord underwent for us, so much that the hardest could be moved to tears. When he has read the gospel, the bishop comes out, and is led with hymns to the Cross, and all the people go with him. There one psalm is again recited, and there is a prayer. Then he blesses the faithful, and the dismissal takes place. As the bishop departs, all come to his hand. The bishop then returns to his house.

From that time all the *monazontes* return to the *Anastasis* and psalms and antiphons are recited until daybreak, and after each psalm and antiphon there is a prayer, for the presbyters and deacons take turns in keeping the vigil every day at the *Anastasis* with the people. Some of the laity also, men and women, who wish stay there until daybreak, but the others return to their homes and retire to bed.[55]

The last part of this, after the bishop has returned to his house, is obviously the normal monastic office which we have already encountered on weekdays, though it has had to be deferred to a later hour because of the cathedral vigil. Mateos considers the first part, the wait before the doors are opened at cockcrow, not to be a formal service,[56] and indeed it may be no more than the equivalent of the community hymn-singing which sometimes precedes public events in our own culture. On the other hand, it strongly resembles the monastic service which follows the cathedral vigil—hymns/psalms with prayers between said by deacons and priests—and since that service would otherwise have been considerably shorter than on a weekday because of the intrusion of the cathedral vigil, it is possible that it was begun at this earlier hour and simply interrupted by the vigil so that it might retain its usual length. It is true that Egeria does not suggest that the participants were chiefly monastic, but it may be that more lay people joined in on a Sunday than on a weekday so that the distinction was not so obvious.

It is most improbable that the three psalms which form the first part of the cathedral vigil itself are simply the psalmody of the normal morning office. Since Egeria describes their performance in such detail, we may reasonably conclude that there was a marked difference from the customary weekday form. Moreover, as we shall see,[57] the practice of alternating psalm and prayer is characteristic of the vigil type of prayer rather than of the office proper, where Egeria gives no hint that this was the way in which the psalms were recited. The climax of the vigil is clearly the reading of the gospel, and this is confirmed by the fact that when Egeria refers briefly to the service elsewhere, it is the reading which she mentions and not the other elements in the vigil.[58] It is also clear that the reading included not merely the resurrection narrative but also the passion, since the assembly 'groans and laments and weeps at what the Lord underwent for us'. The procession to the Cross is apparently not a separate devotional addition here, as it is at the evening office, since the blessing and dismissal do not occur until afterwards, but is an integral part of the rite, and Rolf Zerfass has pointed out the similarity between the structure of this and that of the special stational services held in the holy places, in which a reading is followed by a psalm, a prayer, and blessing.[59]

What we have here is something different from the type of formal ministry of the word encountered so far, which we have earlier termed 'didactic',[60] where the purpose was simply to advance the knowledge of the Scriptures and the reading had no relationship to the rest of the rite. Since the same reading was repeated week after week at the vigil, the listeners cannot have failed to be familiar with its contents, and therefore its proclamation had a different purpose—which we may call 'kerygmatic', a description already used by Zerfass[61]—and that was to interpret the significance of the whole act of worship and to elicit a response from the congregation, expressed here in the psalm and prayer at the Cross. Such a use of the ministry of the word in Christian worship seems to have been virtually unknown in the earliest times, probably being confined almost entirely to the Paschal vigil, and its expansion in the fourth century seems to have been the result of the Jerusalem liturgy's attempts to relate the events of the gospel to the time and place of their occurrence, through the development of the calendar and the pilgrimage services in the holy places described by Egeria. The novelty of the custom accounts for her surprise and admiration that 'the hymns, antiphons, and readings, as well as the prayers which the bishop recites, always have such relevance that they are always fitting and appropriate to the day which is being celebrated and to the place in which it is happening'.[62] This particular rite has no historical precedents of which we are certain, and so may well be a fourth-century creation, an imitation of the Paschal vigil in shortened form, originating in Jerusalem as a weekly commemoration of the resurrection in the very place in which it had happened. Alternatively, if the vigils mentioned in the evidence of the first three centuries were a more frequent occurrence than many scholars have thought,[63] this service may be the descendant of a regular weekly vigil kept by Christians from early times.

Whatever its origins, it had spread beyond Jerusalem, since it is mentioned in the *Apostolic Constitutions*, as well as leaving traces in other later rites.[64] *Apostolic Constitutions* speaks of the vigil being held on both Saturday and Sunday, but Mateos believes the reference to Saturday to be a later interpolation,[65] although as we shall see there was also a Saturday vigil of a different kind at Jerusalem during Lent:

> What excuse will be given to God by the man who does not assemble on that day to hear the saving word concerning the resurrection, when we also stand and offer three prayers in memory of him who rose after three days, and when there is the reading of the prophets and the proclamation of the gospel and the offering of the sacrifice and the gift of the holy food?[66]

The 'reading of the prophets and the proclamation of the gospel' belong to the eucharistic rite which follows and not to the vigil itself. We should not conclude from this account that the vigil followed a different order from that at Jerusalem: the reading is mentioned first as it is the most important element, not because it came first in the rite, and the use of 'prayer' to mean a psalm followed by a prayer is common at this period.[67] It is unlikely that the number of the psalms had originally been chosen in order to symbolize the three days of Christ in the tomb, and more probable that it is yet another example of the tendency to group psalms in threes, and that the mystical interpretation given here is no more than a subsequent rationalization. Similarly, Mateos's claim that the incense was intended to represent the spices brought to anoint the body of Jesus[68] is also questionable, though Dix's suggestion that it was probably connected with veneration for the bishop[69] does not explain why it should be used in this service and no other at this time.

At daybreak on Sunday, Egeria tells us, 'they assemble in the great church built by Constantine which is on Golgotha behind the Cross, and all things are done which are customary everywhere on the Lord's Day',[70] but that still leaves us uncertain whether the custom was the Eucharist alone or the normal morning office followed by the Eucharist. Mateos and Zerfass incline to the latter view, but the question is far from closed.[71] At the end of the Eucharist,

> when the dismissal has taken place in the church in the way which is customary everywhere, then the *monazontes* lead the bishop from the church with hymns to the *Anastasis*. When the bishop begins to approach with hymns, all the doors of the *Anastasis* basilica are opened. All the people enter—the faithful only, not the catechumens—and when the people have entered, the bishop

enters and immediately goes inside the screen of the tomb, the cave. First thanks are given to God, and then there is the prayer for all. Next the deacon bids everyone to stand where he is and bow his head, and the bishop blesses them from his place inside the screen, and then he comes out. As he comes out, all come to his hand. And so it is that the dismissal is delayed almost until the fifth or sixth hour. *Lucernare* is held in the same way as on weekdays.[72]

It would thus appear that the services at midday and 3 p.m. were omitted on Sundays, and Egeria confirms that this was the case in her summary of the Sunday services held in Lent:

In the morning they assemble just as they always do on the Lord's Day, and do what it is customary to do on the Lord's Day in the great church which is called the *Martyrium*, which is on Golgotha behind the Cross. Similarly, after the dismissal from the church has taken place, they go to the *Anastasis* with hymns, just as they always do on the Lord's Day. When this is done, it is the fifth hour. *Lucernare* takes place at the same hour as usual at the *Anastasis* and at the Cross and in all the holy places, for on the Lord's Day the ninth hour is [not] kept.[73]

Though 'not' is missing from the text, the sense obviously requires it, and it has undoubtedly fallen out through scribal error.

It is not surprising that the 3 p.m. service is omitted on Sundays, since we have argued earlier that it had been introduced originally as a time of prayer only on days of fasting,[74] and Egeria similarly omits it from her list of daily services in Eastertide, when again there was no fasting: 'from Easter until the fiftieth day, that is Pentecost, not a single person fasts here, not even those who are apotactites. For always on those days just as throughout the year the customary services are held at the *Anastasis* from cockcrow until morning, and similarly at the sixth hour and at *Lucernare*'.[75] On the other hand, we would not expect the midday office to have been omitted—as it is not in Eastertide—and it is possible that the service after the Eucharist, which included thanksgiving to God and the prayer for all, and took place at the *Anastasis* like the other offices, is a primitive form of the midday daily office, without the later incorporation of psalmody. The suggestion that it was a second celebration of the Eucharist is improbable.[76]

There is evidence of a regular celebration of the Eucharist on Saturdays in some places at this period, as regard for the

Sabbath as a memorial of creation grew,[77] and Egeria implies that this was the case at Jerusalem, since she tells us that during Lent it was held at an early hour for the sake of those who had been fasting all week.[78] This Lenten celebration was preceded not by a short vigil, like the Sunday celebration, but by an all-night vigil, beginning after the evening office on Friday: 'throughout the night they alternate responsorial psalms, antiphons, and various readings, and all this lasts until the morning'.[79] This is clearly a vigil of a different kind from that on Sundays. Egeria gives no indication whether it was a monastic or a cathedral service, but as John Cassian (c. 360–435) describes an identical vigil held throughout the year in Palestinian monasticism,[80] it would appear that we have here a parallel situation to that of daily prayer at the third hour, which belonged to the ancient tradition of the Church, but was retained as a regular observance only in monastic communities in the fourth century, except for Jerusalem, where it was a Lenten addition to the cathedral cycle. Cassian believes that this practice derives from the Apostles who, overwhelmed by the crucifixion, stayed awake throughout the Friday night, and he certainly appears to be correct in seeing it as an extension of the observance of Friday rather than a preparation for the Saturday, since in the monastic custom the brethren have a short rest after the vigil ends 'at the fourth cockcrow' before they begin the day, and in winter, when the nights are longer, this rest is extended rather than the vigil being begun later. We have already encountered in the third century the practice of extending the Friday fast to include Saturday, in imitation of the Paschal fast,[81] and though this would have had to be somewhat curtailed when Saturday became a eucharistic day, yet it would have been a natural step for the night to be spent in a vigil modelled on the Paschal vigil, and inevitable that this would have been adopted more widely in the monastic tradition than in the less rigorous secular tradition of the fourth century.

Cassian provides a more detailed description of the structure of the vigil than Egeria. The monks divided it

> into an office of three parts, so that the labour may be distributed by this variety and relieve the tiredness of the body by some relaxation. For when they have sung three antiphons standing, after this sitting on the ground or on very low seats they respond to three psalms chanted by one of them, each psalm being assigned to

a different brother in turn, and to these they add three lessons while remaining seated in silence. So it is that, by reducing the labour of their bodies, they fulfil their vigils with a greater concentration of the mind.

We may presume that this pattern of three antiphonal psalms, three responsorial psalms, and three lessons was repeated throughout the night. Joseph Gelineau has argued that by antiphonal psalmody at this period is not meant the much later Western practice of two choirs singing alternate verses of a psalm, but a development of the responsorial method in which soloists still sang the verses, while the refrain was repeated by two choirs in turn,[82] and it seems to have been introduced into such extended vigils for the same reason as the variation in posture—to stimulate concentration and reduce the tiredness and distraction to which the monotony of responsorial singing would give rise. According to the ancient ecclesiastical historians, this method of psalmody was first adopted in vigils held in Antioch, though they disagree about its precise origin: Theodoret speaks of it being introduced in the night vigils held by a group of ascetics opposed to the Arian Leontius, bishop from A.D. 344 to 357, while Socrates believes that the custom of singing hymns in this manner went back to the time of Ignatius, and he tells us that the Arians began to sing hymns which promoted their heretical beliefs in this way in their weekly vigils on Friday and Saturday nights, and that it was Chrysostom who organized the singing of the canonical psalms in the same mode among the orthodox, though this last claim can hardly be correct since, as we shall see, we have the evidence of Basil for the adoption of antiphonal psalmody in Cappadocia before this time, and the ascription of the origin of antiphonal hymnody to the time of Ignatius is also doubtful.[83] However, if the rest of the account is reliable, it suggests that the weekly vigils had originally consisted simply of readings and prayers, like the Paschal vigil, and that the introduction of psalmody was in response to the Arian use of hymns on such occasions, though it may also have been influenced by the form of the regular monastic night offices.

Apart from the Sunday vigil, this is the first example of a regular ministry of the word which we have encountered outside the Eucharist in the cathedral tradition. Of the services of the word which we discovered in the second and third centuries, the daily instruction survives at Jerusalem in the bishop's *catechesis* of the baptismal candidates during Lent and Easter week, and the formal services of the word on Wednesdays and Fridays continue. According to Egeria, some of the faithful continued to attend the daily *catechesis*, which lasted for three hours after the morning office. During it the bishop went through the whole Bible, beginning with Genesis, and also taught them 'about the resurrection and the faith'.[84] With regard to Wednesday and Friday, Egeria tells us:

> At the ninth hour they assemble on Sion, because it is customary always, that is all the year, to assemble on Sion on Wednesdays and Fridays at the ninth hour, since in these places, unless it happens to be a martyrs' day, there is always fasting on Wednesdays and Fridays even by catechumens, and that is why they assemble at the ninth hour on Sion. But even if a martyrs' day happens to fall on a Wednesday or Friday in Lent, they still assemble at the ninth hour on Sion. On Wednesdays in Lent then, as I said above, they assemble at the ninth hour on Sion as is the custom throughout the year, and do everything which it is customary to do at the ninth hour, except for the oblation; for the bishop and the presbyter preach assiduously so that the people will always learn the law. When the dismissal has taken place, then the people lead the bishop with hymns to the *Anastasis*, and it is already the time for *Lucernare* when they enter the *Anastasis*: the hymns and antiphons are recited, the prayers are said, and the *Lucernare* dismissal takes place at the *Anastasis* and at the Cross, but the *Lucernare* dismissal is always later on those days, that is in Lent, than during the rest of the year.[85]

This service is not just an extension of the normal daily office at the ninth hour, but it takes place in an entirely different location, which implies that it has a separate history. Since Sion was the ancient centre of the Jerusalem church, we may conjecture that the services held there were of long standing, while the public celebration of the daily offices, being of more recent origin, took place in a setting more in keeping with the character of fourth-century Christianity in Jerusalem. Since the service is also clearly linked with the practice of fasting on those days, we may see it as the successor of the station day observance described by Tertullian,[86] and at least in Lent its contents are 'everything which is customary . . . except for the oblation', with a strong emphasis on preaching. Whether outside Lent the service was still one of the word alone or a full Eucharist depends on how 'customary' is to be understood: does it mean what was customary for the rest of the year in

Jerusalem, or what was customary in the region from which Egeria came? Certainly in some places the Eucharist on these days had been moved from the morning and fused with the afternoon service,[87] so that the fast included fasting from the Eucharist, and this may be what had happened in Jerusalem outside Lent, since during Eastertide when there was no fasting the service was transferred to the morning.[88] On the other hand, since we have suggested earlier that the service of the word had been inherited from Judaism as a morning service,[89] as on Sundays, and had been moved to the afternoon to form the conclusion of the fast on Wednesdays and Fridays, its appearance here as a morning service when there is no fasting may again be another example of Jerusalem's continued adherence to primitive liturgical traditions, and we need not therefore conclude that the service was necessarily eucharistic.

The same service is found elsewhere. In Alexandria it remained as a service of the word throughout the year: Socrates tells us that there 'on Wednesdays and Fridays the Scriptures are read, and the teachers interpret them, and all of the *synaxis* takes place except for the celebration of the mysteries'.[90] Epiphanius knows of *synaxes*, which he believes to have been instituted by the Apostles, held on Wednesdays, Fridays, and Sundays, but he does not make clear whether these were all eucharistic or not. The services on Wednesdays and Fridays were at the ninth hour because of the fast, except during Eastertide when they were in the morning; and he also tells of a further development, apparently not adopted at Jerusalem at the time of Egeria's visit, in which the service was held every weekday during the Lenten fast.[91] The same custom is also attested for Antioch by John Chrysostom: his sermons on the book of Genesis were delivered at this Lenten daily service, and the choice of Genesis suggests that here the baptismal *catechesis*, which as we have seen began with this book at Jerusalem, had been conflated with this afternoon service. Moreover, because here, unlike Jerusalem, the service of the word was held in the same place as the evening office, the two successive services were inevitably tending to become linked together, a process which was completed in later centuries when they became fused into a single rite.[92] Finally, Socrates also speaks of the unusual custom at Caesarea and in Cyprus where 'on Saturdays and Sundays the presbyters and bishops regularly interpret the Scriptures in the evening at the lamplighting',[93] but the origin of this is obscure.

5. *The Monastic Office in the East*

In the early Christian tradition there were always those who regarded the observance of fixed times of prayer in the course of the day as no more than a second-best way of fulfilling the apostolic injunction to 'pray without ceasing': the ideal was truly continuous prayer day and night. We have already encountered this attitude, for example, in Clement of Alexandria,[1] and it was inherited by the eremetic and monastic movements in the fourth century and lay at the heart of their spirituality. There was, however, an important difference in their understanding of ceaseless prayer from that of former generations, as Alexander Schmemann makes clear:

> What was new here was the idea of prayer as the sole content of life, as a task which required separation from and renunciation of the world and all its works. In the early Christian understanding prayer was not opposed to life or the occupations of life, prayer penetrated life and consisted above all in a new understanding of life and its occupations, in relating them to the central object of faith—to the Kingdom of God and the Church. 'Everything you do, do heartily, as for the Lord and not for man' (Col. 3.23). 'And so whether you eat or drink or do any other thing, do all to the glory of God, since the earth is the Lord's and all that is therein' (1 Cor. 10.26,31). Therefore, 'pray at all times by the spirit' (Eph. 6.18). Work was controlled, enlightened and judged by prayer, it was not opposed to prayer. And yet monasticism was a departure out of life and its works for the sake of prayer. . . .
>
> If in the first early Christian view every undertaking could become a prayer, a ministry, a creating of and bearing witness to the Kingdom, in monasticism prayer itself now became the sole undertaking, replacing all other tasks. The labour prescribed by the monastic rules (the weaving of baskets, making of rope, etc.) was in this sense not a 'task'. It had no significance in itself, was not a ministry or vocation. It was necessary only as a support for the work of prayer, as one of its means. This is not the illumination of life and work by prayer, not a joining of these things in prayer, not even a turning of life into prayer, but prayer as life or, more properly, the replacement of life by prayer.[2]

For the nourishment of their prayer the hermits and monks meditated on the Psalter, as earlier generations had done, but there were significant differences in the way they used it. Firstly, it was the Psalter alone that they used, not because they lacked anything else but because there was a growing conviction in the fourth century in both secular and monastic circles that the 'songs of the Spirit', as they were considered to be, were to be preferred to mere ecclesiastical compositions,[3] a conviction encouraged by the fact that non-canonical hymns and psalms were often used to promote heretical ideas. We can see this attitude reflected, for example, in canon 59 of the Council of Laodicea: 'No psalms composed by private individuals or uncanonical books may be read in the church, but only the canonical books of the Old and New Testaments'. Secondly, this attitude towards the inspiration of the Psalter coupled with the fact that the aim was to fill day and night with unbroken prayer meant that, whereas previously it had been used selectively, appropriate psalms for different occasions and situations being drawn from it, it was now to be committed to memory and for the first time used in its entirety, and it came to be regarded as a great and worthy accomplishment to be able to go through the whole Psalter in the space of twenty-four hours: in effect, the hymn book of the secular Church became the prayer book of monasticism. Thirdly, whereas previously the psalms had been used chiefly in communal situations, sung by one to others at meals and in prayer in groups, now they were also to be used to feed the prayer of individuals, though in accordance with the reading habits of the time they were still recited aloud even in private meditation. Thus, for example, Palladius arriving in the desert could hear the psalmody of the hermits in their individual cells.[4] Fourthly, whereas previously the listeners had responded to the psalm with Alleluia or some other refrain, the monk usually responded with his own silent prayer. Thus, for example, Julian the hermit of Abiadene (c. 350) instructed his disciples to go out into the desert in pairs at dawn and there 'while one knelt to offer to God the worship due to him, the other stood and recited fifteen psalms of David; and this having been done, they would change roles, the one would stand to sing, the other throwing himself on the ground would worship. And having gone out from the early morning, they did this assiduously until the evening'.[5] The alternation of psalmody and prayer is a characteristic of the ceaseless vigil of early monasticism, the psalms constituting a source of meditation which stimulated and fed the prayer. According to Athanasius (c. 296–373), even the custom of singing had been adopted not for its musical effect but in order to allow more time for meditation on the meaning.[6] As he advanced spiritually, the monk was expected to

> begin to take in to himself all the thoughts of the psalms and sing them in such a way that he utters them with the deepest emotion of the heart not as the compositions of the prophet but as if he himself were their author, as his own prayer, or certainly consider them to have been directed at himself and recognize that their words were not only already fulfilled through the prophet or in the prophet but are realized and accomplished daily in himself.[7]

It is therefore hardly surprising that in the earliest and most rigorous eremetic tradition of Egypt there were no set times of prayer at all during the day but simply the practice of continuous prayer.[8] The night too was spent in prayer, sometimes with a vigil lasting the whole night, but because it was not possible to go entirely without sleep every night, more often the vigil occupied only a part of the night. Thus the hermit Palamon told his postulant Pachomius, 'I keep watch as I have been taught, always one half of the night in prayer and meditation on God's words and often the whole night'.[9] This half-vigil might be performed in different ways: St. Antony divided the night into three parts, the first and last for prayer and the middle for sleep,[10] while Palamon taught that 'either we pray till midnight and rest the remainder till morning, or we sleep till midnight and pray till morning, or again we do alternately a time of prayer and a time of sleep till morning'.[11] Fifty, sixty, or even more psalms might be recited in the course of such a vigil.[12]

The continuous prayer of the hermit was impractical, however, in a community which had to work at a variety of tasks, and so in Pachomian coenobitism it was replaced by frequent individual moments of prayer throughout the day.[13] Here, moreover, after the day's work ceased the monks would gather together for communal worship. A first evening assembly was held for the whole monastery as soon as work was over at 4 p.m., and a second one followed later in each individual house. Both had the same structure and consisted of six psalms with prayers at the end of each psalm. We are also told of one occasion when monks happened to be away from the monastery and both were said together, forming a single office of twelve psalms and prayers. After a period for sleep the corporate night vigil began about 2 a.m. and finished in the early morning before sunrise.[14]

John Cassian gives us a more detailed picture of this practice as it later developed. He believes that, although elsewhere considerable variety is found in the arrangement of psalmody in the offices between different monasteries, throughout Egypt a uniform custom is observed, and this is because, according to tradition, the number of psalms was fixed by the direction of an angel. He recounts the story, also known to us in more elaborate versions in other sources,[15] how as the monks discussed the number of psalms which ought to be included in each *synaxis*, the time came for their evening assembly and when the twelfth psalm had been completed the cantor disappeared out of the sight of all. 'Thereupon the venerable assembly of the fathers, understanding that by the providence of the Lord a general rule had been fixed for the congregations of the brethren through the direction of an angel, decided that this number would be observed both in the evening and in the nocturnal services.'[16] Clearly in his time, therefore, the two evening assemblies were now regularly fused together to form a single office, and the vigil had adopted an identical structure. It must be stressed that the nocturnal assemblies to which Cassian refers were vigils and not a morning office, as some have erroneously concluded: they were the descendant of the half-night vigils earlier described, beginning apparently at cockcrow,[17] and not of the ancient morning prayer, as for example Mateos thinks,[18] since this was unknown in the Egyptian monastic tradition, and Cassian consistently describes them as *nocturni vigili*, *nocturni sollemnitates*, *nocturni conventiculi*, and *nocturni congregationes*.

It is possible that the legend of the angel grew up in order to justify what was by normal standards an extremely small number of psalms in the night, and Cassian tells us that the monks

consider that a moderate number of obligatory prayers was divinely arranged so that for those more ardent in faith there might be left time in which their indefatigable course of virtue might be extended, and equally for wearied and weak bodies no aversion might be produced through excess. And so, when the discharge of the obligatory prayers has customarily been completed, everyone returns to his own cell ... and they again celebrate with greater attentiveness the same office of prayers as their special sacrifice, nor does anyone of them give himself up any further to rest and sleep until as the brightness of day dawns the activity of the day succeeds the labour and meditation of the night.[19]

In a later version of the legend in which Pachomius objects that the prayers are too few, the angel says, 'I arranged it this way so as to ensure that even the little ones might keep the rule and not grieve. But those who are perfect need no rule, for they have surrendered themselves entirely to the contemplation of God in their cells. I have made rules for such as do not have a discerning mind, so that, like house-servants fulfilling the duties of their station, they may live a life of freedom'.[20] Later sources also tell of further developments—the formalizing of the frequent individual prayers during the day at the number of twelve, and the addition of an office of three prayers at the ninth hour.[21]

At the evening assembly and the night vigil one of the monks stood up in the middle and chanted the psalm while the rest 'sitting on very low seats follow the voice of the singer with a very attentive heart. For they are so worn out with fasting and labour all day and night that, unless they were aided by some such indulgence, they would not be able to fulfil this number standing up'.[22] In order to retain concentration long psalms were broken up into sections, and the psalms were distributed among the brethren so that normally one man would sing only three psalms. Where fewer than four brethren were present at the office the psalms were evenly distributed between them, but where there were more than four, the arrangement of a group of three psalms to each cantor was retained.[23] We have already encountered the tendency to group psalms in threes elsewhere in the early Church,[24] and its persistence here in Egyptian monasticism, where nearly all other liturgical practices seem to be different, points towards it being an ancient and deep-rooted ecclesiastical tradition. The twelfth psalm was concluded by the response 'Alleluia', and this was always one of those psalms which had 'Alleluia' marked in its title in the Bible.[25] The psalms did not follow immediately one after the other, but at the end of each psalm all rose to their feet and stood in silent prayer; then, having prostrated themselves on the floor for a brief moment, they rose again for further silent prayer, concluded by a collect, and so on to the next psalm, thus alternating psalm and prayer.[26] On Sundays and throughout Eastertide they omitted the prostration in accordance with established ecclesiastical custom which forbade kneeling at those times.[27] Cassian is also the first to tell us of the use of the *Gloria Patri* as the conclusion to the psalms, though it may be a much older custom. A doxology of this nature was the traditional ending of prayer, and its use in relation to the psalms was simply a development from this, the precise wording of it being a source of dispute between Catholics and Arians.[28] In Egypt it was not sung at the end of each psalm but only at the end of what Cassian calls the *antiphona*, which here must mean either the whole psalmody of the service or the group of three psalms.[29]

Finally, mention must be made of one other feature which Cassian alone records as part of the daily offices of the Egyptian monks—the addition of two scriptural readings to the end of each service. One lesson was taken from the Old Testament and one from the New, except on Saturdays and Sundays and throughout Eastertide when both came from the New Testament. That these are a later addition to the services is shown not only by the fact that they are mentioned in no other source but also by the structure of the office— they are placed at the very end, without any sort of prayer or responsorial psalm to follow them—and also by Cassian's own admission: whereas he believes that the number of psalms was fixed by an angel, the 'assembly of the fathers' decided to add the two readings 'as an extraordinary element, on a voluntary basis for those who wished by assiduous meditation to retain the memory of the divine scriptures'.[30] Obviously this is once again a didactic ministry of the word, very similar to the addition of the lessons to the synagogue service in Judaism.[31]

What we have here, therefore, is a radically different concept of the office from that found in the secular Church. There is no corporate expression of praise in hymn or canticle, no communal response to the psalmody, except for the Alleluia, no ceremonial lighting of the lamp or offering of incense, no selection of psalms appropriate to the hour—for time was of no consequence to the monk—but simply the continuation in common of the individual meditation on the word of God which filled every waking hour of the monk and which nothing, not even the liturgical tradition of the Church, was allowed to interrupt. Similarly the prayers which follow the psalms are not intercession for the needs of the world but petition for the ascetical growth of the monk himself, for although inter-cession was acknowledged as a legitimate form of prayer in the monastic tradition, it was not regarded as the highest kind of prayer to which one should attain.[32] Thus the office had become inward and not outward looking. As Schmemann says,

> Devotional rules and an ordo of prayer did indeed appear in monasticism (of both types: cenobitic and anchorite) at a very early time. But for the liturgiologist it is essential to understand that these rules developed not as an ordo of worship, but within what might be called a 'pedagogical' system. They were needed to guide the monk on his way toward 'spiritual freedom'. Their origins are completely different from the origins of the liturgical ordo or what we have been calling the *lex orandi*, which is essentially the embodiment or actualization of the *lex credendi* of the Church's faith and life. The purpose of the liturgical ordo is to make worship the expression of the faith of the Church, to actualize the Church herself; the purpose of the monastic devotional rules is to train the monk in constant prayer, to inculcate in him the personal work of prayer. In the liturgical ordo there are no categories of 'long' or 'short' prayers, while its relation to seasons, times and hours is rooted in a definite understanding of these times and hours. In monasticism, however, times and hours as such have no great significance. What is important is the division of prayer in such a way that it will fill up the whole of life, and for this reason it is set in a framework of time. But time itself has no meaning at all other than as the 'time of prayer'. The monastic rule knows only the rhythm of prayer, which due to the 'weakness of the flesh' is interrupted occasionally by sleep and the reception of food.[33]

Outside Egypt, however, the picture tended to be rather different. Monastic communities elsewhere in the East which were more closely associated with the life of the secular Church around them not only adhered to the observance of the times of daily prayer inherited from the early centuries—morning, third, sixth, and ninth hours, evening, and night—but also because of the nature of their life were able to celebrate them all corporately. We are presented with a picture of the practices of the monastic communities of Cappadocia in the writings of St. Basil (c. 330–79), though there is some discrepancy between the *Sermo Asceticus* which is attributed to him and his Longer

Rule. The former document either belongs to an older period than Basil or it reflects an earlier stage in the development of his monastic system,[34] since it prescribes only the six daily offices of the early Church and does not include the office of Compline, which makes its first appearance in his Longer Rule. Nevertheless, the author still contrives to arrive at the ideal of seven times of prayer each day enunciated in Ps. 119.164 by the strange device of directing that the midday prayer be divided, part being said before, and part after, the taking of food.[35]

The other writings of Basil enable us to fill in a few details of the contents of the different offices. The morning office was composed of 'hymns and songs', though Basil does not specify what these were. He does, however, use the expression 'imitate on earth the choruses of angels' in his reference to this service, and may by this be alluding to the use of the canticle Gloria in Excelsis which is explicitly mentioned by other writers.[36] Of the other hours of the day, all we know is that Ps. 91 formed a regular feature of both the midday office and Compline.[37] Since Compline was a new addition to the cycle, the probability is that the psalm had first been appointed for the midday office, because of its reference to 'the destruction that wastes at noonday', and then subsequently included in Compline because of its reference to 'the terror of the night'. Apparently, however, the contents of the different offices were not completely unchanging, for Basil says that 'I think that diversity and variety in the prayers and the psalmody which occur at the fixed hours is useful, because when there is monotony, the soul often becomes weary and is a prey to distraction, but when there is variation and change in the psalmody and the words at each hour, its desire is renewed and the attention is restored'.[38]

Basil also provides in one of his letters a full description of a vigil, defending his practice against some who objected to his use of 'psalms and a kind of music varying from the custom which has obtained among you'.[39] He goes on to say:

Now as to the charge relating to psalmody, with which our calumniators particularly frighten the simpler people, I have this to say. The customs which now obtain are in agreement and harmony with all the churches of God. Among us the people go at night to the house of prayer and, in distress, affliction, and continual tears making confession to God, they at last rise from their prayers and begin to sing psalms. Then, divided into two parts, they sing antiphonally with one another, thus at once confirming their study of the Scriptures, and at the same time producing for themselves a heedful temper and a heart free from distraction. Afterwards they again allow one to begin the song, and the rest respond; and so after passing the night in a variety of psalmody, praying in between, as the day begins to dawn, they all together, as with one voice and one heart, raise the psalm of confession to the Lord, each making for himself his own expressions of penitence. If for these reasons you renounce us, you will renounce Libyans, Thebans, Palestinians, Arabians, Phoenicians, Syrians, and dwellers by the Euphrates, in a word all those among whom vigils and prayers and common psalmody have been held in honour. But, it is said, these things were not observed in the time of the great Gregory. But nor were the litanies which you now practise. I do not say this to find fault with you, for I would pray that all of you should live in tears and continual penitence. For we do nothing else but offer supplication for our sins, but we propitiate our God not in the words of mere man, as you do, but in the songs of the Spirit.[40]

Recent scholars have tended to assume that Basil is here describing the regular midnight office which had been extended into a vigil, following the Egyptian model and lasting until morning, the 'psalm of confession' (Ps. 51) forming the beginning of the morning office, as in other rites.[41] However, this may not be the case. Firstly, he seems to be talking of something in which the ordinary laity are involved, although Mateos has tried to argue that by 'the people' what he has in mind are ascetics who are following a monastic pattern of worship.[42] Secondly, the Longer Rule seems to suggest that the monks generally retired to bed after the midnight office, for after referring to that hour, Basil says: 'again we must rise for prayer, preventing the dawn, so that we are not caught by the day sleeping in bed'.[43] Thirdly, the inclusion of antiphonal psalmody as well as the more traditional responsorial method suggests that it is an occasional vigil of longer duration rather than a regular nightly office, since all our early references to this new way of rendering the psalms refer to such occasions, where it seems to have been adopted in order to introduce some variety and thus reduce tiredness and distraction in such extended observances.[44] If this is true, then it would help to explain the opposition encountered by Basil. We have seen earlier how the weekly vigils appear to have become the scene of conflict between the Arians and the orthodox in Antioch, the former singing their heretical hymns at them, and the latter responding by singing psalms and imitating the antiphonal method of the Arian hymnody. A very similar situation appears to lie behind this letter. Basil's opponents celebrate 'litanies'— a term often used to denote vigils[45]—at which they use hymns ('the words of mere man'), in contrast to Basil who uses the canonical psalms ('the songs of the Spirit'). They, however, attack his use of psalms on these occasions, and the antiphonal way of singing them, as innovations, charges which Basil does not deny, but instead he argues that what he is doing is the common practice of churches throughout the East. It is true that no mention is made here of readings, which elsewhere had a place in these weekly vigils, but that may simply be because their use was undisputed by both parties and not because they were absent from the vigil.

On the other hand, in the work entitled *De Virginitate*, originally ascribed to Athanasius but now often considered to be of Cappadocian rather than Alexandrian origin and to date from the latter half of the fourth century,[46] the midnight time of prayer has certainly been extended to form a regular vigil throughout the night, for as long as the virgin is able to continue, following the Egyptian pattern. For the hours of prayer it prescribes:

> Night and day let not the word of God be absent from your mouth. Let your work always be meditation on the sacred Scriptures. Have a Psalter and learn the psalms. Let the rising sun see the book in your hands and after the third hour perform a *synaxis*, because at this hour the wood of the cross was prepared. At the sixth hour likewise make your prayers, with psalms, weeping, and petition, because at this hour the Son of God hung on the cross. At the ninth hour again in hymns and praises, confessing your sins with tears, supplicate God, because at that hour the Lord hanging on the cross gave up the spirit. . . .
>
> If you come in at the twelfth hour, celebrate a greater and longer *synaxis* with your sister virgins. If you do not have a companion, celebrate it alone, for God is present and listening. . . .
>
> Rise at midnight and hymn the Lord your God, for at that hour our Lord rose from the dead and hymned the Father; therefore at that hour we were commanded to hymn God. Having risen, first say this verse: 'At midnight I rose to praise you because of your righteous ordinances', and pray and begin to say the fiftieth psalm [Ps. 51] until you complete it, and let these things remain fixed for you every day. Say as many psalms as you can say standing, and

after each psalm let there be a prayer and genuflexion, confessing your sins with tears to the Lord and asking him to forgive you. After three psalms say the Alleluia. If there are virgins with you, let them also sing psalms and perform prayers one by one. Towards dawn say this psalm, 'O God, my God, I seek you, my soul thirsts for you', and at sunrise, 'Bless the Lord, all works of the Lord', and 'Glory to God in the highest, and in earth peace, goodwill to men. We praise you, we bless you, we worship you', and the rest.[47]

It is interesting to see that such vigils might be observed individually as well as corporately. As in Egypt a prayer and genuflexion are to follow each psalm, and where the vigil was performed communally, one person was to recite the psalm while the rest listened. Similarly, the psalms are grouped in threes, and each group is concluded with the Alleluia. The first part of the vigil is constant—Ps. 119.62, followed by a prayer and then Ps. 51. The first two elements may well be the remains of the original midnight prayer, but Ps. 51 elsewhere forms the beginning of the morning office, and it would seem that the fact that vigil and morning office tend to run on as a continuous act of worship, together with the fact that the former has here acquired a very strongly penitential character, has led to this psalm being moved back to stand at the head of the whole rite. The morning office proper begins with the traditional morning psalm, Ps. 63, and includes the Benedicite and Gloria in Excelsis. Mateos claims that these are only indications of the beginning and end of the office, and that between the psalm and the Benedicite would come the rest of the office, which was so well known that it did not need explicit mention. This unexpressed element he believes may well have been Pss. 148–50.[48] However, this is an unwarranted assumption, since, as we shall show below, what evidence there is suggests that these psalms originally belonged to the conclusion of the night vigil in the East and not to the heart of the morning office.[49]

Syria and Palestine constitute a midway position between Egypt and Cappadocia, not only geographically but also liturgically. Monastic and ascetic practices there on the one hand included the lesser hours of prayer, as in Cappadocia, while on the other hand adopted a vigil beginning at cockcrow, as in Egypt, more commonly instead of the midnight hour of prayer, it seems, rather than in addition to it. For although Jerome in his *Tract on Ps. 119*, which was addressed to Eastern monks, refers to both midnight and cockcrow, as does the *Apostolic Tradition* of Hippolytus in its final form,[50] all our other sources simply refer to a single night office beginning at cockcrow. Thus, for example, *Apostolic Constitutions* 8.34 directs: 'Offer up your prayers in the morning, at the third hour, the sixth, the ninth, the evening, and at cockcrow'. According to John Chrysostom, this vigil began at Antioch with a fixed element consisting of Ps. 134 and Is. 26.9f. Then followed the variable psalmody, and this appears to have been regularly concluded with Pss. 148–50:

> the songs themselves are suitable and full of love for God. 'In the night', they say, 'lift up your hands to God.' And again, 'in the night my soul yearns for you, O God, because your precepts shed light on earth'. And the hymns of David which cause fountains of tears to flow. . . . And again when they sing with the angels, for angels too are singing then, saying, 'Praise the Lord from the heavens', while we are yawning, scratching, snoring, or simply lying on our backs, meditating endless deceits. Think what it is for them to spend the whole night in this way.[51]

The monks then retired for a short rest before celebrating the morning office, which appears to have closely resembled the secular rite, although the element of intercession seems to have given way to prayer for spiritual progress:

> As soon as the sun is up, or rather even long before its rise, they rise from their beds . . . and having made one choir, with their conscience bright, with one voice all, like as out of one mouth, they sing hymns to the God of all, honouring him and thanking him for all his benefits, both individual and common. So, if it seems good, leaving Adam, let us ask how this choir of those who sing on earth and say 'Glory to God in the highest, and on earth peace, goodwill towards men' differs from the angels. . . . Then after they have sung those songs, they bow their knees and entreat the God who was the object of their hymns for things to the very thought of which some do not easily arrive. For they ask nothing of things present, for they have no regard for these, but that they may stand boldly before the fearful judgement seat, when the only begotten Son of God comes to judge living and dead, and that no one may hear that fearful voice which says, 'I do not know you', and that with a pure conscience and many good deeds they may pass through this troublesome life, and sail over the angry sea with a favourable wind.[52]

Cassian tells us that Palestine, Mesopotamia, and the whole East followed one and the same tradition in assigning three psalms to the offices at the third, sixth, and ninth hours, and later speaks of it as an 'order anciently fixed . . . to signify the confession of the Trinity'. As we have seen, this has it roots at least as early as the end of the second century.[53] He justifies the observance of these hours first by reference to Daniel and then by reference to New Testament events at these times: at the third hour the Spirit was poured out on the Apostles; at the sixth hour Christ was crucified and Peter received his vision; and at the ninth hour Christ died and descended into hell, Cornelius received his vision, and Peter and John went up into the Temple. For the morning and evening offices he refers to the daily sacrifices prescribed in the Old Testament, and to verses in the Psalter thought to allude to morning and evening prayers (Pss. 141.2; 63.1,7; 119.147–8). Finally, he believes that the hours mentioned in the Parable of the Labourers in the Vineyard (Mt. 20.1–6) were intended to correspond to these five times of prayer during the daytime.[54]

The psalms at all these hours were each followed by prayer in the Egyptian manner, just as they were in the vigil,[55] and this contrasts with the practice at Jerusalem, where, as we have seen, the religious shared in the hours of prayer during the day with the secular church, and only celebrated their night office separately.[56] Here the psalms at the day hours were grouped in a block, with intercession at the very end in the secular manner, and only the night office, which began at cockcrow, followed the monastic pattern of alternating psalm and prayer. At the end of this office the participants did not retire for a rest as they did at Antioch, but instead the vigil led directly into the morning office, as in the De Virginitate, and thus in effect formed a preamble to it. We have also seen that there was a similar element of preliminary psalmody attached to the Jerusalem evening office prior to the arrival of the bishop.[57] Since the expansion of night prayer into a vigil had been the result of the influence of the Egyptian practice, it is probable that this addition too is an imitation of the Egyptian evening assembly, and may have been widely adopted in Eastern monasticism at this time, although we have no explicit evidence. What is indisputable is that in later centuries, because of the strong influence exercised over the Church by monasticism, both morning and evening offices in Eastern churches everywhere came to have this preliminary psalmody, derived from the desert monks, prefixed to them, and this strongly suggests that it was already a part of the monastic pattern at this time. It is easily identifiable because the psalms are arranged consecutively, following one another in their Biblical order as the monks sought to work their way through the Psalter, rather than selectively—the psalms being chosen for their appropriateness to the particular time of day—as in the older tradition.[58]

Outside Jerusalem attempts were also made to encourage the ordinary laity to maintain the old times of prayer of the primitive Church, and to share in the corporate celebration of them with the monastic communities. Chrysostom, for example, exhorted the people to come and join in the night prayer,[59] or at least to wake their children and pray at home,[60] and also to take part in the hours of prayer during the day: 'You say, "How is it possible for a secular man detained at court to pray at the three hours of the day and run to church?" It is possible, and it is very easy. For even if it is not easy to run to church, it is possible to pray standing there while still detained at court'.[61] His efforts to persuade the laity to join in the night prayer apparently met with opposition from the clergy, who resented the pressure which was consequently put upon them to forego a full night's sleep and to participate in the service.[62] Though this reaction was widespread in the East, yet so strong was the influence of monasticism that in A.D. 528 the Emperor Justinian passed a decree obliging all clergy in the East to include the night office as well as the morning and evening services in the daily cycle.[63] Less successful, however, was the attempt to persuade the laity to maintain the ancient practice of private Bible study at home: they complained that they were being turned into monks.[64] They considered such things were no longer for them, but only for the ascetic and monastic members of the Church.

The situation in Cassian's monastery at Bethlehem has been the cause of some considerable dispute between liturgical scholars. He describes how a brief morning rest there had become a somewhat prolonged sleep, extending up to the third hour of the day, and this laxity led to the introduction of a *novella sollemnitas* or *matutina sollemnitas* at sunrise in order to limit the sleep and mark the beginning of the day's work. It has traditionally been assumed—and this view is still defended by some today—that Cassian was here speaking of a rest after the celebration of the morning office, and so was referring to the introduction of the office of Prime into the monastic cycle.[65] This view was, however, challenged by J. Froger in 1946,[66] but his thesis, that the new office was not Prime but the morning office, was at first strongly contested by other scholars,[67] and this led Froger to modify his interpretation of Cassian's evidence in some respects, though not in its essentials.[68] Since then his general position has found support from other liturgical scholars.[69]

Cassian begins by describing how

> this morning service (*matutinam*), which is now observed very generally in western countries, was first appointed as a canonical office in our own time and in our own monastery . . . For up till that time we find that when this morning office (*matutina sollemnitate*)—which is customarily celebrated in the monasteries of Gaul a short time after the nocturnal psalms and prayers are completed—was finished at the same time as the daily vigils (*cum cotidianis vigiliis pariter consummata*), the remaining hours were assigned by our elders to bodily refreshment.

When, however, this rest was abused, it was decided that they should get up at sunrise

> and by reciting three psalms and prayers according to the manner which was anciently fixed for the observance of the third or sixth hour to signify the confession of the Trinity, they should by a uniform arrangement at the same time mark an end to sleep and a beginning to work.[70]

One of the main reasons why Froger's thesis has been attacked is that it is quite obvious that the morning office did not originate in Bethlehem late in the fourth century but existed elsewhere from early times, and so it has been concluded that Cassian must therefore be referring to the introduction of some other service. However, that does not necessarily follow. We have seen that Egyptian monasticism did not know a morning office but simply a night vigil and also that this tradition exercised a strong influence over other Eastern monastic practices. It should not surprise us therefore that there were some places which followed this Egyptian pattern more closely still and did not include a morning office after their vigil, for Cassian adds that there were other Eastern monasteries like Bethlehem which did not adopt this new service. Indeed it is possible that the two places where we have encountered monastic involvement in morning offices in Syria and Palestine—at Antioch and Jerusalem—may well have been exceptions to the norm, influenced there by secular practice, and this conjecture is considerably reinforced by the signs, which we shall examine later, that the original Western monastic cycle also lacked a morning office. It is also interesting that in the Latin systematic version of the sayings of the desert fathers the abbot of a monastery in Palestine tells its founder, Epiphanius, Bishop of Salamis in Cyprus, that they observe the third, sixth, and ninth hours and the evening office, and makes no mention of the morning, although some manuscripts of the Greek alphabetical version omit the reference to the evening office from the saying, and others add a reference to the first hour.[71] Cassian's mistake, which has misled scholars, was to assume that since a morning service was a recent innovation at Bethlehem, it must have been the progenitor of all other morning offices everywhere.

If that is the case, why then does Cassian speak of the morning office as having been previously 'finished at the same time as the daily vigils'? Does this not imply that the office existed already and that the new service is not to be identified with it? This difficulty can be resolved when one turns to what he has to say later about the contents of the new service:

> no change was made in the ancient arrangement of psalms by our elders who decided that this morning service (*matutinam sollemnitatem*) should be added, but the dismissal (*missam*) was always celebrated in the same order as before in their nocturnal assemblies. For the hymns which in this country they use at the morning service at the end of the night vigils (*ad matutinam sollemnitatem in fine nocturnarum vigiliarum*), which they are accustomed to end after cockcrow and before dawn, they still sing today, that is Psalm 148, the beginning of which is 'Praise the Lord in the heavens', and the rest which follow, but Psalms 50 [51], 62 [63], and 89 [90] have been assigned to this new service. Lastly, throughout Italy at this day, when the morning hymns are ended, the 50th [51st] psalm is sung in all the churches, which I have no doubt can only have been derived from this source.[72]

This translation follows the traditional interpretation—that the new service is Prime—and has to assume that the expression *matutinam sollemnitatem* is being used to describe both the new service and also a pre-existent morning office. But this is not the only, nor perhaps the most natural, interpretation of the passage. If the phrase 'at the end of the night vigils' is not attached to the subordinate clause but to the main clause of the sentence, a very different sense ensues: 'For the hymns which in this country they use at the morning service they still sing today at the end of the night vigils, which they are accustomed to end after cockcrow and before dawn, that is Psalm 148 . . .'. What we have now is a contrast between the practice found in Cassian's home territory of Gaul ('in this country'), where Pss. 148–50 were included in the morning office, and that at Bethlehem, where these psalms continued to be used at the end of the night vigils, just as they were at Antioch according to Chrysostom,[73] while Pss. 51, 63, and 90 were assigned to the newly instituted morning office. This in turn sheds light on the meaning of the earlier passage: it is because the contents of the Western morning office, i.e. Pss. 148–50, are found at the conclusion of the night vigil at Bethlehem that Cassian can speak of the morning office there as being 'finished at the same time as the daily vigils' before it was instituted in a separate form. The contents of this new service are clearly derived from the secular morning office: we have already encountered Pss. 51 and 63 there, and 90 is a natural choice with its reference to morning in verse 14, and may even have been used in the secular form. The structure, however, is modelled on the monastic hours of prayer during the day, with a prayer following each psalm, and this has misled scholars into seeing it as the forerunner of Prime.

Cassian's account also throws some illumination on the original place of Pss. 148–50 in the daily office. It has come to be treated as an unquestioned fact that these psalms have always formed the nucleus of the morning office in the cathedral tradition and were derived from the usage of the synagogue. However, like many other such 'facts' this rests upon nothing stronger than constant repetition by successive scholars. As we have indicated earlier, the evidence for the use of these psalms in the first-century synagogue liturgy is very flimsy indeed,[74] and claims for their inclusion in the secular morning office in the East in the fourth century rely solely upon supposition. On the other hand, both Cassian and Chrysostom are witnesses to the fact that they formed the conclusion of the monastic night vigil in Syria and Palestine, and we must not forget that the Egyptian vigil always ended with one of the psalms which had Alleluia marked in its title in the Bible, which would include these psalms. What evidence there is, therefore, points to the original place of the three psalms as being the fixed conclusion of the night vigil, perhaps arising out of the practice of early ascetics who recited the whole Psalter in the course of 24 hours, and so would have reached these psalms at the end of their vigil.

How then did they come to occupy a central position in the morning office in later centuries? This is not hard to explain. We have already seen how in some places, as for example Jerusalem, the monastic vigil led directly into the morning office. This juxtaposition of the two could very easily have led to Pss. 148–50 being thought of as the beginning of the latter rather than the conclusion of the former, and the strong influence exercised by monasticism in the Church would account for their being adopted as the beginning of the morning office even in the cathedral tradition. This was the position which they apparently had throughout Italy in Cassian's day, since he tells us in the above quotation that there 'when the morning hymns are ended the 50th [51st] psalm is sung in all the churches', an arrangement which he again mistakenly attributes to the influence of the Bethlehem morning office. There can be little doubt from the context that by 'morning hymns' he means Pss. 148–50, and these now form the beginning of the office, with Ps. 51, the original beginning, coming second. A similar arrangement is found in the morning office of the Chaldean rite, which is thought to have remained in many ways closer to the ancient pattern than other Eastern rites: here Pss. 148–50 precede Ps. 51 on weekdays.[75] In all other rites known to us, however, these psalms form the climax of the morning office, and this seems to have been a further stage of development: we have already seen how in *De Virginitate* Ps. 51 had been drawn back to stand at the head of the whole rite.[76] It would have been perfectly natural for a similar movement to have taken place in the opposite direction so that Pss. 148–50 formed the conclusion not just of the vigil psalmody but of the whole of the hymns and psalms of the combined night and morning offices, and once again the influence of monasticism in the Church as a whole would have ensured that this practice was generally followed.

6. The Cathedral Office in the West

Evidence for the earliest form of the daily office is even more limited in the West than in the East, since we do not possess such a full description as that given by Egeria, but instead as our sources of information we have to rely upon more fragmentary references in the writings of various authors, upon brief injunctions in conciliar documents, and upon liturgical texts of a much later period, reflecting a highly advanced stage in the development of the office from which it is almost impossible to disentangle primitive elements. Thus for North Africa, for example, we have only the briefest of allusions in the works of Augustine (354–430). He tells us that 'day by day I rise, go to church, sing there a morning and an evening hymn, and sing a third and fourth in my house. Thus each day I bring a sacrifice of praise and offer it before my God'.[1] From this we learn not only that daily morning and evening services existed in the churches at this time, but that their character was strongly that of praise, and that apparently here at this stage there was only a single psalm at each office and not a group of psalms. In another passage Augustine speaks of his mother 'omitting on no day the oblation on your altar, coming to your church twice a day, morning and evening, without any intermission, not for idle chatter and old wives' tales, but so that she might hear you in your words and you might hear her in her prayers'.[2] The reference to 'words' (*sermonibus*) does not necessarily mean that the offices included readings: it could refer to the ministry of the word in the Eucharist or more probably to listening to the verses of the psalms. On the other hand, Augustine elsewhere says, comparing the zealous Christian with the ant who makes provision for winter, 'he runs daily to the church of God, he prays, he listens to a reading, he sings a hymn, he chews over what he has heard'.[3] He could here be referring to attendance at a daily Eucharist, though there is no explicit mention of it, or it could be to a daily assembly for instruction such as we have found existing elsewhere in the second and third centuries (and surviving in Lent and Eastertide in the East in the fourth century).[4] It is most improbable that what is in mind is the daily office proper, since all other evidence indicates that this did not include readings anywhere, except in the monastic customs of Egypt, until a later date.

Ambrose (c. 339–97), Bishop of Milan, has a little more to say on the subject of daily prayer in his region. He expects Christians to attend church each morning:

> in the morning hasten and bring to church the first-fruits of your prayer, and afterwards if secular business calls you, you will be able to say, 'my eyes anticipated the morning that I might meditate on thy words', and you will proceed safely to your affairs. How pleasant it is to begin the day with hymns and canticles, with the Beatitudes which you read in the Gospel. How beneficial it is that the words of Christ should bless you, and while you recite the benedictions of the Lord, you should acquire zeal for some virtue, so that even in yourself you may recognize the merit of the divine benediction.[5]

The only surprise here is the mention of the recitation of the Beatitudes as apparently a regular constituent of the morning office, something for which we have no other evidence at all.[6] Ambrose also has stern words for those who neglect their daily duty:

> Woe to those who in the morning seek the draught which inebriates, who ought to offer praises to God, to anticipate the light, and to meet with prayer the Sun of Righteousness, who visits his people and rises to us if we rise to Christ and not to wine and strong drink. Hymns are being recited, and are you holding the harp? Psalms are being sung, and are you taking up the lute or the timbrel?[7]

The ending of the day was to be similarly observed: 'the dawn of the day resounds with the psalm, and with the psalm re-echoes the sunset'.[8] This evening office he terms 'the evening sacrifice' and 'the hour of incense',[9] expressions which suggest that the service included Ps. 141 with its reference to prayer being like incense and the evening sacrifice, though the assumption made by several scholars that Milan knew a literal offering of incense at this early date goes beyond the evidence.[10] On the other hand, there may conceivably be a reference to the remnant of an old regular midday time of prayer in one place: Ambrose says that 'there are very many days on which punctually at the midday hours one may come to the church for the singing of hymns and the celebration of the oblation'.[11] This twofold expression has been thought to indicate that there was an office preceding the actual Eucharist, and it has also been suggested that Ps. 119 was used at this midday office, as it certainly was in the later tradition at Milan, for Ambrose calls the 22 sections of this psalm 'hymns' and compares it to 'the sun in the fullness of its light glowing with midday heat', which may possibly be an allusion to the time of day at which it was regularly recited.[12]

Ambrose wrote metrical hymns for use in the services at Milan, but because of the suspicion with which non-biblical compositions were then generally regarded, they met with opposition: he tells us that his critics complained that the people had been beguiled by them.[13] He also indicates, like Augustine, that psalms were used not only in church but also in the daily life of Christians: 'the psalm is sung at home, and repeated outdoors'.[14] Furthermore, Augustine tells us in his *Confessions* how under Ambrose at Milan there was a development in the use of psalmody: special vigils were held day and night in opposition to the Arian heresy at which 'it was introduced that hymns and psalms should be sung according to the custom of the Eastern parts lest the people should faint through the tediousness of grief; and this custom, which is retained to this day, is imitated by many, by almost all your congregations throughout the world'.[15] A similar account is given by Paulinus in his life of Ambrose: 'at this time antiphons, hymns, and vigils first began to be celebrated in the Milan church, and the devotion of this celebration remains until today not only in that church but in nearly all the provinces of the West'.[16] It has traditionally been thought that what Ambrose introduced here from the East was the custom of antiphonal singing, but this has been challenged by Helmut Leeb, who has suggested that the innovation was actually responsorial psalmody, chiefly on the dangerous ground of an argument from silence: there are no other references to antiphonal singing in Ambrose's writings.[17] On the other hand, it is hard to believe that the responsorial method was unknown in the West before this time, and it seems quite probable that what was novel was not so much a particular way of rendering the psalms as the whole idea of filling the period of a vigil with psalm-singing at all. We have seen earlier the opposition encountered by Basil when he introduced the use of psalms in this way in the East.[18] Nevertheless, as Ambrose in his own reference to this event mentions that the vigils also included readings as well as psalms,[19] it is not unreasonable to conclude that the Eastern model on which they were based was the weekly all-night vigil which consisted of both antiphonal and responsorial psalms and readings.

We have evidence for the existence of this type of vigil on a more regular basis at this period at Remesiana in what is now Yugoslavia. Its bishop, Niceta, who died sometime after A.D. 414, tells in his writings of vigils composed of psalms, readings, and prayers which lasted for 'a part of the night' on Saturdays and Sundays and were opposed by some who thought them 'superfluous or idle or, what is worse, indecorous'.[20] From this opposition it would seem likely that such vigils were not native to this part of the world but had again been introduced in imitation of the Eastern practice, Remesiana lying on the main route between East and West and so no doubt being subject to Eastern influence sooner than the rest of the West. On the other hand, Niceta also says that he knows 'of some not only in our part of the world but also in the East who consider the singing of psalms and hymns superfluous and not fitting for divine religion',[21] which suggests that even in the East the observance of such regular vigils may not have been widespread away from places strongly influenced by monasticism, as we have earlier suspected,[22] and certainly in the West all other evidence for their adoption comes from the monastic world.[23] The only vigils which are found in the cathedral tradition in the West are those held on the eves of festivals, in imitation of the Paschal vigil,[24] and it is very likely the inclusion of psalmody in these which is the almost universal custom attributed by Augustine and Paulinus to the influence of Ambrose.

Apart from Milan, for the rest of Italy at this period we have only a very few scattered references to the daily office. The account of the death of Paulinus written by Uranius in the fifth century refers to the celebration of mattins (*matutinum*) and to the 'time of the evening devotion' (*lucernariae devotionis tempus*).[25] There is also the statement by Cassian, quoted earlier,[26] that in Italy Pss. 148–50 preceded Ps. 51 in the morning office, which implies that in his native Gaul the order was different, and Arnobius the younger, a fifth-century African monk, says that Ps. 148 was sung throughout the world at dawn.[27] As we shall see, certain Gallican synods speak of the use of the response *Kyrie eleison* in the Roman office, and the later sacramentaries contain collects for the morning and evening hours, at least some of which may have formed the concluding prayers of the daily services from an early date.

For the office in Gaul and Spain our information comes mainly from the canons of the various provincial synods, though this evidence must be treated with some caution, partly because some of the councils had jurisdiction over a very limited geographical area and partly because we cannot be certain that their decrees necessarily reflect what was actually happening in the churches: the very fact that they found it necessary to make regulations about the office implies that there was some considerable diversity in the existing liturgical practice which was thought to require limitation, and the fact that such regulations had often to be repeated by successive synods shows that they did not always achieve the uniformity of usage which they desired, but that the individual churches continued to follow their own, perhaps very different, customs. Thus canon 15 of the Council of Vannes in Britanny (A.D. 465) directs that 'in our province there shall be one ritual and custom of psalmody'; canon 1 of the Council of Gerona (A.D. 517) insists that 'both the ritual of the mass itself as well as the custom of psalmody and ministering which has been observed in the Metropolitan church shall be followed in the whole province of Tarragona'; a similar regulation appears in canon 27 of the Council of Epaon in the same year; and canon 1 of the Council of Braga (A.D. 561) decreed that 'one and the same order of psalmody is to be observed in the morning and evening offices; and neither individual variations nor monastic uses are to be interpolated into the ecclesiastical rule'. Calls for uniformity continued to be made in the seventh century: the Fourth Council of Toledo (A.D. 633) demanded that, 'in all Spain and Gaul one and the same method of prayer and psalmody, celebration of mass, vespers, and mattins shall be observed' (canon 2); and this was reiterated by the Eleventh Council of Toledo in A.D. 675 (canon 3).

The earliest evidence for the office in this region comes from the First Council of Toledo in A.D. 400, which directed that the

Lucernarium might not be held, except in church, unless a bishop, priest, or deacon were present (canon 9). This seems to imply that prior to this the lighting of the lamp had continued to be observed as a domestic ceremony alongside its celebration in church, but that now there was a desire to bring it under ecclesiastical control. Canon 14 of the Council of Vannes prescribes a period of seven days exclusion from communion for a city cleric who is absent from the 'morning hymns' (*matutinis hymnis*) without sufficient cause, and canon 14 of the Second Council of Orleans (A.D. 533) directed that clerics who failed to attend when duty required should be deposed from office. There may well have been a rota by which the clergy of a church took turns in officiating at the daily services, since according to canon 7 of the Council of Tarragona (A.D. 516) in country churches where there was both a priest and a deacon as well as other clerics in minor orders, these two might be responsible for the morning and evening offices in alternate weeks. On Saturdays, however, all the clerics had to appear at the evening service, so as to be the more certain to be present on Sunday, and the Third Council of Orleans (A.D. 538) required all priests to be present at the evening office on principal feasts (canon 14). The permission for a deacon to officiate at the daily offices represents an advance on the situation we encountered in Jerusalem where the prayers were always said by the bishop or a priest and the deacons simply pronounced the biddings.

Canon 30 of the Council of Agde in A.D. 506 laid down in detail the order to be followed in the daily offices:

> Because it is fitting that the order of the Church should be kept equally by all, care must be taken that, just as is the case everywhere, after the antiphons the collects should be recited in order by bishops or priests; that the morning and evening hymns should be sung every day; that at the end of the morning and evening services (*missarum*) after the hymns the *capitella de psalmis* should be said; and that after the concluding prayer the people should be dismissed at vespers by the bishop with a blessing.

The various parts of this call for further consideration. The expression 'just as is the case everywhere' (*sicut ubique fit*) should not be taken too literally, but it does suggest that there was thought to be a recognizable norm for the structure of the office in this region to which appeal might be made. The direction that 'after the antiphons the collects should be recited in order by bishops or priests' (*post antiphonas collectiones per ordinem ab episcopis vel presbyteris dicantur*) immediately recalls the monastic office at Jerusalem described by Egeria, where again each psalm was followed by a prayer recited by a priest.[28] As at Jerusalem each collect also seems to have been preceded by a bidding pronounced by a deacon: Caesarius, Bishop of Arles from 502 to 542, who presided over this council, tells in one of his sermons how the deacon said, 'Let us bow the knee'.[29] Various collections of such 'psalm-collects' from different regions in the West—Spain, Africa, and Italy—have survived,[30] and in general the prayers pick up a verse or phrase within the psalm, and expand it with a Christian interpretation.[31] The custom of appending collects to the psalms and canticles of the office is often considered to be a native part of the cathedral tradition. However, since all our earliest evidence for their use is monastic, and there is a complete absence of any reference to them in the earlier cathedral tradition of the East, it seems more likely that the practice had been taken over by the secular Church from the monastic custom. Such monastic influence on the cathedral tradition should not surprise us when we remember that not only Caesarius but also many other bishops were themselves monks, and we must therefore beware of imaging, as scholars have tended to do, that we have before us in the West the remains of a 'pure' cathedral tradition. Indeed, at least part of the purpose of the Agde canon may have been to bring about the adoption of this monastic custom in the secular office, and in two of his sermons Caesarius seems to suggest that there was a reluctance among the laity to join in the prayer after the psalm, which may possibly indicate that they regarded it as an innovation in their tradition, or alternatively it may just indicate that they were becoming lazy and inattentive during the celebration of the office.[32] It is not immediately clear from the canon whether the term 'antiphon' is meant to be understood in a more general sense and refers to responsorial singing, as at Jerusalem, or whether it denotes antiphonal psalmody proper. Since, however, when we encounter the word in the monastic rules drawn up by Caesarius, it is used with the latter meaning,[33] the probability is that it has the same sense here. Similarly, since in those rules antiphonal psalms are usually fixed and not simply taken in consecutive order from the Psalter, this again is likely to have been the case here.

'The morning and evening hymns should be sung every day' (*hymni matutini vel vespertini diebus omnibus decantentur*). Here we reach what is obviously the heart of the offices, but what were these hymns? Although some scholars have concluded that metrical hymns were intended,[34] this is most unlikely to have been the case. Because of the reverence accorded to the divine inspiration of the Psalter and the suspicion directed towards non-canonical compositions as often embodying heretical beliefs, which we have already encountered in the East and at Milan,[35] metrical hymns were slow in gaining acceptance in the West, and canon 12 of the Council of Braga in A.D. 561 refused to allow any 'poetical composition' to be sung in church. They seem to have been accepted in monastic circles sooner than in the secular practice, and the Second Council of Tours (A.D. 567), which was very strongly influenced by monasticism, declared that 'besides the Ambrosian hymns which we have in the canon, others also may be sung which are worthy of it, if the authors are named' (canon 23), while the Fourth Council of Toledo in 633 reversed the earlier attitude of the Council of Braga and welcomed the use of non-biblical compositions (canon 13). As we have observed already,[36] it was quite usual for the psalms to be described as 'hymns', and Jungmann in his study of the morning office in this area argued that what was meant by the expression *hymni matutini* were Pss. 148–50.[37] We have already seen how Cassian called these psalms the 'morning hymns' and indicated that they were used not only in Italy but also in his native Gaul,[38] and we shall later see that they continued to form a regular part of the monastic morning office in this region in the sixth century.[39] Further confirmation of their place in the secular morning office is provided by Gregory of Tours (*c.* 540–94) who tells how his uncle, Bishop Gallus of the Auvergne, heard psalm-singing coming from a church on a Sunday morning and, when told that they were singing the *Benedictio* (i.e. the Benedicite), he himself recited Ps. 51, the *Benedictio*, the *Alleluiaticum*, and the *capitellum*, and completed the morning office.[40] By *Alleluiaticum* must be meant Pss. 148–50, and presumably Ps. 51 and the canticle formed at least part of the *antiphonae* mentioned at Agde, even if that council intended further monastic additions to this cathedral nucleus. Caesarius tells us in sermons that Ps. 51 was a regular daily component of the morning office,[41] but that the Benedicite was a festal addition: 'You have heard in the

Benedictiones, and you do hear on every feast day when they are said, how all thing celestial and terrestrial praise God'.[42] What replaced it on weekdays may well have been the Te Deum, since canon 1 of the Council of Barcelona (*c.* A.D. 540) directs that Ps. 51 is to be recited 'before the canticle', as though some canticle were a normal element in the office, and a letter from Cyprian, Bishop of Toulon, to Maximus, Bishop of Geneva, written sometime between 524 and 533, says of the Te Deum: 'we say daily in the hymn which every church in the whole world has received and sings ...'.[43] Once again 'every church in the whole world' should be treated with caution, but it does imply that its use was widespread in the regions known to the author of the letter. What the 'evening hymns' were is more problematic, since there is no obvious equivalent to Pss. 148–50. Winkler has attempted to find traces of an originally regular use of Psalm 141 in the later Mozarabic tradition,[44] but the evidence is not very conclusive and there is certainly no mention of it in earlier writings. Caesarius, on the other hand, refers to the use of Psalm 104 at Duodecima—a monastic name for the evening office: 'that psalm, dearest friends, which is said throughout the world both in churches and in monasteries at Duodecima is so well known to everybody that the greatest part of the human race have memorized it'.[45] Though there is a complete absence of any mention of the lighting of the lamp in the sources of this period, the evidence of later texts[46] suggests that it was retained, at least on festal occasions.

The *capitella de psalmis* mentioned in the Agde canon are verses taken from the Psalter and used in the form of versicles and responses—what in the Roman tradition came to be called the *preces*—and are the remains of the intercessions which once formed a substantial second half of the early cathedral office. Scholars have distinguished two different types of *capitella* in existence in the sixth century, and these have been termed Gallican and Celtic respectively, those being the regions in which the earliest examples of each type are found, although in reality they represent two different stages in the evolution of the same type of prayer. We have seen how in Jerusalem the intercessions at the evening office were in the form of a series of biddings, to each of which the response *Kyrie eleison* was made, with a collect concluding the whole litany.[47] This also seems to have been the earliest practice in Rome. The 'Celtic' version of this, the earliest example of which is found in the late sixth-century monastic office of Columbanus,[48] substitutes individual verses from the psalms for the *Kyrie* response, while the 'Gallican' entirely omits the biddings, and the psalm verses simply follow one after another, each now being divided into a versicle and response, with a collect at the end of the series, as is prescribed at Agde.[49]

The decrees of later synods indicate how the form laid down at Agde was gradually expanded. Canon 10 of the Council of Gerona (A.D. 517) directed that the Lord's Prayer should be added to the end of the morning and evening office every day, but this innovation was apparently slow to gain acceptance since canon 10 of the Fourth Council of Toledo (A.D. 633) criticized some priests who said it only on Sundays and insisted that it be used every day. The inclusion of the Lord's Prayer here seems to be an imitation of monastic practice. We have seen earlier how at Jerusalem it was thought necessary to have priests to say the collects at the monastic office, and we shall see later how in the Western monastic tradition, presumably because a priest was often not available, it became the regular custom for the concluding prayer of the office to be the Lord's Prayer instead of a collect.[50] No doubt in time the absence of the Lord's Prayer in the cathedral tradition came to be seen as a deficiency, when compared with the monastic office, and so it was added at the end of the collect. Canon 3 of the Second Council of Vaison (A.D. 529) sought to introduce the custom of saying *Kyrie eleison*, already adopted 'not only in the Apostolic See but also throughout all the provinces of the East and of Italy', and prescribed its use at the morning and evening offices and at mass. Once again it would appear that this foreign innovation was not greeted with great enthusiasm, as we have no trace of its adoption, except in the monastic offices of Aurelian.[51] This council also directed that 'since not only in the Apostolic See but also throughout the whole East and all Africa and Italy, on account of the deceit of the heretics who blasphemously maintain that the Son of God has not always existed with the Father but came into being subsequently, in all conclusions [of the psalms] after the *Gloria* "as it was in the beginning . . ." is said, so also this must be said in all our churches' (canon 5). More than a century later in Spain, however, canons 13 and 15 of the Fourth Council of Toledo (A.D. 633) reveal that the wording of the *Gloria* at the end of the psalms was: 'Glory and honour to the Father and to the Son and to the Holy Spirit, world without end'. Finally, canon 2 of the Council of Barcelona (A.D. 540) ordered that the blessing should conclude the morning office as well as the evening.

So far the evidence has suggested that the Western morning and evening offices resembled substantially those found in the East, and there has not been the slightest indication that they regularly included any Scripture reading. Jungmann, however, believed that the Gallican morning office did include a daily reading from the Bible, and he reached this conclusion almost entirely on the basis of the evidence of the homilies of Caesarius.[52] It cannot be denied that Caesarius does refer to a morning service at which there was the reading of Scripture, and frequently also a sermon, but that does not necessarily mean that it was a regular feature of the normal cathedral office in this region. We have already suggested that Caesarius' monastic background may have influenced to some extent the form of service which he advocated at Agde, and there is other evidence that he tried to introduce monastic practices into the worship over which he presided: according to his biographer he had the hours of Terce, Sext, and None chanted daily in his cathedral,[53] and in his homilies he encourages the people to attend these services, especially in Lent.[54] Morever, he uses the term *vigilia* to designate the morning service, which again suggests that it was not the usual morning office which he was advocating, but an expanded version incorporating features of the monastic vigil, which in Gaul included Bible reading, as we shall see.[55] The references in the homilies suggest that, while such vigils went on all the year round, Caesarius particularly encouraged the laity to attend them during Lent, and also in Advent, and that they were composed of psalms followed by collects in the monastic manner and of 'sacred readings', *lectiones divinas*, as well as the customary morning hymns.[56] He also tried to persuade people to adopt a similar practice at home, and to use part of the winter nights for Bible reading, or at least to undertake it as a Lenten observance: 'when the nights are longer, who will there be who can sleep so much that he cannot either read himself or listen to others reading *lectionem divinam* for three hours?'[57] If this seems rather a tall order, it should be remembered that before the advent of electric light there were relatively few other tasks which might be done during the long hours of darkness. Since they were required to assemble earlier for the vigil than for the usual morning office, at least some of the laity apparently did not welcome an extension to their traditional custom, and instead kept to the normal time, so that they are criticized by Caesarius both for coming late to the vigils and for leaving 'when the word of God has begun to be recited'.[58] When there was also to be a sermon, which came at the very end of the morning office,[59] the vigil was curtailed and the morning office proper, beginning with Ps. 51, started sooner, so that the service might still finish at the usual time.[60] This sermon may well be the vestigial remains of the bishop's *catechesis* after the morning office which we have seen earlier in the East, and similarly the sermons which Caesarius is also said to have delivered frequently at the evening office may be the remnants of the afternoon services of the word on station days, now fused with the office proper, as they also eventually were in the East.[61]

The influence of monasticism on the cathedral office was by no means confined to Arles at this period. According to Gregory of Tours, Bishop Injuriosus of Tours (bishop from 529 to 546), had Terce and Sext adopted as a part of the daily cycle in his cathedral city,[62] and the Council of Tours in A.D. 567 sought to impose a monastic *cursus* of psalmody (canon 18). At Auxerre in the fifth century the bishops established daily vigils in their cathedral, which were celebrated in turn by the various ecclesiastical and monastic communities in the city.[63] We have already seen how in the East in A.D. 528 the Emperor Justinian imposed on the reluctant clergy the obligation to take part in the monastic vigil as well as the morning and evening offices,[64] and we find the same obligation being placed upon the clergy in parts of the West at almost exactly the same date: sometime between 523 and 532 Fulgentius, Bishop of Ruspe in North Africa, required his clergy 'to be present at the daily vigils, and the morning and evening prayers',[65] and according to the *Cautio Episcopi* of the *Liber Diurnus*, which was composed by 559 at the latest,[66] a bishop consecrated in Rome had to promise that he would 'celebrate the vigils every day in church from first cockcrow until morning with every order of my clergy'.[67] This requirement was no more popular here with the clergy than it had been in the East, and a decretal of the sixth century shows the protestations of the clergy of a presbyteral church in Rome against the introduction of these daily vigils as part of their duty.[68]

Nevertheless, the dominance of monasticism in the Church was such that in the end the monastic office triumphed over the cathedral, and the latter became more and more conformed to the former, until ultimately it was supplanted by it altogether throughout the West. Such changes in the office meant that, though the laity might continue to attend the services for some time afterwards, at least on occasions, yet because of the increased range of psalmody now used and the growing complexity of the music, to say nothing of the widening gap between the ancient Latin of the liturgy and the new vernacular Latin in everyday use, they found it more difficult to be as actively involved as before but were increasingly becoming the spectators of the professional clergy and religious who sang the office, and, according to Caesarius, were tending to spend the service gossiping among themselves.[69] He also complains that they have no problem in remembering and singing devilish love songs, and so they should be able to learn 'some antiphons' as well as Pss. 51 and 91.[70] Apparently he was able to get the people to take a more active part and join in the singing of the psalms and hymns,[71] but such success was only temporary: the effect of monasticism was to spell the end of the cathedral office as the prayer of the people. As Balthasar Fischer has remarked, 'we are witnessing the arrival of the Middle Ages'.[72]

7. *The Monastic Office in the West*

Western monasticism grew out of that in the East, and hence its forms of daily prayer were derived from those of the East. The oldest extant formalized Western monastic rule is probably the *Ordo Monasterii*, which appears as part of what has traditionally been called 'The Rule of St. Augustine'. Its actual origin has been the subject of some debate, and an Italian, or even Gallican, provenance has frequently been proposed, but the latest editor of the rule, Luc Verheijen, has suggested that the *Ordo Monasterii* does come from North Africa and was drawn up by one of Augustine's followers in the middle of the fifth century.[1] For the daily office it prescribes:

> at Mattins three psalms are to be said: 62 [63], 5, and 89 [90]. At Terce the first psalm is to be said responsorially, then two antiphons, the reading, and the concluding prayer (*completorium*); in the same way Sext and None, but at Lucernarium one responsorial psalm, four antiphons, then one responsorial psalm, the reading, and the concluding prayer. At a convenient time after Lucernarium, all sitting, lessons are read, and after this the customary psalms are to be recited before sleep. At night prayers in November, December, January, and February there are to be twelve antiphons, six psalms, and three readings; in March, April, September, and October ten antiphons, five psalms, and three readings; in May, June, July, and August eight antiphons, four psalms, and two readings.[2]

This has a strong resemblance to the Eastern pattern as described by Cassian. The allocation of three psalms each to the offices at the third, sixth, and ninth hours is what he maintains to be the universal practice of the East, and the night office, in its shortest form, follows the Egyptian arrangement of twelve psalms and two readings.[3] The morning office closely resembles that said by Cassian to have been introduced at Bethlehem, and quite clearly does not adhere to the model followed by the rest of the offices, as it has fixed psalms prescribed for it, and apparently no reading or concluding prayer. This suggests that it was a later addition, introduced after the pattern of the rest had been established, and thus it lends support to our earlier contention that a morning office did not form part of the original daily cycle of Eastern monasticism.[4] Compline, which was also not a part of the formal daily cycle in the East, similarly consists here merely of fixed, but unspecified, psalms and no concluding reading or prayer, while the evening office on the other hand, in spite of the name 'Lucernarium', is a wholly monastic service, conforming to the structure of the other day hours, with simply the psalmody doubled. Was this doubling also perhaps the Eastern pattern at the evening office, about which we have no detailed evidence? However, the choice of psalms at the morning office does not correspond exactly with the Bethlehem selection, which according to Cassian was 51, 63, and 90. Verheijen claims that it has preserved the authentic Bethlehem tradition here and that Cassian included Ps. 51 in error, because of his desire to explain how that psalm came to be in the Italian morning office,[5] but it seems at least as likely a conjecture that the compiler of the rule has amended the Bethlehem pattern to produce what he considered to be a more suitable selection of psalms. It is interesting that Ps. 5 appears out of numerical order, and Verheijen has suggested that the arrangement 63—5—90 instead of the more natural 5—63—90 was deliberately chosen in order to give expression to a development of thought in the three psalms, from the 'de luce' of 63.1, through the 'mane' of 5.3, to the reference to the evening and the brevity of human life in Ps. 90.[6]

On the other hand, although the offices seem to be based on the Eastern model, they have also undergone other changes, besides the arrangement of the psalms at Mattins. With the exception of Mattins and Compline, they all include both antiphonal and responsorial psalmody, as well as the reading of Scripture. The Eastern tradition, as we have seen, generally did not include any readings in the office, apart from Egypt where two readings were attached to the evening and night offices, and the only place where the combination of antiphonal psalmody, responsorial psalmody, and readings is found is in the weekly all-night vigil of Syria and Palestine.[7] It has therefore been suggested that the structure of the daily services in the *Ordo Monasterii* has been greatly influenced by the form of that vigil.[8] If this is the case, the compiler has rejected the equal division of antiphonal and responsorial psalms found in the East in favour of the predominance of one over the other, and always in the same ratio: two antiphonal psalms to one responsorial. This arrangement was perhaps necessitated by the desire to retain the traditional number of three psalms at the day hours. He has also rejected the Eastern practice of repeating the combination over and over again, and instead, apparently using the Egyptian pattern of twelve psalms and two readings as his base, he has included exact directions as to how the length of the night office, and of the different elements within it, should vary according to the variation in the length of the night through the year, a contrast to the East where the regular night office had either remained constant throughout the year or been much more indeterminate as to its length. In so doing, he has tried as far as possible to maintain the same ratio between the number of psalms and the number of readings (12/2; 15/3; 18/3), and similarly has prescribed only one reading for the day offices in order to keep roughly the same proportion of psalms to readings there. All this reveals the marks of the more precise, mathematical, and legislative mind of the West, which is to be a major characteristic of other Western monastic offices, as we shall see.

Elsewhere in the West, however, the relative simplicity displayed in this document was abandoned, and we find a wide variation between the different monastic patterns and a considerable elaboration of the contents of each office, especially in the Gallican and Mozarabic regions, where there was also a tendency for the number of offices in the daily cycle to increase, so that in some places the attempt was even made to maintain a more or less continuous round of worship, with offices following one another every hour of the day.[9] Cassian indicates that already in his day there was a diversity of practice:

> We have found that many in different countries, according to the fancy of their mind (having indeed as the Apostle says 'a zeal for God but not according to knowledge'), have made for themselves different rules and arrangements in this matter. For some have appointed that each night 20 or 30 psalms should be said, and that these should be prolonged by the music of antiphonal singing and by the addition of some modulations as well. Others have even tried to go beyond this number. Some use eighteen. And in this

way we have found different rules appointed in different places, and the systems and regulations that we have seen are almost as many in number as the monasteries and cells which we have visited. There are some too to whom it has seemed good that in the day offices of prayer, Terce, Sext, and None, the number of psalms and prayers should be made to correspond exactly to the number of the hours at which the services are offered up to the Lord. Some have thought fit that six psalms should be assigned to each service of the day.[10]

Sixth-century monastic practice in Southern Gaul is revealed to us through the rules for monks and nuns at Arles drawn up by Caesarius, in which the directions concerning the daily office are derived, according to the author, 'for the most part' from the rule of the monastery at Lerins.[11] Though lengthy and complex, these directions are not very systematically arranged, and are often imprecise or even contradictory. The rules were subsequently amplified, and to some extent clarified for us, by his successor Aurelian, bishop from 546 to 553.[12] In these rules the number of daily offices has risen to nine: a night office called Nocturns; Mattins; Prime; Terce; Sext; None; Lucernarium; Duodecima; and Compline (the last only mentioned by Aurelian, and so evidently not considered a formal part of the cycle in the time of Caesarius). This is the first sure appearance of Prime and it is a feature of the festal office alone in Caesarius, only becoming part of the regular daily pattern in Aurelian. It looks as if its introduction may have had a similar purpose to that of the *novella sollemnitas* at Bethlehem—to put an end to the traditional custom of retiring for a further period of sleep after rising for the night office, for Aurelian directs that 'after the morning prayers there must not be a return to sleep, but when Mattins has been completed, Prime should be said immediately, and then all should have time for reading until the third hour'.[13] The practice of a second period of sleep, however, which had earlier been criticized by Cassian,[14] continued to flourish elsewhere in Gaul and Spain in the seventh century and even later.[15]

The inclusion of both Lucernarium and another evening office of the twelfth hour, Duodecima, is interesting and suggests that there has been a fusion of two traditions here, monastic and secular. Duodecima, as we shall see, is identical in structure to the night office and is thus clearly monastic in origin, while both Mattins and Lucernarium differ from all the other offices of the day, except Compline, in having no reading attached to them, and the contents of Mattins, and probably Lucernarium, are fixed and unvarying. Moreover, as we shall see, the psalms at these two offices are sung in a different manner—'with antiphons'—from those at the rest of the services. Once again, therefore, we are pointed towards an original monastic cycle of the type we have suggested was usual in the East, consisting of evening and night offices, together with the third, sixth, and ninth hours, as well as relatively informal prayers before sleep, to which both morning and evening services adopted from the secular custom have been added. It may well be significant that the description of the daily cycle begins not with Mattins or Prime but with Terce, as though that were traditionally regarded as the first service of the day.

Four of the daily offices, those which might be considered as the major hours of the day—Nocturns, Mattins, Lucernarium, and Duodecima—begin with a fixed psalm *directaneus*, that is, recited entirely by one person without any response from the community, and its function may have been that of an 'assembling psalm', intended to fill the time during the gradual arrival of the remainder of the brothers or sisters. Cassian reports that it was the Eastern custom to allow late arrival at an office up to the end of the first psalm without penalty.[16] The *directaneus* at Nocturns is Ps. 51, which also forms the beginning of the night office in the *De Virginitate* ascribed to Athanasius,[17] and at Mattins it is Ps. 145. Those at Lucernarium and Duodecima are only mentioned in the description of the Eastertide form of the office: both Caesarius and Aurelian refer to the Lucernarium psalm as 'short' (Caesarius *brevis*, Aurelian *parvulus*), but only Aurelian specifies that it is to be Ps. 68.32f., with Ps. 113 on alternate days, while both state that the beginning of the Duodecima psalm is to be 104.19b, Aurelian again terming it *parvulus*. Since, as we have seen, Caesarius maintains in one of his sermons that Ps. 104 was regularly sung 'throughout the world' at the evening office in both secular and monastic usage,[18] it is probable that these psalms were used not only at Eastertide but in the ferial office also.

The main psalmody of the offices was apparently recited in the Egyptian manner: according to Aurelian the psalms were arranged in the traditional groups of three, and a different member of the community recited each group, with the Alleluia response being added to the third psalm.[19] Although this is only said to be the case in the description of the Eastertide offices, it almost certainly also applied generally to all the offices throughout the year,[20] except for Mattins, Lucernarium, and Compline, about which more will be said later. Although neither the *Ordo Monasterii* nor the rules of Caesarius and Aurelian explicitly mention prayer following each psalm, the custom obviously continued, as it is referred to, as we have seen, by Caesarius in his sermons and by the Council of Agde,[21] and it is also spoken of by Cassian, who contrasts the Egyptian practice, where such prayer was made standing, with only a brief genuflection, with the practice in Gaul which was to kneel for the prayer. Cassian also informs us that, in contrast to the East, the *Gloria Patri* was used at the conclusion of each psalm.[22] At least in some places, however, the prayer after the psalm appears to have been entirely silent, without any concluding collect, perhaps because no priest was present to say one.[23]

Duodecima and Nocturns are simply extended versions of the Egyptian evening and night offices: in addition to the initial *directaneus*, they consisted of eighteen psalms and two lessons. The increase from twelve to eighteen psalms each night was a practice already known in Cassian's day, as our earlier quotation showed, and was the number prescribed in the winter form of the night office in the *Ordo Monasterii*. Attached to the psalmody at both offices was a further element of expansion, again already known to Cassian, three 'short antiphons' (Caesarius, *antiphonae minores*; Aurelian, *antiphona parvula*), by which are probably meant fixed portions of certain psalms sung antiphonally.[24] These are only mentioned by Caesarius in his description of the Eastertide offices, but are explicitly said to be used throughout the year in Aurelian's version. A new feature of monastic services is the inclusion of a metrical hymn in each office, and the fact that its position varies in the different offices throughout the day—sometimes coming before the lessons, sometimes after[25]—coupled with the fact that the rules carefully prescribe which hymn is to be used at each service, suggests that it was a recent innovation, and very likely not a traditional part of the office at Lerins. Moreover, we have seen earlier the hesitancy felt about metrical hymns in this region.[26] Each office concludes with a *capitellum*, a practice obviously derived from the secular custom,[27] although the use of the singular instead of the plural may indicate that it had been reduced to a single versicle and response: only in Aurelian's reference to Compline do we find the plural, *capitella*.[28]

The hours of Terce, Sext, and None each have six psalms, an antiphon, a hymn, a reading, and the *capitellum*. The inclusion of a reading and of some antiphonal singing follows the practice in the *Ordo Monasterii*, and may be derived from it, although the number of psalms has been doubled from the traditional three, again an arrangement mentioned by Cassian in the quotation above. For some mysterious reason Caesarius orders a further doubling in the festal form of Terce, but not of Sext and None: he does this in the Saturday and Sunday office by placing a group of three lessons after the first block of six psalms, and following this with a second block of six psalms, an antiphon, hymn, and the *capitellum*, but in the Eastertide version by contrast he has a single block of twelve psalms followed by three antiphons and the three lessons. Prime has six psalms like Sext and None, but two readings instead of one. Aurelian increases the number of psalms in the Eastertide Sext and None to twelve, in line with Terce, but also increases the number of antiphons at Terce to six, and in his rule for monks, but not that for nuns, prescribes that twelve psalms instead of six be used at the offices of Prime, Terce, Sext, and None throughout the year. By contrast Compline remains extremely simple at all times—a sign of its less formal nature. It consists not of a number of psalms, as in the *Ordo Monasterii* and elsewhere, but of a single psalm, 91, recited in the simplest manner possible, *directaneus*, and followed by the 'customary prayers' (*capitella consuetudinaria*).

As we have said above, the contents of Mattins were unvarying from day to day. When speaking of the ordinary weekday office, Caesarius simply says that the introductory *directaneus* is Ps. 145, and 'then the whole of Mattins is recited in order antiphonally', implying that its contents were sufficiently established and familiar to everyone to need no description, but Aurelian supplies further details: first, according to him, there is an antiphonal canticle (unspecified), and then the *directaneus*, followed by seven psalms—43, 63 (the traditional morning psalm), 147a, 147b, 148, 149, 150—a hymn, and the *capitellum*. To the *capitellum* he adds a twelvefold

Kyrie eleison, following the Roman custom advocated by the Council of Vaison in 529,[29] but as neither this nor his opening canticle appear in the festal form of the office, nor in Caesarius' references to it, they are quite possibly innovations made by him, in spite of the prominent part which Caesarius had himself played in the Council of Vaison, as may also be the addition of a threefold *Kyrie* to three points in each of the daily offices—at the beginning, after the psalms, and at the end—which Aurelian specifies. The festal form of Mattins is an elaborated version of the ferial office, and this is described by both authors: 'Alleluia' replaces the antiphonal response throughout, and into the weekday contents are inserted *Confitemini Domino* (by which Ps. 118 is probably meant), *Cantemus Domino* (by which the canticle from Exod. 15 is probably intended), Ps. 146, the Benedicite, the Te Deum (according to Caesarius) or the Magnificat (according to Aurelian), and the Gloria in Excelsis, resulting in a structure of three groups of three psalms, each followed by a canticle, in addition to the opening *directaneus* and the concluding hymn, Gloria in Excelsis. Some of the elements from both ferial and festal forms we have already encountered in the secular Gallican office. By comparison, Lucernarium is very brief, consisting at all times of the *directaneus*, three antiphons, with the Alleluia response to the third, and a hymn: no further details are given. As we have commented earlier, it is interesting that the psalmody in these two offices is antiphonal, in contrast to the 'Egyptian method' adopted in the rest of the daily round, and this suggests that the psalms for Lucernarium as well as Mattins were fixed rather than variable.

In winter the night office is not extended in length, but instead a second nocturns, consisting similarly of a *directaneus* (Ps. 57), eighteen psalms, two readings, and a hymn, follows the first. Moreover, in order to fill the long hours of darkness until the time for Mattins, three *missae* are to be added after the double office each night. The meaning of the term *missa* in this context is most clearly explained by Aurelian:

One brother shall read three or four pages, depending on the size of the book . . . and then there shall be a prayer. Again he shall read the same amount, and there shall be another prayer. A third time he shall read the same amount. Then you shall rise, recite an antiphon from the psalms in order, then a responsory, then an antiphon. Again another brother shall read, and when you have thus completed the three *missae*, you shall say Mattins. . . .

Each *missa* therefore was a unit of worship, comprising three readings, each followed by a prayer, and three psalms, rendered in the same proportions as the psalmody in the offices of the *Ordo Monasterii*—two antiphonal psalms to one responsorial. The inclusion of the phrase 'from the psalms in order' with reference to the antiphons, expressed more clearly by Caesarius as 'in the order of the Psalter', implies, as we have suggested earlier, that the antiphonal psalmody at the offices was usually on a selective and not consecutive basis, and hence this comment was required here in order to indicate the different arrangement in the *missae*. On Friday evenings throughout the year, winter and summer alike, there were to be six such *missae* after Duodecima, and then a further three followed between Nocturns and Mattins (two in summer according to Aurelian), thus creating an all-night vigil. Similarly on Sundays throughout the year six *missae* were added after the night office, though as the length of the reading was controlled by the abbot they were no doubt much shorter in summer than in winter. Whilst on weekdays the books of the Old and New Testaments were to be read 'in their order', on Sundays:

> the gospels are to be read, but always in the first *missa* one resurrection [narrative] is to be read, on another Sunday another resurrection [narrative], and similarly the third and fourth. While that first *missa* of the resurrection is being read, and one resurrection [narrative] is always read at the first *missa*, no one should presume to sit, but afterwards in the five *missae* which follow, all sit as usual.

At festivals of the martyrs, the first *missa* was to be from the gospels, and the rest from the passion of the martyr.

The Friday night–Saturday morning vigil is obviously the descendant of the weekly all-night vigil we have already encountered in the East, each *missa* being merely a condensed version of the unit of three antiphonal psalms, three responsorial psalms, and three lessons of which that vigil was composed. The Sunday group of *missae* is similarly the descendant of the cathedral vigil in which the resurrection narrative was read, although its shape here has been determined by the form of the Friday–Saturday vigil. However, the extension of such vigils in which Scripture reading played a prominent part into a regular daily practice is a new departure, without Eastern precedent. It would appear therefore that the practice of night prayer both here and also, as we shall see later, generally in Western monasticism has been affected by two separate traditions stemming from the East. Firstly, the model of Egyptian night prayer has caused the extension of the old midnight hour of prayer into a longer office of psalms. Secondly, the Eastern custom of a daily vigil from cockcrow until dawn has given rise to a further observance, although this follows the structure not of the Eastern *daily* vigil but of the Eastern *weekly* vigil. The latter is almost certainly a later development than the former, since it does not appear in the *Ordo Monasterii* where instead the length of the night office is made to vary according to the time of year, although the weekly vigil does seem to have had some effect here on the shape of all its daily offices.

In contrast to Southern Gaul, Celtic monasticism, as revealed in the late sixth-century rule of Columbanus, preserved a relatively simple and primitive cycle of daily worship,[30] although the author admits that he is aware of a wide diversity of monastic practice in this regard. The day hours, which probably comprised only Terce, Sext, and None, though this is not explicitly stated, consisted of three psalms each, adhering to the custom observed apparently everywhere except in Gaul, with intercessions appended to them, about which we have spoken earlier.[31] Additionally there was an office 'at the beginning of the night', which Columbanus calls Duodecima elsewhere,[32] and an office at midnight, each composed of twelve psalms—without doubt imitating the Egyptian pattern, and also a further office, described as '*ad matutinam*'. This was to vary in length according to the length of the night, gradually increasing from a shortest form in summer of twenty-four psalms to a maximum in winter of thirty-six psalms, while at the weekends more psalms were prescribed, no doubt the vestigial remains of the weekly longer vigils: the minimum in the Saturday and Sunday offices was thirty-six psalms, and this gradually increased until half of the Psalter, seventy-five psalms, was recited on each of the two nights in winter, which together with the psalms at the evening and midnight offices produces a staggering total of ninety-nine psalms a night. The psalms were recited in the traditional groups of three, two without antiphons and the third with, and we learn from elsewhere in the rule that a genuflection for a short silent prayer followed each psalm, though there is no mention of a collect concluding this.[33] In spite of the name *ad matutinam*, the contents and the variable nature of this service proclaim it to be a vigil and not a genuine morning office, the absence of which from this cycle provides further confirmation of our earlier contention that it had no place in the original monastic round. The inclusion of two night offices—the midnight and the *ad matutinam*—is once again to be attributed to the influence of two parallel traditions, one extending the old midnight hour of prayer into an office of twelve psalms on the Egyptian model, the other adding a vigil of variable length on the Eastern model, here composed entirely of psalmody as in the East. The author also refers to 'some catholics' who had, in place of this pattern, four offices of twelve psalms each, at the beginning of the night, at midnight, at cockcrow, and *ad matutinam*, though the last was increased to thirty-six psalms on Saturdays and Sundays. He gives no further information, but we may conjecture that the cockcrow and morning offices are simply a later division into two parts of a vigil of the type described by Columbanus, which in its shortest form had the same number of psalms as these two services ($2 \times 12 = 24$).

A similar dual tradition about night prayer is also evidenced in Roman monasticism, which like the Celtic form preserved many primitive traits. In contrast to what we have suggested was the general trend of Western monasticism, the earliest ascetic practice at Rome seems to have been to observe all the traditional five times of prayer inherited from the pre-Nicene period, and not to omit the morning hour. On the other hand, the observance not only of the ancient midnight hour of prayer but also alongside this of a vigil for some part of the night, in which again, as in the *missae* of the rules of Caesarius and Aurelian, the reading of Scripture and not simply psalmody played a substantial part, seems to have been envisaged. Thus Jerome, writing at Rome in A.D. 384, says: 'prayers, as everyone knows, ought to be said at the third, sixth, and ninth hours, at dawn, and at evening. No meal should be begun without prayer, and before leaving the table thanks should be returned to the Creator. We should rise two or three times in the night and go over the parts of Scripture which we know by heart'.[34] He similarly writes in 403 to advise a Roman

134

lady, Laeta, to accustom her daughter to keep the hours of prayer from her childhood: 'she ought to rise at night to recite prayers and psalms; to sing hymns in the morning; at the third, sixth, and ninth hours to take her place in the line to do battle for Christ; and lastly to kindle her lamp and to offer the evening sacrifice. So let the day be passed, and so let the night find her at her labours. Let reading follow prayer, and prayer again succeed to reading'.[35] Again he writes in 404 to another Roman lady, Demetrias, who has embraced a life of virginity: 'in addition to the rule of psalmody and prayer which you must always observe at the third, sixth, and ninth hours, at evening, at midnight, and at dawn, you should determine how much time you ought to give to the learning and reading of Scripture, not as a labour but for the delight and instruction of your soul. When you have completed this period, and the concern of your soul has roused you frequently to bend your knees . . .'.[36]

Further north in Milan Ambrose was commending a similar practice to his people: he urged that 'the greater part of the night' be devoted to prayer and to reading,[37] and seems to imply that cockcrow was the proper time to rise,[38] while in his advice to those dedicated to a life of virginity he counselled a vigil of psalmody instead: 'in your bedchamber itself I would have you join psalms in frequent interchange with the Lord's Prayer, either when you wake up or before sleep bedews your body'.[39] To this he adds the instruction that 'we ought also specially to repeat the creed as a seal upon our hearts daily before light'.[40] Augustine too teaches catechumens to adopt the practice of reciting the creed daily 'before you go to sleep, before you go forth'.[41] On the other hand, there is in the writings of Ambrose, perhaps surprisingly, no reference to the other hours of daily prayer, not even in his advice to virgins, and it is interesting that, though he several times refers to the psalm verse 'seven times a day do I praise thee',[42] he never suggests a literal application of it.

By the middle of the fifth century the basilica churches of Rome began to have attached to them religious communities which were responsible for singing the full round of daily offices there, and thus monasticism came to exercise a strong influence upon the worship of the city.[43] At one time it was thought that the Roman monastic office as it was known to us was derived entirely from that in the rule of St. Benedict and hence we could know virtually nothing about its pre-

Benedictine form. Today, however, largely as a result of the research of C. Callewaert,[44] it has become clear that the dependency is the other way round: it was Benedict who drew upon the ancient Roman monastic office when framing his rule. Nevertheless, since this early monastic pattern has to be disentangled from very much later documents which have felt the influence of Benedict's adaptation, any reconstruction must be to some degree tentative, and must also be conscious that there would probably have been variations between different monastic communities in Rome.

It has been concluded that the Roman office as it was known to Benedict in the sixth century consisted of eight daily hours of prayer—Nocturns, Mattins, Prime, Terce, Sext, None, Vespers, and Compline. The term Lucernarium seems to have been unknown in the Roman monastic tradition.[45] The night office was celebrated at midnight and was composed of twelve psalms, a versicle, three lessons with three responsories (i.e. responsorial psalms or parts of psalms), and very probably a concluding litany. On Sundays the number of psalms was increased and distributed over three nocturns, each ending with three lessons and three responsories. Mattins and Vespers both consisted of five psalms, followed by a versicle, Gospel canticle (i.e. Benedictus or Magnificat), litany, and at least in some Roman monastic communities if not in all, the Lord's Prayer instead of the collect found in secular practice.[46] Although at Vespers the five psalms were apparently taken in consecutive order from the Psalter, as were the psalms at the night office, at Mattins they were fixed and were (a) Ps. 51, (b) a psalm proper to each day of the week and appropriate to the morning hour, (c) Pss. 63 and 67 under a single *Gloria*, (d) an Old Testament canticle proper to each day of the week, and (e) Pss. 148–50 under a single *Gloria*. Ps. 119, divided into sections and repeated each day, provided the psalmody for the lesser hours, except for Compline, for which Pss. 4, 91, and 134 were appointed, and possibly also Ps. 31.1–6, though this is more likely a later addition.[47] These lesser hours are thought to have consisted at this time of an opening versicle, though this is uncertain,[48] three psalms, a lesson, a responsory, a versicle, *Kyrie eleison*, and Lord's Prayer. Metrical hymns were unknown.

There are, however, reasons to doubt that the offices, and especially the night office, were in precisely this form in the time of Benedict. Firstly, although it has been a common belief among liturgical scholars that two introductory elements—an opening versicle and Ps. 95—were not yet included in the night office but were taken over into it subsequently from Benedict's office, the basis of this hypothesis is very fragile, and it seems more likely that the process was in the reverse direction, Benedict adopting them from the Roman tradition, especially in view of the fact they are present in the *Regula Magistri*, which as we shall see was similarly dependent upon the Roman tradition, and also the fact that Benedict includes two other introductory elements—Ps. 3 and a hymn—which do not appear in the Roman office, as one might have expected if it were dependent on Benedict at this point.[49]

Secondly, and much more importantly, there is evidence to suggest that the second part of the night office—comprising the lessons and responsories—was not an integral part of it at this stage. One piece of this evidence is a letter sent by Theodemar, Abbot of Monte Cassino from 777 to 797, to the Emperor Charlemagne, but actually composed by Paul the Deacon, which says: 'If anyone wonders why blessed Benedict prescribed only one lesson from the Old Testament to be read at the night office on weekdays in summer, let him understand that it was not yet the custom at that time for Holy Scripture to be read in the Roman Church, as it is now, but this was instituted some time later, either by blessed Pope Gregory or, as is claimed by some, by Honorius'.[50] Unless the author is completely mistaken in his historical facts, which of course cannot be entirely ruled out, this raises doubts about the presence of the lessons not only in the night office but also in the lesser hours of the day, and it is interesting to note that there is evidence that even in the ninth century there was still no lesson or responsory in Prime or Compline.[51] Another piece of evidence comes from the *Cautio Episcopi* of the *Liber Diurnus*, to which we have already referred earlier.[52] This imposes upon the secular clergy the obligation to join in the monastic night vigils, but what it prescribes is that during the summer these shall consist of 'three lessons and three antiphons and three responsories' and during the winter of 'four lessons with their responsories and antiphons, but on Sundays throughout the year nine lessons with their antiphons and responsories'. This of course is not the classical Roman night office, and it is significant that that Roman office is never described as a vigil, nor does the length of its psalmody vary in the course of the year, and moreover it is celebrated at midnight. We have already seen that both the traditional midnight prayer and also some form of vigil involving the reading of Scripture were known to Jerome, and it would therefore appear that even in the sixth century both these continued to exist as independent elements—the midnight prayer now consisting of twelve psalms, doubtless the result of Egyptian influence, and the vigil of readings and psalmody being similar in form to the *missae* of the rules of Caesarius and Aurelian (which were also independent of the office proper), and even more similar to the structure of the Eastern weekly vigils mentioned by Egeria and Cassian.[53] This independence of office and vigil also helps to explain why the *Regula Magistri* and the Rule of St. Benedict have a different arrangement of lessons at the night office both from each other and from the Roman pattern—they simply had no model to follow in this respect—and why the Roman pattern ultimately differed from the vigil described in the *Cautio Episcopi*—its source was not that but instead the winter arrangement of the Rule of St. Benedict. We may suppose, as in the case of the *missae* of Caesarius and Aurelian, that the oldest vigil is the Sunday version, and there is at least some evidence to suggest that originally it consisted simply of three psalms and a gospel reading, like the Sunday vigil in Jerusalem,[54] and was only subsequently conformed to the pattern of the Friday–Saturday full vigil of the East. This would then have been imitated on the weekdays in an abbreviated form, and somewhat extended in the winter months.

Nevertheless, though this may have been the structure of the Roman office in Benedict's time, it is still not its most primitive form. Prime may already have been established in the daily cycle at Rome at this period, but there were other places in Southern Italy which were still resisting its introduction, and so we can hardly imagine that it had been a part of the Roman pattern for very long before this.[55] Moreover, Joseph Pascher has detected behind the evening office of five psalms an even older version which had six psalms in consecutive order, as in the *Ordo Monasterii*, and he has suggested that there was similarly an earlier form of Mattins composed of six psalms, Pss. 51, 63, 67, 148, 149, and 150.[56] Why then were they subsequently reduced to five? It is a principle of the Roman monastic office that the whole Psalter is used in the course of a single week, but, as is also the case in the Eastern rites, the consecutive recitation of the psalms is limited to the evening and night offices, without doubt following the model of Egyptian monasticism, the other hours having fixed psalms. In contrast to the Eastern practice, however, the psalms which are used in the other offices of the day are not repeated when they occur in the consecutive recitation but are omitted. The evidence suggests that this was not always the case, but that originally, like the East, Rome recited the Psalter in full without omissions at the evening and night offices. This explains, for example, why the evening psalms begin at Ps. 109: this leaves forty-two psalms to the end of the Psalter, which provides six psalms each day for seven days. Since twelve psalms were prescribed for each of the weekday night offices, from Pss. 1–108, this would have left thirty-six which were presumably used at the longer Sunday office, though our evidence is weakest at this point and we only have traces of an office of twenty-five psalms.[57] The reduction of the evening office from six psalms to five, and of the Sunday psalms by stages down to eighteen,[58] therefore, seems to have come about as a result of the desire to avoid repetition. It would appear that at first those psalms which were used at the other hours were simply omitted from the consecutive *cursus*, and other psalms recited twice, in order to retain the original number, but eventually the number was reduced to obviate this necessity. The reduction of Mattins from six psalms to five seems to have followed in order to keep the morning and evening offices parallel, but this process was complicated by the fact that at some stage both a variable daily canticle and a daily proper psalm were inserted into this office, and this resulted in Pss. 63 and 67 being grouped under a single *Gloria* and Pss. 148–50 also being grouped under a single *Gloria*, in order to keep the number to five.

It is out of this Roman monastic tradition that the offices of both the Rule of St. Benedict and the *Regula Magistri*, 'Rule of the Master', grew. There has been a long debate as to the relationship between these two monastic texts,[59] but the evidence does seem to point strongly in the direction of seeing the *Regula Magistri* not as an elaborated development of Benedict's rule but as the earlier of the two documents, of which Benedict's work is a revision, mitigating, simplifying, and reverting to the more ancient tradition in many respects. This is the conclusion reached by the latest editor of the two rules, Adalbert de Vogüé, and is the one which will be adopted here.

The *Regula Magistri* knows of eight offices each day— Nocturns, Mattins, Prime, Terce, Sext, None, Lucernarium, and Compline. The dual tradition about night prayer is here reflected in the fact that in winter the night office was celebrated at midnight and completed by cockcrow so that the brethren might return to sleep before Mattins, though the author encourages them to read or meditate or do something useful instead, while in summer it was celebrated at cockcrow, and Mattins then followed immediately, although the brethren were allowed to rest until Prime if they wished.[60] Both these periods of rest seem to have been current in different forms of Roman monasticism at this period.[61] All the offices had the same basic structure, differing only in length, as this table shows:

	Nocturns	Mattins & Lucernarium	Prime, Terce, Sext, & None	Compline
	Opening versicle			
	Ps. 95			
Ant. Pss. without Alleluia:	(9): winter[62]	4	2	2
	6 : summer			
Responsorial Psalm:	1			
Ant. Pss. with Alleluia:	(4): winter[62]	2	1	1
	3 : summer			
Responsorial Psalm:	1 with Alleluia	1	1	1
		Versicle		
Lesson:	Apostle	Apostle	Apostle	Apostle
Lesson:	Gospel	Gospel	Gospel	Gospel
	Versicle		Versicle	
	Prayer	Prayer	Prayer	Prayer
				Closing versicle

The main differences from the early Roman monastic custom are in having a night office of variable length and in attaching lessons to each office, practices we have already found in other Western monastic uses, from which the author of this rule has very probably derived them. He follows the Egyptian custom in prescribing two lessons for each office, but differs from it in drawing both lessons from the New Testament. There are also reasons for believing that the 'Gospel' at Mattins and Lucernarium may always have been the gospel canticles Benedictus and Magnificat and not a variable reading.[63] The opening versicle and Ps. 95 at the beginning of Nocturns may have been an innovation in this rule or may have been derived from earlier Roman practice.[64] The nature of the 'prayer' with which each office ended is uncertain, and so again may or may not have been derived from Roman usage. It is merely called *rogus Dei*, 'petition to God', and may have been a collect, or a litany, or the Lord's Prayer, or simply silent prayer.[65]

There are also two features of these offices which are not only departures from Roman practice but also entirely new developments in Western monasticism. The first is that nearly all the psalmody is antiphonal: the *Ordo Monasterii* showed a preference in this direction (two antiphonal psalms to one responsorial), but in the rules of Caesarius and Aurelian it is only found at Mattins and Lucernarium, in the *missae* during the night, and in the subsidiary psalmody of the other offices, while the main psalms were recited in the Egyptian manner, as they also appear to have been in the earliest form of the Roman monastic office.[66] Moreover, such responsorial psalms as there are in the *Regula Magistri* seem to be subsidiary additions to the main psalmody, just as the antiphonal psalms are in the rules of Caesarius and Aurelian. This is suggested not only by the fact that the responsorial psalms are additional to the traditional multiples of three in which the antiphonal psalms are generally arranged, but also by the fact that whilst, with the exception of Mattins and Compline, the antiphonal psalms are to be recited always in the Biblical order (*currente semper psalterio*), no such directive is included in the case of the responsorial psalms, implying that these may have been fixed and selected for their appropriateness to the particular office, and at Prime, Terce, Sext, and None they consist of only two verses.[67]

The second new development is that, whilst we have already encountered in the East in the *De Virginitate* and in the West in the rules of Caesarius and Aurelian the practice of appending Alleluia to each third psalm, here at Nocturns, Mattins, and Lucernarium the psalms are grouped in two separate blocks, all those with Alleluia following those without, though maintaining the same proportions—two psalms without Alleluia to one with. Some precedent for this is, however, provided by the *Ordo Monasterii*, where the responsorial and antiphonal psalms at the night office were arranged in two distinct blocks, one after the other, and in the same proportions—two antiphonal psalms to one responsorial. As in Gaul, each psalm was followed by the *Gloria Patri* and by prayer, though apparently silent prayer alone, without a concluding collect,[68] and this suggests that the Roman monastic practice may have been similar, a conjecture supported by the absence of any surviving collection of Roman, as distinct from Italian, psalm-collects.[69]

As we have indicated above, the antiphonal psalms at the offices are always recited in the Biblical order, except for Mattins and Compline: apparently the use of selected psalms at these two services was too firmly established to allow the author to restore in its entirety what he presumably saw as the 'pure' monastic tradition of going through the Psalter in order at all the offices, in contrast to the Roman custom which included both selective and consecutive psalmody. At Mattins, however, he seeks to minimize what we have seen was felt to be a problem in the Roman office—the repetition of psalms already used in the consecutive *cursus*—by prescribing that, in addition to Ps. 51 and the *laudes* (i.e. Pss. 148–50), canticles alone should be used to make up the total of six psalms.[70] We have noted above that at some stage a series of daily canticles was included in the Roman morning office, and it may have been this which inspired the author of the rule to use canticles in his office, although it may equally be that it was their use in the *Regula Magistri* which gave rise to the Roman practice. On Sundays and feasts the Benedicite was to be used, apparently in place of Ps. 51. The psalms at Compline are not specified, but were presumably those used in the Roman tradition. The fact that the rule finds it necessary to put forward a justification for the use of the antiphonal method at this service is a sign that this was an innovation: 'the seven times a day when the prophet says that we ought to offer praise to God are all sung in the same manner because of the sevenfold Spirit who is not divided in some way'.[71]

In addition to the regular daily office, the *Regula Magistri* also prescribes a weekly all-night vigil from evening until second cockcrow, followed by Mattins, after which the brethren may rest, but on a Saturday night and not the traditional Friday night. Contrary to the claim made by de Vogüé,[72] there is no evidence that the early Roman tradition ever knew a weekly all-night vigil at all, and this therefore seems to be an invention of the author of the rule, who appears to have extended the shorter Sunday vigil practised at Rome and elsewhere into an all-night observance, in imitation of the full vigils held on the eves of festivals, because he believes that 'to justify the name "vigil" the brethren should give up their sleep and sing psalms and listen to the reading of lessons',[73] and he reserves the term 'vigil' for this occasion alone and does not use it of the night office generally.

Benedict's work on the office was, as we have already indicated, to reform the pattern set in the *Regula Magistri*, mitigating its severity and returning in some respects to the more ancient traditions. One of the biggest changes which he made was in the night office. Unlike the *Regula Magistri* he did not reserve the term 'vigil' for an all-night vigil, but regarded all night offices as vigils, and thus made no attempt to retain the midnight hour for their celebration, since that time had no special significance for a vigil. In both summer and winter, therefore, Benedict mitigates the severity of the *Regula Magistri* by allowing about two hours more to the period of sleep in each case: in winter the monks rise at 2 a.m. instead of midnight, and in summer rise about two hours later still so that the morning office can follow on directly at daybreak. Benedict similarly extends the 'summer' period of later rising so that it ends at the beginning of November and not on 24 September, as in the *Regula Magistri*. On the other hand, the second period of sleep, permitted in that rule, appears to be abolished by Benedict, quite possibly because it had been so severely criticized by Cassian as contrary to the ideal of Egyptian monasticism, and thus the real motive behind the change in the hour of the night office may very well have been that sufficient rest might be provided in the first period of sleep.[74]

Benedict also modified the contents of the night office, as the table overleaf shows. The addition of Ps. 3 to the introductory part of the office seems again to have been the result of Benedict's fidelity to the ideals of Cassian, who describes how in the East it is permitted to arrive late at the night office up to the end of the second psalm without penalty.[75] Benedict has therefore provided not just one 'assembling psalm', as in the

Early Roman	Regula Magistri	Rule of St. Benedict
? Versicle	Versicle	Versicle
		Ps. 3
? Ps. 95	Ps. 95	Ps. 95
		Hymn
12 psalms	6 pss. (9 in winter)	6 pss.
		Versicle—blessing
	1 responsory	Summer: 1 lesson + responsory
		Winter: 3 lessons
		+ 3 responsories
	3 pss. + Alleluia	6 pss. + Alleluia
	(4 in winter)	
	1 responsory + alleluia	
	Apostle	Apostle
	Gospel	
Versicle	Versicle	Versicle
? Litany	*Rogus Dei*	*Kyrie eleison*

rules of Caesarius and Aurelian,[76] but two, and he later directs that punishment shall only be given to one who arrives at the office after the *Gloria Patri* of Ps. 95, 'a psalm which, with this in mind, we wish to be recited very slowly'.[77] The use of Ps. 3 to introduce the night vigil is very widespread in monastic custom and so probably very ancient, and it derives from the mention of waking in verse 5.[78] The inclusion of metrical hymns in the office is simply following the development we have already observed in Gaul, though there the hymns came towards the end of the offices and not near the beginning.[79] Benedict retains the division of psalmody into two blocks found in the *Regula Magistri*, but he makes them of equal proportions, and returns to the Roman monastic office for the quantity—twelve psalms, the number unchanging throughout the year. Once again he may well have been influenced by the ideal of Egyptian monasticism here, as well as by the fact that he wished to retain the Roman principle of reciting the whole Psalter each week, and a varying number of psalms at the night office would have made this very difficult to achieve.

In order to retain the difference in length between summer and winter found in the *Regula Magistri* and other rules, he introduces variation in the lessons. For the winter office he draws on the pattern of the Roman vigil, which we have suggested was independent of the night office there at this stage, and incorporates three lessons 'from the book' and three responsories—the summer prescription of the Roman usage—no doubt again anxious not to overburden his monks. In the summer he reduces this to a single short lesson from the Old Testament, recited 'by heart' and not read, and a single responsory. The two lessons at the end of the office in the *Regula Magistri* are reduced to one lesson 'out of the Apostle, to be said by heart'. Thus in a sense in his summer office Benedict is closer to the Egyptian model than the *Regula Magistri* in prescribing that the first lesson shall be from the Old Testament and the second from the New, but departs from that, and from the *Regula Magistri*, in placing the first lesson, or group of lessons in winter, between the two blocks of psalmody and not at the end. Such an unusual position has something of a precedent in the office of Terce on Saturdays and Sundays in the rules of Caesarius and Aurelian, where three lessons intervene between two blocks of six psalms (though this appears to be a doubling of the weekday office of six psalms rather than the division of a group of twelve psalms),[80] but it does not explain why Benedict should choose to adopt it here, and it has been suggested that his motive was to extend the break in the middle of the psalmody, which the responsorial psalm provided in the *Regula Magistri*, in order to give a substantial rest to the monks and so maintain their concentration better.[81] Finally, the *Kyrie eleison* mentioned by Benedict as the conclusion of the office is a litany shorn of its biddings and consisting of the response alone: he reserves the full form for the morning and evening offices.

For the Sunday night office Benedict rejects the all-night vigil of the *Regula Magistri*, which we have suggested was a peculiarity of that rule and not a traditional observance, and he reverts to the model of the Roman custom, which had prescribed an increased number of psalms followed by a vigil made up of three groups of three lessons, three antiphonal psalms, and three responsories. Benedict, however, does not increase his weekday number of twelve psalms, thus remaining faithful to the Egyptian ideal, but achieves the lengthening of the office in the same way as he had done on weekdays—by varying the number of lessons. He prescribes a group of four lessons and responsories (the Roman winter weekday pattern), in place of his weekday three, and he repeats this three times as in the Roman custom. Whether intentionally or not, this brings the total of lessons to the sacred number of twelve. The first group of lessons is placed after the first half of the psalmody, as on weekdays, the second group similarly follows the second half, and three canticles are provided to precede the third, so as not to increase the total number of psalms, as this table shows:

> 6 antiphonal psalms
> Versicle—blessing
> 4 lessons
> 4 responsories
> 6 antiphonal psalms
> Versicle—blessing
> 4 lessons
> 4 responsories
> 3 canticles with Alleluia
> Versicle—blessing
> 4 lessons
> 4 responsories
> Te Deum
> Gospel
> Hymn: Te Decet Laus
> Blessing

The inclusion of the gospel reading at the end appears to have been the result of the influence of the ancient Sunday cathedral vigil, although there is nothing to indicate whether or not it was always to be one of the resurrection narratives which was read, as in the rules of Caesarius and Aurelian,[82] and possibly also the choice of three canticles has the same origin, since the use of canticles instead of psalms in the Sunday vigil has parallels in the Ambrosian, Armenian, and Chaldean rites.[83]

For the morning office Benedict again abandons the pattern of the *Regula Magistri* and follows closely the later form of the Roman rite, which was by then current, as this table shows:

Early Roman	Regula Magistri	Later Roman	Benedict
			Ps. 67
Ps. 51	Ps. 51	Ps. 51	Ps. 51
Ps. 63	Canticle	Variable Ps.	Variable Ps.
Ps. 67	Canticle	Pss. 63 & 67	Variable Ps.
Ps. 148	Ps. 148	Canticle	Canticle
Ps. 149	Ps. 149	Pss. 148–50	Pss. 148–50
Ps. 150	Ps. 150		
			Apostle
	Responsory		Responsory
			Hymn

Versicle	Versicle	Versicle	Versicle
	Apostle		
Gospel canticle	Gospel (canticle)	Gospel canticle	Gospel canticle
Litany	*Rogus Dei*	Litany	Litany
Lord's Prayer		Lord's Prayer	Lord's Prayer

Because Benedict wished to retain the Roman principle of completing the whole Psalter in a single week, and yet at the same time wanted to adhere to the Egyptian practice of reciting only twelve psalms each night, including Sunday, and of dividing the longer psalms, he did not require all the nocturnal psalms of the Roman rite, and thus he utilized some of them in the morning office by increasing the variable series of psalms to two each day. The details of this arrangement are as follows:

	Sunday	Monday	Tuesday	Wednesday	Thursday	Friday	Saturday
Roman:	118	5	43	65	90	143	92
Benedict:	118	5	43	64	88	76	143
	63	36	57	65	90	92	Canticle

He thus retains each Roman psalm on its day, except for Pss. 143 and 92, which he places in their numerical order, though it is possible Benedict's order may reflect the Roman usage current in his day, which was later changed.[84] Ps. 92 is used on Saturday in the Roman rite presumably because of its title 'For the Sabbath', while Ps. 143 is particularly appropriate for Friday, the day of the crucifixion. The psalms which Benedict adds to the Roman cycle are chosen in such a way that not only do they all have some reference to morning, except for Ps. 64, but the numerical progression of the psalms is also kept throughout the week, except for Sunday, where he introduces the Roman daily psalm, 63, and for Friday, where he introduces Ps. 76 for some inexplicable reason: clearly he could not use Ps. 91 here, as that was traditional at Compline and inappropriate to the morning, but he could perhaps have found a suitable psalm between 92 and 143, as for example Ps. 97 with its reference to light in verse 11. The selection of Ps. 64 was presumably because he could not find anything more suitable between Pss. 57 and 65. Ps. 67 has the function of an 'assembling psalm', and is recited *directaneus*; the inclusion of a metrical hymn in the office follows the Gallican custom; and the only point of dependence on the *Regula Magistri* is the insertion of a reading from the Apostle and a responsory, although the arrangement of these immediately after the psalmody seems to be modelled on his summer version of the night office.[85] Benedict insists that the Lord's Prayer at the end of the morning and evening offices is to be said aloud, in contrast to the other hours of the day where it is said silently, and this suggests that this custom is an innovation in the tradition from which he came.

The evening office is parallel in structure to the morning, except that there is no 'assembling psalm' and, apparently out of a desire not to overburden the monks, the number of psalms is reduced from five to four, taken in consecutive order from the Psalter and with the longer psalms divided. For the other hours of the day—Prime, Terce, Sext, and None—the order is: the versicle *Deus in Adiutorium* followed by a *Gloria*; hymn; three psalms or sections of psalms; one lesson; versicle; *Kyrie eleison*; and silent Lord's Prayer. Compline differs from this only in that there is apparently no opening versicle, the hymn comes after the psalms instead of before them, and a blessing is added to the end of the service, the first two of these being also features of the morning and evening offices. The use of an initial versicle with a *Gloria* at the other hours may perhaps be intended as a very abbreviated form of 'assembling psalm',[86] and the choice of this particular verse from Ps. 70 may have been influenced by Cassian, who makes much of it as a formula for contemplation,[87] or it may already have existed as a versicle in the Roman rite. Benedict follows the *Regula Magistri* in introducing Bible reading, though he has only one lesson, as in the morning and evening offices, instead of the two in the *Regula Magistri*. For the psalmody at these hours he uses the traditional Roman psalm, 119, but instead of dividing it between Prime, Terce, Sext, and None, and repeating it each day, he distributes it between Prime, Terce, Sext, and None on Sunday, together with Terce, Sext, and None on Monday, thus reducing the total number of verses at each hour to a very moderate level. For Prime on weekdays he utilizes the remainder of the Roman nocturnal psalms no longer required in his night office (Pss. 1, 2, 6–20, dividing 9/10 and 18), and for Terce, Sext, and None on other days psalms no longer required in his shortened evening office, Pss. 120–8, divided into threes, and repeated each day. For Compline, however, he retains the traditional three psalms of the Roman rite, 4, 91, 134, repeated each day and recited in the traditional manner, *directanei*. With regard to the execution of the psalms at the other hours, although those in the night, morning, and evening offices are to be antiphonal, for the lesser hours he appears to hesitate between the *directanei* of the early Roman practice and the antiphonal mode of the *Regula Magistri*, and prescribes that the latter is to be adopted only if the community is numerous enough to sustain it. There is no sign anywhere in the rule of the use of psalm-collects, which we have earlier suggested were not a part of the Roman tradition, but equally there is no clear indication of a period of silent prayer after each psalm. In the later monastic tradition this tended to be abbreviated and it ultimately disappeared, the psalms following straight on after one another, but it seems unlikely that this had already happened at such an early date.[88]

Conclusion

The writing of a conclusion, though usually welcomed by the reader, poses an acute problem for an author. He can easily be tempted to distort the evidence he has presented in order to fit some preconceived notion about the subject under consideration and bring his work to a neat and tidy end, or to select from the material in an arbitrary manner in order to make some point which he feels to be relevant to the situation of the Church today, and thereby neglect other considerations which may be equally valid, even if they have no such immediate practical application. In one sense, therefore, the evidence must speak for itself, and the reader draw from it whatever lessons seem to be pertinent. On the other hand, one cannot devote years of study to a subject without finding that certain questions are continually raised by it which relate to one's own beliefs and practices. Thus what now follows is not so much a conclusion as an indication of the main issues which have appeared as of significance to the author in his journey through the prayer-life of the Church in the early centuries.

1. The variety of practice in this early period raises the question as to whether any particular authority can be claimed for any specific arrangement of times of prayer. The emergence of the morning and evening hours as pre-eminent was, as we have seen, a fourth-century development which came about partly because of practical convenience and partly because they were seen as the fulfilment of the Old Testament pattern of daily sacrifice. If, however, the Christians of the first three centuries were right in seeing the true fulfilment of these sacrifices in the ceaseless prayer and praise of the Church, is there any particular justification in retaining these two offices as somehow normative for the Church at all times and in all places? Their dominant position has frequently been defended in recent years by the claim that they are the most ancient of the regular Christian times of prayer, but, as we have seen, if antiquity is to be the criterion for selection, then both night and noon have equal claim to be considered as of cardinal

importance. Night prayer in particular, which has so often been neglected in the later traditions of the Church, at least as regards the hour of its celebration, is so intimately related to New Testament eschatological thought that it cannot easily be regarded as of secondary significance in comparison with the morning and evening hours. Similarly the ninth hour, too, cannot be lightly dismissed, since it is the one time of prayer which owes its origin directly to an event of supreme importance to the Christian. Far and above all this, however, what is fundamental to the early understanding of daily prayer is that the real aim is unbroken communion with God, and the adoption of specific times of prayer is only a means to that end. This therefore suggests that there is no particular normative pattern of Christian daily prayer but that the times and frequency of such prayer may very well vary in accordance with the spiritual needs of the Christian, as well as his or her cultural and pastoral situation. Set hours of prayer are not so much an obligation imposed upon us as a guide and aid towards the practice of ceaseless prayer, and when they fail to fulfil this function, their continued use may rightly be questioned.

2. A major characteristic of the set times of daily devotion in the first few centuries was prayer, and especially intercession for the needs of the Church and the world. This may seem too obvious to warrant mention, and yet it is the very element in the daily offices which steadily declines almost to the point of extinction. As often happens in the history of liturgy, secondary elements, in this case psalmody, gradually adopt a dominant role, and what were originally the primary elements assume a subsidiary place, and are abbreviated in order to give more time to the newer additions. In this instance the process was encouraged by the emphasis in monasticism on the office as intended for the individual spiritual growth of those involved in it rather than as a corporate act of the Church for the benefit of all mankind. Recent reforms of the office have not succeeded in reversing this trend, perhaps in part because of a widespread loss of faith in the power of intercession. All too often the concluding prayers and intercessions are regarded as an optional appendage to the office rather than its heart, and are the first thing to be omitted when the service has to be abbreviated or combined with some other rite.

3. The influence of monasticism was also responsible for the emergence of psalmody as the dominant element in the daily

office. This, as we have seen, grew out of a belief in the particular inspiration of the Psalter in comparison with non-biblical compositions and was built upon the Christological interpretation of the psalms adopted by the first Christians. Such an understanding of prophecy and its fulfilment does not easily accord with that commonly held today, and thus it is hardly surprising that the recitation of psalms has been found to present considerable difficulties for contemporary Christian worship, especially since revisions of the office have clung tenaciously to the principle that the whole Psalter must continue to be used in worship, in accordance with the monastic ideal. The problem becomes even worse where those saying the psalms are unaware of the tradition of Christological interpretation, and where no provision is made by way of solo recitation, appropriate congregational response, period of silent reflection and prayer, or concluding collect to express and encourage this attitude towards the Psalter, and thus they are left struggling with the sentiments of many of the compositions as they attempt to see them as articulating their own praise and prayer to God. All this is not to deny that many psalms can still be found to embody profound Christian aspirations, or that the Christological understanding may not be an entirely legitimate way of interpreting some others, and one which has insights to contribute to our apprehension of the nature and work of Christ, but it does challenge both the extent and the method of the use of psalms in Christian daily prayer and their dominance over other sources of meditation and forms of prayer and praise, especially non-canonical poems and hymns.

4. Like the use of psalms, the inclusion of Bible readings in the daily office was mainly the product of monasticism, and especially of Western monasticism, and again like the psalms its place there appears open to question. In the course of our study we have sought to identify three different functions which the reading of Scripture, or of non-scriptural material for that matter, may have, and these we have termed didactic, kerygmatic, and paracletic. The didactic is essentially the orderly study of the Bible, undertaken in order to become familiar with its contents and to interpret its meaning, which in ancient times had generally to be done by public reading aloud, because of the illiteracy of many of the hearers and the scarcity of copies of the text, and for the sake of convenience

was often attached to an act of worship, though it had no intrinsic connection with it. The kerygmatic ministry of the word, on the other hand, uses selected extracts from the Bible within an act of worship in order to express and interpret the significance of the occasion which is being celebrated, and to elicit a response from the congregation, while the paracletic ministry of the word consists again of selected extracts, but this time chosen because of their appropriateness not so much to the particular occasion as to the individual spiritual needs of those assembled together, to encourage and stimulate them in their faith. It is principally the first of these functions which Bible reading in the daily offices was intended to fulfil, although the use of psalms there originates from the informal paracletic ministry of the word in the *agape*, and the proper lessons of festivals are the development of a kerygmatic liturgy of the word. In the present day, however, it is doubtful whether this is the most sensible and effective form of Bible study, when copies of the Scriptures are plentiful and illiteracy generally not such the problem that it was in the past, and it may be thought desirable for this to be pursued in other ways and in other situations than that of the daily meetings for prayer, as indeed it was in the secular Church in the early centuries, lest it should overshadow their primary purpose, as it has tended to do in the Anglican daily office. This again is not to deny that there may be a proper place for both a paracletic and a kerygmatic ministry of the word within the office itself, but it does suggest that we need to be more aware of why we are including readings within the daily prayers and consequently of what readings are appropriate in order to fulfil that function, and not simply perpetuate the practice as being a venerable institution handed down from the past.

All these considerations are not meant to be destructive of the daily office but are intended as possible pointers towards its renewal. It is essentially a monastic pattern of office which we have inherited from the past, and so it is hardly surprising that it does not meet the needs of those of us who are not of that tradition, and it may even be doubted whether it accords with contemporary monastic spirituality. We need to discover and create a truly 'cathedral' office, not necessarily by reconstructing what was done at Jerusalem or Antioch or wherever in the fourth century, but by using the insights provided by historical study in order to establish the essentials of our pattern of daily prayer and spirituality, and then express these in forms appropriate to our own age. If we have the courage to do this in a bold and thorough way, what may emerge may be radically different in outward appearance from what has gone before in both cathedral and monastic traditions, but it may more truly embody the spirit of the practice of daily prayer in the early Church, and thus rescue the divine office from the oblivion into which it is in real danger of falling in many churches, and restore it to its proper place as the backbone of catholic Christianity.

Notes

1. Its original form was no doubt very much shorter: see Dugmore, pp. 18–20.
2. *Ber.* 1.1–2.
3. *Pseudo-Aristeas* 160.
4. Philo, *De Spec. Leg.* 4.141; Josephus, *Ant.* 4.212.
5. 1 QS 10.10: 'At the coming in of day and night I will come into the covenant of God, and at the going out of evening and at morning I will recite his statutes'.
6. *Ber.* 3.3.
7. *Ber.* 1.4
8. Dugmore, pp. 20–1.
9. *j. Ber.* i.8.3c; *b. Ber.* 12a.
10. See Dugmore, p. 105; H. Schneider, 'Der Dekalog in den Phylakerien von Qumran', *Biblische Zeitschrift* 3 (1959), pp. 18–31; F. E. Vokes, 'The Ten Commandments in the New Testament and in First Century Judaism', *SE* 5, pp. 147–8.
11. *Ber.* 4.1; S.–B. II, p. 697.
12. *Pesah.* 5.1; Josephus, *Ant.* 14.65.
13. See H. Danby, *The Mishnah* (1933), p. 794; Dugmore, pp. 16, 43, 60; J. Jeremias, *The Prayers of Jesus* (1967), pp. 70–1.
14. *Ta'an.* 4.2.
15. *Ber.* 3.3.
16. Jeremias, *Prayers of Jesus*, p. 71.
17. 'Between the two evenings' (Exod. 29.39,41; Num. 28.4,8): see R. de Vaux, *Ancient Israel: Its life and Institutions* (1965), p. 182.
18. Dugmore, pp. 63–4.
19. Jeremias, *Prayers of Jesus*, p. 71.
20. *Ta'an.* 4.3–4.
21. I. Sonne in *Interpreter's Dictionary of the Bible* (1962) IV, p. 479b. On the origin of the synagogue see H. H. Rowley, *Worship in Ancient Israel* (1967), pp. 213f.; J. Weingreen, *From Bible to Mishna* (1976), pp. 115–31.
22. *Ber.* 4.1.
23. *Sukk.* 5.5; *Tam.* 7.3.
24. See also S.–B. II, pp. 697–9.
25. Ibid. II, pp. 697–700. For Dan. 6.10 and Ps. 55.17 see pp. 8–9.
26. See Dugmore, pp. 121–2: 'Be merciful, O Lord our God . . . towards thy Temple and thy habitation. . . . Accept us, O Lord our God, and dwell in Zion; and may thy servants serve thee in Jerusalem . . .'.
27. S. Holm-Nielsen, *Hodayot* (Aarhus 1960), pp. 202–3.
28. A. R. C. Leaney, *The Rule of Qumran and its meaning* (1966), pp. 239–41.

29. See above, n. 5. Leaney himself, p. 245, accepts this, not differentiating between the two activities.

30. 1 QM 14.12–14: 'But we, your holy people, will praise your name because of the works of your truth. We will exalt your splendour because of your mighty deeds [in all the] seasons and appointed times for ever, at the coming of day and at nightfall and at the departure of evening and morning'. See J. van der Ploeg, *Le Rouleau de la Guerre* (Leiden 1959), pp. 160–1.

31. G. Vermes, *The Dead Sea Scrolls in English* (1962; 2nd edn, 1975), pp. 89, 188; M. Delcor, *Les Hymnes de Qumran* (Paris 1962), pp. 246–7.

32. Philo, *De Vita Contemplativa* 27.

33. C.-H. Hunzinger, 'Aus der Arbeit an den unveröffentlichten Texten von Qumran', *Theologische Literaturzeitung* 85 (1960), col. 152.

34. S. Talmon, 'The Manual of Benedictions of the Sect of the Judean Desert', *Revue de Qumran* 2 (1960), pp. 475–500.

35. J. A. Jungmann, 'Altchristliche Gebetsordnungen im Lichte des Regelbuches von 'En Fescha', *Zeitschrift für katholische Theologie* 75 (1953), pp. 215–9.

36. Josephus, *Jewish War* 2.128–32.

37. T. H. Gaster, *The Scriptures of the Dead Sea Sect* (1957), pp. 123, 179, 199.

38. See B. Gärtner, *The Temple and the Community in Qumran and the New Testament* (1965), pp. 44–6.

39. Holm-Nielsen, p. 202.

40. See for example Vermes, loc. cit.; P. Wernberg-Moeller, *The Manual of Discipline* (Leiden 1957), p. 141.

41. See for example B. S. Childs, *Exodus* (1974), p. 603; John Mauchline, *1 and 2 Samuel* (1971), p. 48.

42. See for example de Vaux, p. 190.

43. See for example R. H. Charles, *The Book of Daniel* (Century Bible), pp. 63–4; Jeremias, *Prayers of Jesus*, p. 69; D. S. Russell, *The Jews from Alexander to Herod* (1967), p. 233.

44. The fact that Elijah was able to run the seventeen miles from Carmel to Jezreel after the time of the evening oblation (1 Kgs. 18.36,46) does not necessarily mean that it was offered at 3 p.m.

45. Jeremias, *Prayers of Jesus*, p. 71, n. 25.

46. In I. Singer (ed.), *The Jewish Encyclopedia* VIII (1904), p. 132.

47. Dugmore, p. 65.

48. See D. S. Russell, *The Method and Message of Jewish Apocalyptic* (1964), p. 61.

49. See for example J. Daniélou, *The Theology of Jewish Christianity* (1964), p. 16.

50. See pp. 47f.

51. See Leaney, *Rule of Qumran*, pp. 75–7; W. Rordorf, *Sunday* (1968), pp. 181–2.

52. See Leaney, *Rule of Qumran*, pp. 37–41, 77–90.

53. Josephus, *Jewish War* 2.128.

54. Philo, *De Vita Contemplativa* 27, 89.

55. S.-B. IV, pp. 220–1.

56. Cf. 1 Kgs. 8.29f.; Ps. 5.7; 28.2; 138.2; Dan. 6.10; 1 Esd. 4.58. The Mishnah directed that if a man 'was riding on an ass, he should dismount; if he cannot dismount he should turn his face; and if he cannot turn his face, he

should direct his heart toward the Holy of Holies. If he was journeying on a ship or a raft he should direct his heart toward the Holy of Holies' (*Ber.* 4.5–6).

57. Cf. Ezek. 8.16; 11.1; *Sukk.* 5.4.

58. See W. H. Brownlee, 'Messianic Motifs of Qumran and the New Testament', *NTS* 3 (1956/7), pp. 198–207.

59. See Is. 60.19–20; Ps. 27.1; 84.11; Mic. 7.8; Mal. 4.2

60. Testament of Levi 18.2–4: 'Then shall the Lord raise up a new priest. And to him shall all the words of the Lord be revealed; and he shall execute a righteous judgement upon the earth for a multitude of days. And his star shall arise in heaven as of a king, lighting up the light of knowledge as the sun the day, and he shall be magnified in the world. He shall shine forth as the sun on the earth . . .'. Cf. Ibid. 4.3; Testament of Judah 24.1.

61. 'O cause a new light to shine upon Zion, and may we all be worthy soon to enjoy its brightness. . . .'

62. Erik Peterson, 'Die geschichtliche Bedeutung der jüdischen Gebetsrichtung', *TZ* 3 (1947), p. 7.

63. For other forms see Joseph Heinemann, *Prayer in the Talmud* (Berlin 1977).

64. This is true for example of J. P. Audet, 'Literary Forms and Contents of a Normal *Eucharistia* in the First Century', *SE* 1, pp. 643–62, which appeared in an expanded form as 'Esquisse historique du genre littéraire de la "bénédiction" juive et de 1' "eucharistie" Chrétienne', *Revue Biblique* 65 (1958), pp. 371–99. See the criticism of his approach in T. J. Talley, 'The Eucharistic Prayer of the Ancient Church According to Recent Research: Results and Reflections', *SL* 11 (1976), pp. 139–41.

65. Gen. 24.27. For other examples of this type of *berakah* see Exod. 18.10; 1 Sam. 25.32; 2 Sam. 18.28; 1 Kgs. 5.7.

66. See also 2 Chron. 2.12, where the simple form of 1 Kgs. 5.7 has been expanded by both a further descriptive phrase and additional narrative.

67. J. M. Robinson, 'The Historicality of Biblical Language', in B. W. Anderson (ed.), *The Old Testament and Christian Faith* (1964), p. 142.

68. See for example 2 Macc. 10.38; 15.34; Tob. 13.1; 1 Esd. 8.25.

69. See H. Ringgren, *The Faith of the Psalmists* (1963), p. 77.

70. See for example 1 Kgs. 8.33,35; Neh. 9.2; Dan. 9.20.

71. See for example Is. 25.1–5; Ecclus. 51.1–12; and the Qumran *hodayoth* (1 QH).

72. O. Michel, *TDNT* 5, p. 204; see also R. J. Ledogar, *Acknowledgement: Praise-verbs in the early Greek Anaphoras* (Rome 1968), pp. 70–6.

73. Judith 8.25; 2 Macc. 1.11; 10.7 (*v.l.*); 3 Macc. 7.16; and the noun *eucharistia* in Wisd. 16.28. See H. Conzelmann, *TDNT* 9, pp. 409–410; Ledogar, pp. 94–106; J. M. Robinson, 'Die Hodajot-Formel in Gebet und Hymnus des Früchristentums', in W. Eltester (ed.), *Apophoreta. Festschrift für Ernst Haenchen* (Berlin 1964), pp. 198–9.

74. Josephus, *Ant.* 8.111–13: see W. C. van Unnik, 'Eine merkwürdige liturgische Aussage bei Josephus', in O. Betz, Klaus Haacher and Martin Hengel (eds.), *Josephus-Studien* (Göttingen 1974), pp. 362–9. See also Josephus, *Ant.* 6.145.

75. See H. Cazelles, 'L'Anaphore et l'Ancien Testament', in *Eucharisties d'Orient et d'Occident* I (Lex Orandi 46, Paris 1970), pp. 11–21.

76. See also Neh. 1.5–11; Jer. 32.17–25; 1 Macc. 7.37–8, 41–2; 2 Macc. 14. 35–6; 3 Macc. 2.2–20.

77. And not for the *hodayah*, as is supposed by Robinson, 'Historicality of Biblical Language', p. 132, n. 19.

78. Ibid., p. 134.

79. For the earliest form of this see L. Finkelstein, 'The Birkat Ha-Mazon', *JQR* 19 (1928/9), pp. 211–62.

80. See for example 1 Esd. 4.60 (combined with a *hodayah*); Tob. 3.11f.; 8.5–8; S. of III Ch. 3.29–34; 1 Macc. 4.30–3.

81. See Robinson, 'Die Hodajot-Formel', pp. 231–2.

82. See Heinemann, *Prayer in the Talmud*, pp. 77–103; Talley, pp. 141–5.

83. See for example Eric Werner, *The Sacred Bridge* (1959), p. 5.

84. Text in Dugmore, pp. 114–27.

85. *b. Meg.* 17b.

86. S.–B. I, pp. 406f.; II, p. 186; IV, pp. 233f.

87. L. Bouyer, *Eucharist: Theology and Spirituality of the Eucharistic Prayer* (1968), p. 71.

88. See for example Dugmore, pp. 22–5; A. Marmorstein, 'The Oldest Form of the Eighteen Benedictions', *JQR* 34 (1943/4), pp. 137–59.

89. Heinemann, *Prayer in the Talmud*, p. 37.

90. Ibid., pp. 37–51; see also pp. 218–24, 284–7.

91. *Sot.* 7.1; Jeremias, *Prayers of Jesus*, p. 76, n. 34.

92. *Ber.* 1.3: 'The School of Shammai say: In the evening all should recline when they recite, but in the morning they should stand up, for it is written, "and when you lie down and when you rise up". But the School of Hillel say: They may recite it every one in his own way, for it is written, "And when you walk by the way". Why then is it written, "And when you lie down and when you rise up"? It means the time when men usually lie down and the time when men usually rise up'.

93. Kneeling is indicated in Ez. 9.5; Ps. 95.6; Is. 45.23; Dan. 6.10; standing in 1 Sam. 1.26; 1 Kgs. 8.22 (cf. 8.54: kneeling); 2 Chron. 6.12 (cf. 6.13: kneeling); Jer. 18.20. See also Mt. 6.5; Lk. 18.11f.

94. 1 Kgs. 8.22,54; 2 Chron. 6.12,13; Ez. 9.5; Ps. 28.2; Is. 1.15; Lam. 2.19.

95. Dugmore, p. 43.

96. Josephus, *Jewish War* 2.128–9; 1 QS 6.3.

97. Philo, *De Vita Contemplativa* 30.

98. A. Guilding, *The Fourth Gospel and Jewish Worship* (1960), pp. 6–44, argues for a lectionary which completed the Pentateuch once every three years, M. D. Goulder, *The Evangelists' Calendar* (1978), pp. 19–72, for an annual cycle. The theory of a triennial cycle has been challenged by J. R. Porter, 'The Pentateuch and the Triennial Lectionary Cycle', in F. F. Bruce (ed.), *Promise and Fulfilment* (1963), pp. 163–74; L. Morris, *The New Testament and the Jewish Lectionaries* (1964); L. Crockett, 'Luke 4.16–30 and the Jewish Lectionary Cycle', *JJS* 17 (1966), pp. 13–46; J. Heinemann, 'The Triennial Lectionary Cycle', *JJS* 18 (1968), pp. 41–8.

99. See Guilding, pp. 20–3; Goulder, *The Evangelists' Calendar*, pp. 105–40.

100. Rowley, pp. 235–7.

101. *Meg.* 3.6.

102. Lk. 18.12; Mk. 2.18//Mt. 9.14//Lk. 5.33. Public fasts were held on these days only if the autumn rains had not begun by the seventeenth day of the month of Marheshvan: see *Ta'an.* 1.3–7; 2.9.

103. On the use of this blessing see Rowley, p. 237.

104. Bouyer, p. 60.

105. See p. 66.

106. See p. 86.

107. 1 QS 6.6–8a. See also p. 7.

108. *Tamid.* 7.4. The psalms were 24, 48, 82, 94, 81, 93, 92.

109. See Guilding, pp. 38f.; J. A. Lamb, *The Psalms in Christian Worship* (1962), pp. 14–15.

110. See for example David Hedegard, *Seder R. Amram Gaon* (Lund 1951), Pt. I, pp. 32f.

111. See for example Anton Baumstark, *Comparative Liturgy* (1958), p. 38.

112. See Richard S. Sarason, 'On the Use of Method in the Modern Study of Jewish Liturgy', in William Scott Green (ed.), *Approaches to Ancient Judaism: Theory and Practice* (Missoula, Montana, 1978), p. 130.

113. Translation of these in Vermes, pp. 150–201.

114. Philo, *In Flaccum* 121–2.

115. Philo, *De Vita Contemplativa* 29.

116. Ibid. 80, 83, 84.

117. The Rabbinic schools of Shammai and Hillel disputed as to whether 'light' or 'lights' should be said: see *Ber.* 8.5.

Chapter 2

1. W. Grundmann, *TDNT* 3, p. 619.

2. Jeremias, *Prayers of Jesus*, p. 79.

3. Jeremias, *The Eucharistic Words of Jesus* (2nd edn, 1966), pp. 118–19. See the criticism of his view by E. Haenchen, *The Acts of the Apostles* (1971), p. 191.

4. F. J. Foakes Jackson & Kirsopp Lake, *The Beginnings of Christianity* (1933), IV, pp. 10–11.

5. Mk. 1.2//Lk. 4.31; Mk. 1.39//Mt. 4.23//Lk. 4.44; Mk. 3.1//Mt. 12.9//Lk. 6.6; Mk. 6.2//Mt. 13.54; Mt. 9.35; Lk. 4.15–30; 13.10; Jn. 6.59; 18.20.

6. See for example Dugmore, pp. 1–8; Lamb, p. 21; C. F. D. Moule, *Worship in the New Testament* (1961), p. 15; A. Schmemann, *Introduction to Liturgical Theology* (1966), p. 46. On the *Birkath ha-Minim* see W. D. Davies, *The Setting of the Sermon on the Mount* (1964), pp. 275–6; but cf. Peter Schäfer, 'Die sogennante Synode von Jabne zurtrennung von Juden und Christen in ersten/zweiten Jh. n. Chr.', *Judaica* 31 (1975), pp. 54–64, 116–24.

7. Acts 5.12–13; see also 3.11; 5.21,42.

8. Rordorf, pp. 124–5.

9. Mt. 4.23; 9.35; 10.17; 12.9; 13.54; 23.34. See also Jas. 2.2; and for the continued use of the term 'synagogue' in Christianity see Dugmore, p. 5.

10. M. D. Goulder, *Midrash and Lection in Matthew* (1974), pp. 152, 280.

11. G. J. Cuming, 'The New Testament Foundation for Common Prayer', *SL* 10 (1974), p. 91.

12. See p. 18.

13. Mt. 18.20: see Cuming, 'New Testament Foundation', p. 96.

14. See F. E. Vokes, 'The Didache—still debated', *Church Quarterly* 3 (1970), pp. 57–62.

15. Cf. the instances in Luke's gospel where the motif of prayer is added to the accounts in the other gospels: Lk. 3.21//Mt. 3.16//Mk. 1.10; Lk. 5.16;

6.12//Mk. 3.13; Lk. 9.18//Mt. 16.13//Mk. 8.27; Lk. 9.28–9//Mt. 17.1–2//Mk. 9.2–3; Lk. 11.1; 23.46//Mt. 27.50//Mk. 15.37.

16. See pp. 47f.

17. See pp. 4–10.

18. Cf. p. 18.

19. The references to standing in Mt. 6.5 & Lk. 18.11f. concern Jews at prayer.

20. Prostration, falling on one's face, is not an attitude of prayer but an act of reverence: see D. G. Delling, *Worship in the New Testament* (1962), pp. 104–6.

21. See p. 8.

22. See for example Jeremias, *Prayers of Jesus*, p. 81.

23. Mt. 6.9–15//Lk. 11.1–4. See also Jeremias, *Prayers of Jesus*, p. 106.

24. See Goulder, *Midrash and Lection in Matthew*, pp. 297–300.

25. See above, ch. 1, n. 86.

26. Bouyer, p. 61; Jeremias, *Prayers of Jesus*, p. 98.

27. See Heinemann, *Prayer in the Talmud*, pp. 191–2, 251f., and his essay, 'The Background of Jesus' Prayer in the Jewish Liturgical Tradition', in Jakob J. Petuchowski and Michael Brocke (eds.), *The Lord's Prayer and the Jewish Liturgy* (1978), pp. 81–9.

28. Jeremias, *Prayers of Jesus*, pp. 73–4, 79–81.

29. See p. 17, and for variation in order and text in the phylacteries see J. Bowman, 'Phylacteries', *SE* 1, pp. 527–8; Vokes, 'The Ten Commandments in the New Testament and in First Century Judaism', *SE* 5, pp. 147–8.

30. Dugmore, pp. 104–5.

31. See above, ch. 1, n. 10.

32. On the disputed interpretation of this, see pp. 42–3.

33. *Ap. Const.* 7.32–4: see Bouyer, pp. 119–35.

34. See pp. 17–18.

35. Jeremias, *Prayers of Jesus*, p. 26.

36. Ibid., p. 75. What he alleges to be a further quotation from the first of the Eighteen Benedictions in Mk. 12.26//Mt. 22.32//Lk. 20.37 is a quotation from Exod. 3.6: see Cuming, 'New Testament Foundation', p. 92.

37. See p. 35.

38. Dugmore, pp. 78, 107. Cf. Cuming, 'New Testament Foundation', p.94

39. See the examples in Dugmore, pp. 75f.

40. In the Pauline epistles references to this type of prayer are far more numerous than those to any other: see the analysis in G. P. Wiles, *Paul's Intercessory Prayers* (1974), who, however, tends to see rather more such passages than are actually there.

41. A baptismal context has been proposed for the liturgical material in both Ephesians and 1 Peter by a number of scholars, though with significant differences: see F. W. Beare, *The First Epistle of Peter* (2nd edn, 1958), pp. 196–202; J. Coutts, 'Ephesians 1.3–14 and 1 Peter 1.3–12', *NTS* 3 (1956/7), pp. 115–27; F. L. Cross, *1 Peter, A Paschal Liturgy* (1954); N. A. Dahl, 'Adresse und Pröomium des Epheserbriefes', *TZ* 7 (1951), pp. 241–64; J. C. Kirby, *Ephesians: Baptism and Pentecost* (1968); A. R. C. Leaney, '1 Peter and the Passover: an interpretation', *NTS* 10 (1963/4), pp. 238–51; R. R. Williams, 'The Pauline Catechesis', in F. L. Cross (ed.), *Studies in Ephesians* (1956), pp. 89–96. But cf. the criticism by C. F. D. Moule, 'The Nature and Purpose of 1

Peter', *NTS* 3 (1956/7), pp. 1–11, and by T. C. G. Thornton, '1 Peter, A Paschal Liturgy?', *JTS* 12 (1961), pp. 14–26.

42. See R. McL. Wilson, 'Some Recent Studies in the Lucan Infancy Narratives', *SE* 1, pp. 235–53.

43. See pp. 14f.

44. See p. 7.

45. See also Phil. 1.3f.; Col. 1.3f.; 1 Thess. 1.2–3; 2 Thess. 1.3f.; Philem. 4–6. 1 Cor. opens with a simple thanksgiving, 2 Cor. with the passive *berakah* (but see the reference to a *eucharistia* involving intercession in 1.11), Galatians begins abruptly with no prayer at all, while Ephesians, though probably not Pauline, includes both the passive *berakah* (1.3f.) and also the more characteristically Pauline thanksgiving-intercession formula (1.15f.).

46. See for example H. Conzelmann, *TDNT* 9, pp. 411–12; Kirby, pp. 84–5, 104.

47. In addition to the examples already given, for *eucharisteo* see Acts 28.15; Rom. 1.21; 1 Cor. 1.14; 14.18; Eph. 5.20; Col. 1.12; 3.17; 1 Thess. 2.13; 2 Thess. 2.13; and for *eucharistia* see 2 Cor. 4.15; 9.11–12; Eph. 5.4; Col. 2.7; 4.2; 1 Thess. 3.9; 1 Tim. 2.1. See also the interjection 'thanks be to God' in Rom. 6.17; 7.25; 1 Cor. 15.57; 2 Cor. 2.14; 8.16; 9.15.

48. See Jeremias, *Eucharistic Words*, pp. 97, n. 4, and 175.

49. See Robinson, 'Die Hodajot-Formel', pp. 209–12; Talley, pp. 146–8.

50. See p. 16, and also Robinson, 'Die Hodajot-Formel', pp. 202–3.

51. See p. 15.

52. See Haenchen, pp. 226–8.

53. The phrase 'you made heaven and earth' occurs in Is. 37.16, but in the indicative and not as a participle, as here, and without the ending 'and the sea and everything in them', and in this latter form it is a common expression: see p. 35. The words *gar ep' aletheias*, 'for truly', occur in Is. 37.18, but *ep' aletheias* is a common expression both in the LXX (Deut. 22.20; Tob. 8.7; Job 9.2; 19.4; 36.4; Dan. 2.5,8,47; 8.26) and in the Lucan writings (Lk. 4.25; 20.21; 22.59; Acts 10.34). The phrase *kai ta nun*, 'and now', is peculiar to Acts in the NT (5.38; 17.30; 20.32; 27.22): *kai nun* is a semitism occurring very frequently before imperatives, of which there are numerous instances in the LXX (e.g. 2 Macc. 14.36); Is. 37.20 has *nun de kyrie*, and although the parallel version of this passage in 2 Kgs. 19.19 has *kai nun kyrie*, it lacks the earlier *ep' aletheias*. Both versions have *ide*, 'see', and not *epide*, 'look upon', as in Acts 4.29, and it comes at an earlier point in the prayer.

54. See Kirby, pp. 126–38.

55. Robinson, 'Die Hodajot-Formel', pp. 213–17.

56. Rom. 8.15; Gal. 4.6. For the use of the term *abba* see Jeremias, *Prayers of Jesus*, pp. 11–65.

57. K. H. Rengstorf, *TDNT* 2, pp. 45–8.

58. Lk. 2.29; Acts 4.24; Rev. 6.10; probably of God in Jude 4, but apparently of Christ in 2 Pet. 2.1: see J. N. D. Kelly, *A Commentary on the epistles of Peter and Jude* (1969), p. 252.

59. Rom. 1.25; 9.5; 11.36; 16.27; Gal. 1.5; Eph. 3.21; Phil. 4.20; 1 Tim. 1.17; 6.16; 2 Tim. 4.18; Heb. 13.21; 1 Pet. 4.11; 5.11; 2 Pet. 3.18; Jude 25; Rev. 1.6; 5.13–14; 7.12; *Didache* 8.2; 9.2,3,4; 10.2,4,5; 1 Clement 20.12; 32.4; 38.4; 43.6; 45.8; 50.7; 58.2; 61.3; 64; 65.2. For the Amen response to prayer see also 1 Cor. 14.16; 2 Cor. 1.20.

60. Intercession for the pagan civil power was also known in Judaism: see for example Ez. 6.10; Bar. 1.11; Josephus, *Jewish War* 2.197.

61. Eph. 5.20 should be read in the light of Col. 3.17, which makes it clear that the actual formula used was 'through' and not 'in the name of': see C. L. Mitton, *The Epistle to the Ephesians* (1951), p. 253. Baptism 'in the name of Jesus' (Acts 2.38; 8.16; 10.43,48; 19.5; 1 Cor. 6.11) did not necessarily involve the use of those words as such but only the confession of faith in Jesus, and in any event would have been declaratory rather than precatory, as seems also to have been the case in exorcism and healing: see Acts 3.6,16; 4.7,10,30; 16.18; 19.13; Jas. 5.14.

62. It is possible, though unlikely, that the doxologies in 2 Tim. 4.18; Heb. 13.21; 1 Pet. 4.11; 1 Clement 20.12; 50.7 are also addressed to Christ.

63. See Delling, p. 118; J. A. Jungmann, *The Place of Christ in Liturgical Prayer* (1965), pp. 127–43.

64. See also 1 Thess. 3.11; 2 Thess. 2.16.

65. Rom. 15.13; 1 Cor. 1.4–8; Eph. 1.15–21; Phil. 1.3–11; 4.19; 1 Thess. 1.2–3; 3.11–13; 5.23. See Wiles, pp. 41, 158.

66. See Jeremias, *Prayers of Jesus*, pp. 94–107.

67. See p. 23.

68. See p. 11.

69. See pp. 57–9.

70. Daniélou, *The Theology of Jewish Christianity*, p. 341. See also 'the star in the east' (Mt. 2.2): ibid., pp. 217–19.

71. See such passages as Mt. 17.2; Lk. 1.78; Jn. 1.9; 8.12; Acts 26.13; Rom. 13.11–13; 2 Cor. 4.3–6; Eph. 5.8–14; Col. 1.12–13; 1 Thess. 5.5; 2 Pet. 1.19; 1 Jn 1.5f.; Rev. 1.16; 21.23f.; 22.16. For Qumran, see p. 10.

72. See Mk. 11.25 for a further allusion to the Lord's Prayer in a section on praying.

73. A. E. J. Rawlinson, *The Gospel according to St. Mark* (1925), p. 211, suggested that its aim was to encourage Christians to face martyrdom in the right spirit.

74. Delling, p. 111.

75. Schmemann, pp. 40–59.

76. See also J. J. von Allmen, 'The Theological Meaning of Common Prayer', *SL* 10 (1974), pp. 129–33.

77. See Rordorf, pp. 225–8.

78. See pp. 66f.

79. Rordorf, p. 178.

80. A. Jaubert, 'Jésus et le calendrier de Qumrân', *NTS* 7 (1960), p. 27.

81. Ibid., pp. 1–10; G. R. Driver, *The Judean Scrolls* (New York 1965), pp. 316–30; Rordorf, pp. 183f.

82. Jaubert's designation of them as 'jours liturgiques' is therefore misleading (see Rordorf, pp. 185f.), and the theory of J. Blinzler, 'Qumran-Kalender und Passionschronologie', *Zeitschrift für die neutestamentliche Wissenschaft* 49 (1958), p. 245, that Wednesday and Friday were kept as fast-days by the Essenes, ignores the fact that these days had a festal rather than a penitential character in the solar calendar: see H. Braun, *Qumran und das Neue Testament* (Tübingen 1966), II, p. 51.

83. Not perhaps to the extent suggested by Jaubert that Jesus observed the Passover in accordance with it: see Rordorf, p. 184, n. 4; but cf. Driver, pp. 330–5.

84. See p. 66.

85. See Rordorf, pp. 215–37.

86. That the early Church fasted, in contrast to Jesus himself, is shown by Mt. 9.14–15//Mk. 2.18–20//Lk. 5.33–5.

87. Rordorf, pp. 118–42.

88. Oscar Cullmann, *Early Christian Worship* (1953), pp. 26–9.

89. Usually thought to have been on Saturday evening, but convincingly argued as having been on Sunday evening by Rordorf, pp. 179–80, 200–5, though his thesis has not entirely escaped criticism: see for example Samuele Bacchiocechi, *From Sabbath to Sunday* (Rome 1977), esp. pp. 85–9.

90. See Acts 5.21, where the apostles enter the Temple at daybreak and teach, and Acts 2.1f., the morning assembly on the day of Pentecost, which according to the solar calendar would have been a Sunday.

91. See Rordorf, pp. 250–2.

92. Among these are the works already cited by Goulder, Guilding, & Kirby.

93. See p. 28.

94. Pliny, *Ep.* 10.96.

95. See Cullmann, pp. 22, 28; R. P. Martin, *Carmen Christi* (1967), pp. 1–9; Rordorf, pp. 202–4, 251–61.

96. See for example the list of NT quotations and allusions in C. A. Briggs, *Psalms* (ICC, 1906), I, pp. ci–cii.

97. See Balthasar Fischer, 'Le Christ dans les Psaumes: la devotion aux Psaumes dans l'Eglise des Martyrs', *LMD* 27 (1951), pp. 86–109; 'Les Psaumes, Prière Chrétienne, Témoignages du IIe Siècle', in Mgr. Cassien & Bernard Botte (eds.), *La Prière des Heures* (Lex Orandi 35, Paris 1963), pp. 85–99.

98. See J. D. Crichton, *Christian Celebration: The Prayer of the Church* (1976), p. 60.

99. See John Wilkinson, *Egeria's Travels* (1971), p. 137.

100. Cuming, 'New Testament Foundation', p. 98.

101. C. K. Barrett, *A Commentary on the First Epistle to the Corinthians* (1968), p. 327.

102. Although the general sense of this verse is clear, the syntax is difficult: see Cuming, 'New Testament Foundation', p. 97; C. F. D. Moule, *The Epistles of Paul the Apostle to the Colossians and to Philemon* (1962), p. 125.

103. Barrett, p. 325; Rordorf, p. 249. For the *agape*, see pp. 51, 53, 55–7.

104. See pp. 21–2.

105. Gregory Dix, *The Shape of the Liturgy* (1945), p. 219.

106. See Baumstark, *Comparative Liturgy*, pp. 49–51; Bouyer, pp. 125–9; E. R. Hardy, 'Kedushah and Sanctus', *SL* 6 (1969), pp. 183–8.

107. On this subject see R. Deichgräber, *Gotteshymnus und Christushymnus in der frühen Christenheit* (Gottingen 1967); Martin, *Carmen Christi*; Robinson, 'Die Hodajot-Formel', pp. 213–35; J. T. Saunders, *The New Testament Christological Hymns* (1971).

Chapter 3

1. Dugmore, pp. 10, 47, 70, 112.
2. Clement, *Strom.* 7.7.
3. *Strom.* 2.23: 'We are to rise from our slumbers with the Lord, and retire to sleep with thanksgiving and prayer'; *Pedagog.* 2.4: 'before partaking of sleep it is a sacred duty to give thanks to God, having enjoyed his grace and love, and so go straight to sleep'.
4. *Strom.* 7.12.
5. *Strom.* 7.7; see also *Pedagog.* 2.9: 'we ought often to rise by night and bless God'.
6. See pp. 4–10.
7. Origen, *De Or.* 12.2.
8. Dugmore, pp. 67–8.
9. I.-H. Dalmais, 'Origine et Constitution de l'Office', *LMD* 21 (1950), p. 22.
10. J. H. Walker, 'Terce, Sext and None An Apostolic Custom?', *SP* 5 (1962), p. 209.
11. E. G. Jay, *Origen's Treatise on Prayer* (1954), pp. 115–16.
12. Origen, *Contra Cels.* 6.41.
13. *Strom.* 7.7.
14. See pp. 78, 88, 91–2.
15. Tertullian, *De Or.* 24–5.
16. See for example, J. Mateos, 'The Origins of the Divine Office', *Worship* 41 (1967), p. 479.
17. *Ad Uxorem* 2.5.
18. *De Or.* 25.
19. *De Corona* 3.
20. *Apol.* 39.
21. See p. 22.
22. *Ad Nationes* 1.13.
23. See pp. 21–2, 44. Ps. 133 may possibly have formed a regular element in the *agape:* see Tertullian, *De Ieiun.* 13.
24. Cyprian, *De Dom. Orat.* 34–6.
25. *pace* Walker, 'Terce, Sext and None', pp. 208, 212.
26. *Ep.* 63.16.
27. *Ep.* 1.16.
28. The numbering of the chapters is that of Botte's edition, followed by G. J. Cuming, *Hippolytus: a Text for Students* (1976), whose translation is used here.
29. See A. F. Walls, 'The Latin version of Hippolytus' *Apostolic Tradition*', *SP* 3 (1961), p. 158.
30. See pp. 103–4.
31. *De Ieiun.* 10: see p. 67.
32. Daniélou, *The Theology of Jewish Christianity*, p. 342; see also ibid., pp. 45–52.
33. Henry Chadwick, 'Prayer at Midnight', in *Epektasis: Melanges Patristiques offerts au Cardinal Jean Daniélou* (Paris 1972), pp. 47–9. Reference to prayer by the angels and the whole of creation is also found in Tertullian, *De Or.* 29.
34. Gregory Dix, *The Apostolic Tradition of St. Hippolytus* (1937), p. 83.

35. Dix, *The Shape of the Liturgy*, p. 86.

36. B. Botte, *La Tradition Apostolique de saint Hippolyte* (Münster 1963), pp. xxxi, xxxii.

37. G. Dix, *The Apostolic Tradition of St. Hippolytus* (2nd edn, with preface and corrections by H. Chadwick, 1968), p. j.

38. See p. 51.

39. See Botte, p. 65, n. 1.

40. See p. 64.

41. *Paed.* 2.9.

42. Daniélou, *The Theology of Jewish Christianity*, p. 342.

43. *De Dom Orat.* 35. See p. 52.

44. See pp. 10, 38. On the use of 'Day' as a Christological title, see Daniélou, *The Theology of Jewish Christianity*, pp. 168–72.

45. *Ad Nation.* 1.13; *Apol.* 16.

46. *Strom.* 7.7.

47. *De Or.* 32.

48. Ibid., 31.4.

49. Erik Peterson, 'La croce e la preghiera verso l'oriente', *EL* 59 (1945), pp. 52–68.

50. Daniélou, *The Theology of Jewish Christianity*, pp. 268–9, 341–2. For the later development of the symbolism of eastward prayer, see J. Daniélou, *The Bible and the Liturgy* (1960), pp. 30–2.

51. *Strom.* 7.7: see p. 50.

52. *Strom.* 6.14.

53. *De Or.* 25: see p. 50.

54. *De Ieiun.* 10.

55. Dugmore, pp. 66–7.

56. Walker, 'Terce, Sext and None', pp. 209–10.

57. *De Dom. Orat.* 34: see p. 52. See also Tertullian, *De Ieiun.* 10.

58. Walker, 'Terce, Sext and None', pp. 210–12.

59. See pp. 53–4.

60. *De Dom. Orat.* 34: see p. 52.

61. *De Ieiun.* 10: see p. 67. Cf. Walker, 'Terce, Sext and None', p. 207.

62. Vincent Taylor, *The Gospel according to St. Mark* (1952), p. 590.

63. See pp. 49–50, 78.

64. R. H. Lightfoot, *The Gospel Message of St. Mark* (1950), p. 53.

65. See p. 67.

66. See Tertullian, *De Or.* 18.

67. See pp. 88, 91–2.

68. *De Or.* 10.

69. *Apol.* 39; see also ibid., 30, 32.

70. *Ad. Demet.* 20; see also *Ep.* 7.8; 30.6; *De Dom. Orat.* 17.

71. *Martyrdom of Polycarp* 14.

72. *De Or.* 33.1.

73. See p. 50.

74. Tertullian, *De Anima* 9.

75. Clement, *Strom.* 7.7; Tertullian, *Apol.* 39; Cyprian, *Ep.* 1.16; *Ap. Trad.* 25: see pp. 48, 51, 53, 56.

76. See p. 44.

77. See Jeremias, *Eucharistic Words*, pp. 255–6.

78. The singing of psalms in relation to means also continued in the fourth century: see John Chrysostom, *Expos. in Ps.* 41.2.

79. *De Or.* 27.

80. *Ad Uxor.* 2.8.

81. See for example Lamb, p. 27.

82. *De Or.* 27–8; see also *Apol.* 30.

83. See p. 48.

84. *Hom. in Num.* 23.3; see also *Contra Celsum* 8.17, 21–2.

85. See for example Dugmore, pp. 82–3.

86. See pp. 26–7.

87. *De Or.* 23.

88. See pp. 82, 101.

89. 1 Clement 2, 29; Tertullian, *Apol.* 30.

90. Origen, *De Or.* 31.2–3.

91. Tertullian, *De Or.* 17.

92. Ibid., 14; Origen, *Hom. in Exod.* 3.3.

93. *De Dom. Orat.* 8.

94. Tertullian, *De Or.* 27; *Ad Uxor.* 2.8; *Ap. Trad.* 41. See pp. 54, 64.

95. Justin, *Apol.* 67.

96. See p. 41.

97. See p. 20.

98. See Dix, *The Shape of the Liturgy*, pp. 37f.

99. See p. 40.

100. Clement, *Strom.* 7.12; Origen, *Hom. in Lev.* 10.2.

101. *Shepherd of Hermas, Simil.* 5.1.

102. Tertullian, *De Or.* 19.

103. See for example Dix, *The Shape of the Liturgy*, p. 342; Dugmore, p. 38.

104. Tertullian, *De Ieiun.* 10.

105. *De Corona* 3.

106. *De Or.* 19. See also E. Dekkers, 'La Messe du soir à la fin de l'antiquité et au moyen âge, Notes historiques', *Sacris erudiri* 7 (1955), pp. 106–10.

107. Tertullian, *De Cult. Fem.* 2.11.

108. See pp. 91–2.

109. See p. 19.

110. Dugmore, pp. 28–37; Rordorf, pp. 142–53.

111. Tertullian, *De Ieiun.* 14. See Rordorf, pp. 143–4, for other possible reasons for the emergence of the Saturday fast.

112. Tertullian, *De Or.* 23.

113. Origen, *Hom. in Num.* 23.4: see Rordorf, p. 151, esp. n. 3.

114. *Ap. Trad.* 22: see Dix's edn, p. 43n.; but cf. Dugmore, pp. 33–4; Rordorf, p. 146.

115. See for example Dix, *The Shape of the Liturgy*, p. 325.

116. See p. 39.

117. See p. 91.

118. See also Dugmore, pp. 88–9, for further evidence.

119. Origen, *Hom. in Jes. Nav.* 4.1.

120. Origen, *Hom. in Gen.* 10.3.

121. Dugmore, pp. 47–9.

122. For this see the references in Adolf Harnack, *Bible Reading in the Early Church*, trans. J. R. Wilkinson (1912).

Chapter 4

1. The term was coined by Baumstark, *Comparative Liturgy*, pp. 111f., who first recognized the fundamental distinction between the two types of office.
2. See p. 106.
3. Eusebius, *Comm. in Ps.* 64.10.
4. See pp. 78f.
5. See p. 64.
6. John Chrysostom, *Expos. in Ps.* 140.3.
7. 8.17–18: Eng. trans. in P. W. Harkins, *St. John Chrysostom: Baptismal Instructions* (1963), pp. 126–7.
8. See p. 65.
9. Chrysostom, *Hom. in Matt.* 11.9.
10. *Expos. in Ps.* 140.1.
11. *Hom. in I Ep. ad Tim.* 6.
12. Gregory of Nyssa, *Vita Macrinae* 22.
13. Ibid., 25.
14. Basil, *De Spirit. Sanct.* 29.73.
15. F. J. Dölger, 'Lumen Christi', *Antike und Christentum* 5 (Münster 1936), pp. 1–43; J. Mateos, 'Quelques anciens documents sur l'office du soir', *OCP* 35 (1969), p. 350.
16. Dix, *The Shape of the Liturgy*, p. 87; G. Winkler, 'Über die Kathedralvesper in den verschiedenen Riten des Ostens und Westens', *ALW* 16 (1974), pp. 60–1.
17. See pp. 51, 56.
18. Ephraem, *Carmina Nisibena* 17.37f.; quoted in Dix, *The Shape of the Liturgy*, p. 428.
19. Theodoret, *Quaestiones in Exodum* 28.
20. Mateos, 'Quelques anciens documents', p. 372.
21. See for example G. Winkler, 'L'aspect Pénitential dans les offices du soir en Orient et en Occident', in *Liturgie et Rémission des Peches* (Bibliotheca EL Subsidia 3, Rome 1975), pp. 273–93.
22. *Peregrinatio Egeriae*, Eng. trans. in John Wilkinson, *Egeria's Travels*.
23. See Wilkinson, pp. 39–42, 242–52.
24. *Peregrinatio* 24.1. Egeria's Latin is so bad that a literal translation is not possible, but that given here attempts to stay closer to the original than Wilkinson's rendering.
25. See p. 105.
26. Mateos, 'La vigile cathédrale chez Egérie', *OCP* 27 (1961), p. 283.
27. The absence of any explicit mention of the catechumens at the midday and 3 p.m. services need not necessarily mean that they were excluded from them, and it is even possible that a reference to them has fallen out of the text through scribal error: see Rolf Zerfass, *Die Schriftlesung im Kathedraloffizium Jerusalems* (Münster 1968), p. 13, n. 38.
28. *Peregrinatio* 27.4. See p. 62.
29. See pp. 84f.

30. *Quorum voces sunt infinitae:* This is interpreted as an allusion to the heavenly choir by Balthasar Fischer, 'The Common Prayer of Congregation and Family in the Ancient Church', *SL* 10 (1974), p. 115, n. 43, and rendered 'their voices are innumerable'.

31. *Peregrinatio* 24.2–6. The expression *ad manum accedere*, translated here as 'come to his hand', probably means that they have the bishop's hand laid on them in blessing, not that they kiss his hand: see Mateos, 'Quelques anciens documents', pp. 366–7; but cf. Wilkinson, p. 83, n. 9.

32. *Peregrinatio* 24.9; 31.1f.

33. See Mateos, 'Quelques anciens documents', p. 360.

34. See pp. 63–4, 76.

35. *Ap. Trad.* 25. See p. 56.

36. See pp. 105–6.

37. *Peregrinatio* 24.7.

38. See Mateos, 'Quelques anciens documents', pp. 367–9; Baumstark, *Comparative Liturgy*, pp. 41–2.

39. Epiphanius, *Adv. Haer.* 3.23.

40. See for example Eusebius, *Comm. in Ps.* 60.1; Augustine, *Retract.* 2.11.

41. *Peregrinatio* 25.5.

42. See pp. 63, 84, 87, 97, 103.

43. Mateos, 'Quelques anciens documents', p. 361.

44. See p. 101.

45. Mateos, 'L'office monastique à la fin du IVe siècle: Antioche, Palestine, Cappadoce', *OC* 47 (1963), p. 67.

46. See pp. 65, 73–4.

47. See p. 103.

48. Rufinus, *Second Apology* 35.

49. See pp. 109–10.

50. See for example Mateos, 'Quelques anciens documents', pp. 360, 374.

51. See pp. 43, 63–4.

52. See *Ap. Con.* II.57; Chrysostom, *Hom. in I Cor.* 36; *Expos. in Ps.* 117.1; Council of Laodicea, canon 15.

53. Chrysostom, *Expos. in Ps.* 41.5.

54. Basil *Ep.* 207. See p. 101.

55. *Peregrinatio* 24.8–12.

56. Mateos, 'La vigile cathédrale', pp. 288–9.

57. See pp. 94f.

58. See *Peregrinatio* 27.2; 44.2–3.

59. Zerfass, p. 17.

60. See p. 20.

61. See for example Zerfass, pp. 37–8.

62. *Peregrinatio* 47.5.

63. See pp. 39, 68–9.

64. See Mateos, 'La vigile cathédrale', pp. 302–10; Zerfass, pp. 121–7.

65. Mateos, 'La vigile cathédrale', p. 298.

66. *Ap. Con.* II.59.

67. Mateos, 'La vigile cathédrale', pp. 299–301.

68. Ibid., p. 292.

69. Dix, *The Shape of the Liturgy*, p. 427, n. 5.

70. *Peregrinatio* 25.1.

71. Mateos, 'La vigile cathédrale', pp. 293–5; Zerfass, pp. 47–50.

72. *Peregrinatio* 25.2–4.

73. Ibid., 27.3.

74. See p. 62.

75. *Peregrinatio* 41.

76. See Wilkinson, p. 60.

77. See Rordorf, pp. 146–8.

78. *Peregrinatio* 27.7–9.

79. Ibid., 27.8.

80. John Cassian, *De Inst. Coen.* 3.8–9. See O. Heiming, 'Zum monastischen Offizium von Kassianus bis Columbanus', *ALW* 7 (1961), pp. 107–8.

81. See p. 68.

82. Joseph Gelineau, *Voices and Instruments in Christian Worship* (1964), pp. 101f.

83. Theodoret, *Hist. Eccl.* 2.24; Socrates, *Hist. Eccl.* 6.8; see also Sozomen, *Hist. Eccl.* 3.20. For Basil see pp. 100f.

84. *Peregrinatio* 46.1–47.2.

85. Ibid., 27.5–7.

86. See pp. 66–8.

87. See Dekkers, pp. 99–130.

88. *Peregrinatio* 41.

89. See p. 68.

90. Socrates, *Eccl. Hist.* 5.22.

91. Epiphanius, *Adv. Haer.* 3.22.

92. See Zerfass, pp. 133f.; G. Winkler, 'Der geschichtliche Hintergrund der Präsanktifikatenvesper', *OC* 56 (1972), pp. 184–206.

93. Socrates, *Eccl. Hist.* 5.22.

Chapter 5

1. See pp. 47–8.

2. Schmemann, pp. 105, 107.

3. See J. Gelineau, 'Les psaumes à l'époque patristique', *LMD* 135 (1978), p. 103.

4. Palladius, *Lausiac History* 7.

5. Theodoret, *Hist. Relig.* 2.

6. Athanasius, *Ep. ad Marcellinum de interpretatione psalmorum.*

7. John Cassian, *Coll.* 10.11.

8. See A. van der Mensbrugghe, 'Prayer-time in Egyptian Monasticism (320–450)', *SP* 2 (1957), pp. 435f.

9. *Vit. Pachomii Gr.* I.60.

10. Athanasius, *Vita Antonii* 35.

11. *Vit. Gr.* I.60; see Mensbrugghe, p. 437, n. 3.

12. Cassian, *De Inst. Coen.* 2.5.

13. *Vit. Gr.* I.51–2.

14. Mensbrugghe, pp. 439–44.

15. Ibid., pp. 445f.

16. Cassian, *De Inst. Coen.* 2.5–6.

17. Ibid., 3.5.

18. Mateos, 'L'office monastique', p. 69, n. 45.

19. *De Inst. Coen.* 2.12.

20. Palladius, *Lausiac History* 32.

21. See Mensbrugghe, pp. 449–54.

22. Cassian, *De Inst. Coen.* 2.12.

23. Ibid., 2.11.

24. See pp. 63, 84, 87.

25. *De Inst. Coen.* 2.11.

26. Ibid., 2.7.

27. Ibid., 2.18.

28. See Jungmann, *The Place of Christ in Liturgical Prayer*, pp. 172f.

29. *De Inst. Coen.* 2.8.

30. Ibid., 2.6. See also Zerfass, pp. 51–2.

31. See pp. 19–20.

32. See Cassian, *Coll.* 9.9–25.

33. Schmemann, pp. 107–8.

34. See Mateos, 'L'office monastique', p. 70.

35. Basil, *Serm. Ascet.* 4.

36. Basil, *Ep.* 2. See pp. 75, 103, 104.

37. Basil, *Reg. Fus. Tract.* 37.3–5.

38. Ibid., 37.5.

39. Basil, *Ep.* 207.2

40. Ibid., 207.3–4.

41. See Mateos, 'L'office monastique', pp. 67, 81–3.

42. Ibid., pp. 85–6.

43. Basil, *Reg. Fus. Tract.* 37.5.

44. See pp. 89–90.

45. See for example Palladius, *Dialogus de vita Chrysostomi* 5.

46. See Mateos, 'L'office monastique', p. 71, n. 52.

47. Ps.-Athanasius, *De Virginitate* 12, 16, 20.

48. Mateos, 'Office de minuit et office du matin chez s. Athanase', *OCP* 28 (1962), p. 179.

49. See pp. 109–10.

50. See pp. 54–5.

51. Chrysostom, *Hom. in 1 Ep. ad Tim.* 14.4

52. Chrysostom, *Hom. in Matt.* 68.3.

53. See pp. 50, 52.

54. Cassian, *De Inst. Coen.* 3.3–4.

55. Ibid., 2.8; 3.7.

56. See pp. 77f.

57. See pp. 78–81.

58. See for example Mateos, 'La synaxe monastique des vêpres byzantines', *OCP* 36 (1970), pp. 248–50.

59. Chrysostom, *Expos. in Ps.* 133.

60. Chrysostom, *Hom. in Act.* 26; see also Basil, *Hom. in martyrem Julittem* 4.

61. Chrysostom, *De Anna Sermo* 4.5.

62. See Palladius, *Dialogus de Vita Chrysostomi* 5.

63. *Codex Iustinianus* I. 3. 42. 24(10).

64. Chrysostom, *Hom. in Matt.* 2.5.

65. See for example Crichton, p. 37; W. J. Grisbrooke, 'The Formative

Period—Cathedral and Monastic Offices', in Cheslyn Jones, Geoffrey Wainwright and Edward Yarnold (eds.), *The Study of Liturgy* (1978), p. 361.

66. Jacques Froger, *Les origines de prime* (Rome 1946).

67. See for example Owen Chadwick, 'The Origins of Prime', *JTS* 49 (1948), pp. 178–82; J. M. Hanssens, *Nature et genese de l'office des matines* (Analecta Gregoriana 57, Rome 1952), pp. 43–58.

68. Jacques Froger, 'Note pour rectifier l'interpretation de Cassien, *Inst.* 3,4; 6, proposée dans *Les Origines de Prime*', *ALW* 2 (1952), pp. 96–102.

69. See for example Mateos, 'L'office monastique', pp. 66–7; G. Winkler, 'Das Offizium am Ende des 4. Jahrhunderts und das heutige chaldäische Offizium, ihre strukturellen Zusammenhänge', *Ostkirchliche Studien* 19 (1970), pp. 298–9; Zerfass, p. 53.

70. Cassian, *De Inst. Coen.* 3.4.

71. *Apophthegmata Patrum* 12.6 (*PL* 73.941); cf. J. P. Migne, *Patrologia Graeca* 65.164.

72. Cassian, *De Inst. Coen.* 3.6.

73. See p. 104.

74. See p. 21.

75. See Winkler, 'Das Offizium am Ende des 4. Jahrhunderts', p. 305.

76. See pp. 102–3.

Chapter 6

1. Augustine, *En. in Ps.* 49.23.

2. *Confessions* 5.9.

3. *In Ps.* 66.3.

4. See pp. 69–70, 90–1.

5. Ambrose, *Expos. in Ps. 118*, *sermo* 19.32.

6. See Fischer, 'Common Prayer', pp. 114–15.

7. *De Elia* 55: see also *Expos. in Ps. 118*, *sermo* 19.22,30.

8. *In Ps. 1, enarr.* 9; see also *Hexameron* 5.12.36.

9. *Expos. in Ps. 118*, *sermo* 8.48; *De Virginibus* 3.18.

10. See for example Winkler, 'Über die Kathedralvesper', p. 92.

11. *Expos. in Ps. 118*, *sermo* 8.48.

12. *Expos. in Ps. 118*, *prol.* 1,3. See F. H. Dudden, *The Life and Times of St. Ambrose* (1935), vol. 2, pp. 443–4.

13. *Ep.* 21.34.

14. *In Ps. 1, enarr.* 9.

15. Augustine, *Conf.* 9.7.

16. Paulinus, *Vita Ambrosii* 13.

17. Helmut Leeb, *Die Psalmodie bei Ambrosius* (Vienna 1967), pp. 91–113.

18. See pp. 100–2.

19. *Ep.* 20. 11–13.

20. Niceta of Remesiana, *De Vigiliis* 1,3; see also *De Psalmodiae Bono* 12: critical edn in A. E. Burn, *Niceta of Remesiana: his Life and Works* (1905), pp. 55–82.

21. *De Psalmodiae Bono* 2.

22. See p. 89.

23. See pp. 132f.

24. References in J. A. Jungmann, *Pastoral Liturgy* (1962), pp. 109–10; see also Gregory of Tours, *Hist. Franc.* 7.22.

25. Uranius, *Epistola* 4 (*PL* 53.861–2).

26. See p. 108.

27. Arnobius the Younger, *In Ps. 148*.

28. See p. 77.

29. Caesarius, *Serm.* 77.

30. See Louis Brou (ed.), *The Psalter Collects from V–VIth Century Sources* (1949); Jorge Pinell, *Liber Orationum Psalmographus* (Barcelona 1972: Monumenta Hispaniae Sacra, Serie Liturgica IX).

31. See Crichton, pp. 86–7.

32. *Serm.* 76, 77.

33. See pp. 129f.

34. See for example H. G. J. Beck, *The Pastoral Care of Souls in South-East France during the sixth century* (Rome 1950), p. 115.

35. See pp. 94, 113.

36. See p. 82.

37. Jungmann, *Pastoral Liturgy*, pp. 134–5.

38. See p. 108.

39. See p. 130.

40. Gregory of Tours, *Vitae Patrum* 6.7.

41. *Serm.* 134.1.

42. *Serm.* 69.

43. Quoted in Burn, *Niceta of Remesiana*, p. cviii.

44. Winkler, 'Über die Kathedralvesper', pp. 86f.

45. *Serm.* 136. 1.

46. See Winkler, 'Über die Kathedralvesper', pp. 84f.

47. See p. 79.

48. See p. 133.

49. See J. B. L. Tolhurst, *The Monastic Breviary of Hyde Abbey*, vol. 6 (1942), pp. 19f.

50. See pp. 77–8, 136.

51. See Edmund Bishop, *Liturgica Historica* (1918), pp. 126–7; W. S. Porter, *The Gallican Rite* (1958), pp. 22–3. For Aurelian, see pp. 130–1.

52. Jungmann, *Pastoral Liturgy*, pp. 135f.

53. Caesarius, *Vita* I.13.

54. *Serm.* 86.5; 196.2.

55. See pp. 131f.

56. *Serm.* 72; 86.5; 188.6; 196.2,4.

57. *Serm.* 6.2.

58. *Serm.* 76.3.

59. *Serm.* 212.6: *matutinis explicitis*.

60. This surely is the correct interpretation of *Serm.* 76.3 ('when there is to be a sermon, let us have Ps. 50 [51] said earlier so that not later but always at the usual hour we come out of church'), rather than Jungmann's strange conclusion: 'on days when a sermon follows the lesson he permits the psalm to be recited earlier. Otherwise the psalm obviously was recited after the lesson' (*Pastoral Liturgy*, p. 137). See also *Serm.* 118.1.

61. Caesarius, *Vita* I.45. See pp. 90–2.

62. Gregory of Tours, *Hist. Franc.* 10.31.15.

63. *De gestis episcoporum Antissiodorensium, PL* 138.231–5; 243–5.

64. See p. 106.

65. Ferrandus, *Vita Fulgentii* 29.59.

66. See de Vogüé, *RB* 5, p. 468, n. 59.

67. Th. Sickel, *Liber Diurnus Romanorum Pontificorum* (Vienna 1889), LXXIV.

68. E. Friedberg, *Corpus Iuris Canonici* (Leipzig 1879), vol. I, p. 316.

69. *Serm.* 72.1.

70. *Serm.* 6.3.

71. Caesarius, *Vita* I.15.

72. Fischer, 'Common Prayer', p. 113.

Chapter 7

1. Luc Verheijen, *La Règle de Saint Augustin* (Paris 1967), vol. 2, pp. 125–74.

2. *Ordo Monasterii* 2, in Verheijen, vol. 1, pp. 148–50.

3. See pp. 96–8, 105.

4. See pp. 106–8.

5. Verheijen, vol. 2, p. 136.

6. Ibid., vol. 1, p. 163; vol. 2, p. 136.

7. See pp. 89–90.

8. Heiming, pp. 109–13.

9. See for example W. C. Bishop and C. L. Feltoe, *The Mozarabic and Ambrosian Rites* (Alcuin Club Tracts XV, 1924), pp. 62–6.

10. Cassian, *De Inst. Coen.* 2.2.

11. Caesarius, *Regula ad Monachos* XX, XXI, XXV; *Regula Virginum* 66–9 in G. Morin (ed.), *Sancti Caesarii Opera*, vol. 2 (Maredsous 1942); Eng. trans. in M. C. McCarthy, *The Rule for Nuns of St. Caesarius of Arles: a translation with a critical introduction* (Catholic University of America Studies in Medieval History, New Series, vol. 16, Washington, D.C., 1960).

12. Aurelian, *Regula ad monachos: ordinem quo psallere* (*PL* 68.393–6); *Regula ad virgines: ordinem quo psallere* (*PL* 68.403–6).

13. Aurelian, *Regula ad monachos* 28.

14. Cassian, *De Inst. Coen.* 2.13; 3.5.

15. See de Vogüé, *RB* 5, pp. 427–8.

16. Cassian, *De Inst. Coen.* 3.7.

17. See p. 102.

18. See p. 119.

19. See pp. 97, 103.

20. *Pacé* de Vogüé, *RB* 5, pp. 502–3; cf. Heiming, pp. 121–2.

21. See pp. 116–17.

22. Cassian, *De Inst. Coen.* 2.7–8. For the Eastern practice see p. 98.

23. See de Vogüé, *RB* 5, pp. 582–3.

24. See Heiming, p. 118.

25. Heiming, p. 122, is mistaken in thinking that the variation in position is between offices in Eastertide and those in the rest of the year.

26. See p. 118.

27. See p. 119.

28. See Heiming, p. 121.

29. See p. 120.

30. Critical edn: G. S. M. Walker, *Sancti Columbani Opera* (Dublin 1957), pp. 128–33.

31. See pp. 119–20.

32. Walker, *Sancti Columbani Opera*, p. 146, line 23.

33. Ibid., p. 156, line 2.

34. Jerome, *Ep.* 22.37.

35. *Ep.* 107.9.

36. *Ep.* 130.15.

37. Ambrose, *Expos. in Ps. 118, sermo* 7.32; see also ibid., *serm.* 8.45–52; 19.18; *Expos. ev. Luc.* 7.87,88; *De Abraham* 1.84.

38. *Hexam.* 5.88.

39. *De Virginibus* 3.19.

40. Ibid., 3.20; see also *Exhort. Virginitatis* 58.

41. Augustine, *De Symbolo ad Catechumenos* 1.

42. See for example *De Virginibus* 3.18; *Expos. in Ps. 118, sermo* 21.15.

43. See Guy Ferrari, *Early Roman Monasteries. Notes for the history of the monasteries and convents at Rome from the Vth through the Xth century* (Vatican City 1957, *Studi di antichita cristiana* 23).

44. See C. Callewaert, *Liturgicae Institutiones II: De brevarii romani liturgia* (2nd edn, Bruges 1939), and *Sacris erudiri* (Steenbrugge 1940).

45. See de Vogüé, *RB* 5, pp. 522–5.

46. Ibid., pp. 493–4.

47. Ibid., p. 542.

48. Ibid., pp. 535–6.

49. Ibid., p. 435, n. 4.

50. *PL* 95.1583.

51. See de Vogüé, *RB* 5, p. 539, n. 56.

52. See p. 122.

53. See pp. 89–90, 131–3.

54. See de Vogüé, *RB* 5, pp. 475–7; Mateos, 'La vigile cathédrale', p. 309.

55. See de Vogüé, *RB* 5, pp. 514–15.

56. Joseph Pascher, 'Der Psalter für Laudes und Vesper im alten römischen Stundengebet', *Münchener theologische Zeitschrift* 8 (1957), pp. 256–67; 'De Psalmodia Vesperarum', *EL* 79 (1965), pp. 317–26; see also de Vogüé, *RB* 5, pp. 485–6.

57. See Joseph Pascher, 'Zur Frühgeschichte des römischen Wochenpsalteriums', *EL* 79 (1965), pp. 55–8.

58. For details of this, see de Vogüé, *RB* 5, p. 470, n. 66.

59. Conveniently summarized in M. D. Knowles, *Great Historical Enterprises* (1963), pp. 135–95.

60. *Regula Magistri* 33, 44.

61. See de Vogüé, *RB* 5, pp. 428–30.

62. The winter figures are conjectures, because the text is corrupt at this point: the total number of antiphonal psalms appears to have been thirteen, but we cannot be certain how they were divided between the two blocks: see Adalbert de Vogüé, *La Règle du Maître* (Paris 1964), vol. 1, p. 50, n. 1; p. 52, nn. 1–2.

63. See de Vogüé, *La Règle du Maître*, vol. 2, p. 192.

64. See pp. 136–7.

65. See de Vogüé, *La Règle du Maître*, vol. 2, p. 183.

66. See de Vogüé, *RB* 5, pp. 529–30.

67. *Regula Magistri* 46.8–10.

68. Ibid., 33, 43–5.

69. See de Vogüé, *RB* 5, pp. 581–2. He rightly doubts the suggestion by Heiming, p. 94, that in the *Regula Magistri* the *Gloria Patri* followed the silent prayer and served as its conclusion.

70. *Regula Magistri* 39.4–5.

71. Ibid., 42: see de Vogüé, *RB* 5, p. 530.

72. *RB* 5, pp. 453f.

73. *Regula Magistri* 49.2.

74. Ch. 8: see de Vogüé, *RB* 5, pp. 419–27.

75. Cassian, *De Inst. Coen.* 3.7.

76. See p. 128.

77. Ch. 43.

78. See A. Baumstark, *Nocturna Laus* (Münster 1957), pp. 91–4.

79. See p. 129.

80. See p. 130.

81. De Vogüé, *RB* 5, pp. 443–6.

82. See p. 132.

83. See Mateos, 'La vigile cathédrale', pp. 305–7; de Vogüé, *RB* 5, pp. 474–9.

84. See Heiming, pp. 151–2.

85. And not on the cathedral office, as is claimed by de Vogüé, *RB* 5, p. 492, as there is no evidence for the inclusion of lessons in that tradition.

86. See Heiming, pp. 141, 146; but cf. de Vogüé, *RB* 5, p. 535, n. 38.

87. Cassian, *Coll.* 10.10.

88. See the discussion in de Vogüé, *RB* 5, pp. 577–88.

Select Bibliography

Listed below are only those secondary works which either are directly concerned with the origins and early development of the divine office or are mentioned more than once in the notes. Primary sources can be traced through the index of references.

ANTON BAUMSTARK, *Comparative Liturgy*, 1958.

—— *Nocturna Laus*, Münster 1957.

W. C. BISHOP & C. L. FELTOE, *The Mozarabic and Ambrosian Rites*, Alcuin Club Tracts XV, 1924.

BERNARD BOTTE, *La Tradition Apostolique de saint Hippolyte*, Münster 1963.

LOUIS BOUYER, *Eucharist: Theology and Spirituality of the Eucharistic Prayer*, 1968.

LOUIS BROU (ed.), *The Psalter Collects from V–VIth Century Sources*, 1949.

A. E. BURN, *Niceta of Remesiana: his Life and Works*, 1905.

C. CALLEWAERT, *Liturgicae Institutiones II: De brevarii romani liturgia*, 2nd edn, Bruges 1939.

—— *Sacris erudiri*, Steenbrugge 1940.

MGR. CASSIEN & BERNARD BOTTE (eds.), *La Prière des Heures*, Lex Orandi 35, Paris 1963.

HENRY CHADWICK, 'Prayer at Midnight', in *Epektasis: Melanges Patristiques offerts au Cardinal Jean Daniélou* (Paris 1972), pp. 47–9.

OWEN CHADWICK, 'The Origins of Prime', *JTS* 49 (1948), pp. 178–82.

J. D. CRICHTON, *Christian Celebration: The Prayer of the Church*, 1976.

OSCAR CULLMANN, *Early Christian Worship*, 1953.

GEOFFREY J. CUMING, *Hippolytus: a Text for Students*, 1976.

—— 'The New Testament Foundation for Common Prayer', *SL* 10 (1974), pp. 88–105.

I.-H. DALMAIS, 'Origine et Constitution de l'Office', *LMD* 21 (1950), pp. 21–39.

JEAN DANIÉLOU, *The Theology of Jewish Christianity*, 1964.

E. DEKKERS, 'La Messe du soir à la fin de l'antiquité et au moyen âge, Notes historiques', *Sacris erudiri* 7 (1955), pp. 99–130.

D. G. DELLING, *Worship in the New Testament*, 1962.

GREGORY DIX, *The Apostolic Tradition of St. Hippolytus*, 1937; 2nd edn, with preface and corrections by Henry Chadwick, 1968.

—— *The Shape of the Liturgy*, 1945.

F. J. DÖLGER, 'Lumen Christi', *Antike und Christentum* 5 (Münster 1936), pp. 1–43.

G. R. DRIVER, *The Judean Scrolls*, New York 1965.

C. W. DUGMORE, *The Influence of the Synagogue upon the Divine Office*, 1944; reissued as Alcuin Club Collections No. 45, 1964.

BALTHASAR FISCHER, 'Le Christ dans les Psaumes: la devotion aux Psaumes dans l'Eglise des Martyrs', *LMD* 27 (1951), pp. 86–109.

—— 'The Common Prayer of Congregation and Family in the Ancient Church', *SL* 10 (1974), pp. 106–24.

JACQUES FROGER, *Les origines de prime*, Rome 1946.

—— 'Note pour rectifier l'interpretation de Cassien, *Inst.* 3,4; 6, proposée dans *Les Origines de Prime'*, *ALW* 2 (1952), pp. 96–102.

JOSEPH GELINEAU, *Voices and Instruments in Christian Worship*, 1964.

—— 'Les psaumes à l'époque patristique', *LMD* 135 (1978), pp. 99–116.

M. D. GOULDER, *Midrash and Lection in Matthew*, 1974.

—— *The Evangelists' Calendar*, 1978.

W. J. GRISBROOKE, 'The Formative Period—Cathedral and Monastic Offices', in Cheslyn Jones, Geoffrey Wainwright, and Edward Yarnold (eds.), *The Study of Liturgy* (1978), pp. 358–69.

A. GUILDING, *The Fourth Gospel and Jewish Worship*, 1960.

E. HAENCHEN, *The Acts of the Apostles*, 1971.

J. M. HANSSENS, *Nature et genese de l'office des matines*, Analecta Gregoriana 57, Rome 1952.

O. HEIMING, 'Zum monastischen Offizium von Kassianus bis Columbanus', *ALW* 7 (1961), 89–156.

JOSEPH HEINEMANN, *Prayer in the Talmud*, Berlin 1977.

—— 'The Background of Jesus' Prayer in the Jewish Liturgical Tradition', in Jakob J. Petuchowski and Michael Brocke (eds.), *The Lord's Prayer and the Jewish Liturgy*, 1978.

S. HOLM-NIELSEN, *Hodayot*, Aarhus 1960.

A. JAUBERT, 'Jésus et le calendrier de Qumrân', *NTS* 7 (1960), pp. 1–30.

E. G. JAY, *Origen's Treatise on Prayer*, 1954.

JOACHIM JEREMIAS, *The Prayers of Jesus*, 1967.

—— *The Eucharistic Words of Jesus*, 2nd edn, 1966.

J. A. JUNGMANN, *Altchristliche Gebetsordnungen im Lichte des Regelbuches von 'En Fescha', Zeitschrift für katholische Theologie* 75 (1953), pp. 215–19.

—— *Pastoral Liturgy*, 1962.

—— *The Place of Christ in Liturgical Prayer*, 1965.

J. C. KIRBY, *Ephesians: Baptism and Pentecost*, 1968.

J. A. LAMB, *The Psalms in Christian Worship*, 1962.

A. R. C. LEANEY, *The Rule of Qumran and its meaning*, 1966.

R. J. LEDOGAR, *Acknowledgement: Praise-verbs in the early Greek Anaphoras*, Rome 1968.

HELMUT LEEB, *Die Psalmodie bei Ambrosius*, Vienna 1967.

M. C. MCCARTHY, *The Rule for Nuns of St. Caesarius of Arles: a translation with a critical introduction*, Catholic University of America Studies in Medieval History, New Series, vol. 16, Washington, D.C., 1960.

R. P. MARTIN, *Carmen Christi*, 1967.

J. MATEOS, 'Office de minuit et office du matin chez s. Athanase', *OCP* 28 (1962), pp. 173–80.

—— 'L'office monastique à la fin du IVe siècle: Antioche, Palestine, Cappadoce', *OC* 47 (1963), pp. 53–88.

—— 'The Origins of the Divine Office', *Worship* 41 (1967), pp. 477–85.

—— 'Quelques anciens documents sur l'office du soir', *OCP* 35 (1969), pp. 347–74.

—— 'La synaxe monastique des vêpres byzantines', *OCP* 36 (1970), pp. 248–50.

—— 'La vigile cathédrale chez Egérie', *OCP* 27 (1961), pp. 281–312.

A. VAN DER MENSBRUGGHE, 'Prayer-time in Egyptian Monasticism (320–450)', *SP* 2 (1957), pp. 435–52.

JOSEPH PASCHER, 'Der Psalter für Laudes und Vesper im alten römischen Stundengebet', *Münchener theologische Zeitschrift* 8 (1957), pp. 256–67.

—— 'De Psalmodia Vesperarum', *EL* 79 (1965), pp. 317–26.

—— 'Zur Frühgeschichte des römischen Wochenpsalteriums', *EL* 79 (1965), pp. 55–8.

ERIK PETERSON, 'La croce e la preghiera verso l'oriente', *EL* 59 (1945), pp. 52–68.

—— 'Die geschichtliche Bedeutung der jüdischen Gebetsrichtung', *TZ* 3 (1947), pp. 1–15.

JORGE PINELL, *Liber Orationum Psalmographus*, Barcelona 1972: Monumenta Hispaniae Sacra, Serie Liturgica IX.

J. M. ROBINSON, 'The Historicality of Biblical Language', in B. W. Anderson (ed.), *The Old Testament and Christian Faith* (1964), pp. 124–58.

—— 'Die Hodajot-Formel in Gebet und Hymnus des Frühchristentums', in W. Eltester (ed.), *Apophoreta. Festschrift für Ernst Haenchen* (Berlin 1964), pp. 194–235.

W. RORDORF, *Sunday*, 1968.

H. H. ROWLEY, *Worship in Ancient Israel*, 1967.

A. SCHMEMANN, *Introduction to Liturgical Theology*, 1966.

T. J. TALLEY, 'The Eucharistic Prayer of the Ancient Church According to Recent Research: Results and Reflections', *SL* 11 (1976), pp. 138–58.

S. TALMON, 'The Manual of Benedictions of the Sect of the Judean Desert', *Revue de Qumran* 2 (1960), pp. 475–500.

J. B. L. TOLHURST, *The Monastic Breviary of Hyde Abbey*, vol. 6, 1942.

R. DE VAUX, *Ancient Israel: Its Life and Institutions*, 1965.

LUC VERHEIJEN, *La Règle de Saint Augustin*, 2 vols, Paris 1967.

G. VERMES, *The Dead Sea Scrolls in English*, 1962; 2nd edn, 1975.

A. DE VOGÜÉ, *La Règle de Saint Benoît*, vol. 5, Paris 1971.

—— *La Règle du Maître*, 2 vols, Paris 1964.

F. E. VOKES, 'The Ten Commandments in the New Testament and in First Century Judaism', *SE* 5, pp. 146–54.

G. S. M. WALKER, *Sancti Columbani Opera*, Dublin 1957.

J. H. WALKER, 'Terce, Sext and None An Apostolic Custom?', *SP* 5 (1962), pp. 206–12.

G. P. WILES, *Paul's Intercessory Prayers*, 1974.

JOHN WILKINSON, *Egeria's Travels*, 1971.

GABRIELE WINKLER, 'L'aspect Pénitential dans les offices du soir en Orient et en Occident', in *Liturgie et Rémission des Peches* (Bibliotheca *EL* Subsidia 3, Rome 1975), pp. 273–93.

—— 'Der geschichtliche Hintergrund der Präsanktifikatenvesper', *OC* 56 (1972), pp. 184–206.

—— 'Das Offizium am Ende des 4. Jahrhunderts und das heutige chaldäische Offizium, ihre strukturellen Zusammenhänge', *Ostkirchliche Studien* 19 (1970), pp. 289–311.

—— 'Über die Kathedralvesper in den verschiedenen Riten des Ostens und Westens', *ALW* 16 (1974), pp. 53–102.

ROLF ZERFASS, *Die Schriftlesung im Kathedraloffizium Jerusalems*, Münster 1968.

Index of References

1. OLD TESTAMENT

4. NEW TESTAMENT

5. PATRISTIC LITERATURE

General Index

Africa 50, 57, 111–12, 117, 122, 124–6
Agape 42, 44–5, 51, 53, 55–7, 63, 71, 80–1, 153
Alexandria 9, 47–8, 57, 58, 66, 92, 93, 102
Antioch 18, 74, 83, 90, 92, 101, 104f., 108
Antiphonal psalmody 89–90, 101–2, 113–14, 117, 125–6, 128, 129–32, 134, 137–8, 140–1, 142, 145–6, 149
Benedicite 82, 103, 118–19, 131, 142
Benedictus 30–1, 136, 141
Berakah 12–16, 28, 30–1, 33, 34, 36
Bible reading 48, 71, 102, 106, 121, 134–5; *see also* Word, ministry of
Birkat ha-Mazon 16, 33
Birkat ha-Minim 24
Caesarea 18, 72, 92
Canticle (Old Testament) 131, 136, 139, 142, 146
Cappadocia 75, 90, 99–103
Celtic office 119–20, 133–4
Compline 100, 124–5, 127, 128, 129, 130, 136, 137, 140, 142, 148
Creed 135
Decalogue 2, 28, 43
Eastward orientation 11, 38, 58–9
Egypt 6, 95–9, 124–5, 128, 129, 131, 138, 139, 140, 143, 144, 145, 147
Essenes 7, 10, 11, 19, 24, 37, 57–9
Gaul 115–23, 126–33
Gloria in Excelsis 75, 82, 100, 103, 104, 131
Gloria Patri 98, 120–1, 129, 136, 139, 142, 144, 148
Hodayah 14–16, 21, 31–3, 34, 36, 37, 46
Hymns 21–2, 44–6, 48, 51, 64, 72, 74, 75, 79–83, 84–5, 87–8, 90, 91, 94, 100, 102, 113, 118, 129–31, 144, 146, 147, 148, 152
Incense 76–7, 84, 87, 112

Intercession 13, 14, 15, 30, 31, 34, 35, 39, 62–3, 74, 75, 80–1, 99, 104, 119, 151
Jerusalem 2, 4, 9, 11, 15, 17, 18, 23, 24, 25, 26, 43, 50, 59, 61, 62, 70, 72, 77–92, 105, 108, 117, 119, 120
Justinian 106, 122
Kaddish 27
Kneeling for prayer 18, 26–7, 64–5, 98, 117, 129, 134, 135
Kyrie eleison 75, 79, 115, 119–20, 130–1, 136, 144, 145, 148
Lessons: *see* Word, ministry of
Lighting of the lamp 22, 51, 57, 75–6, 77, 80, 116, 119, 135
Lord's Prayer 26, 27, 28, 37, 38, 45, 49, 62, 75, 120, 135, 136, 141, 147, 148
Ma'amadoth 2–3, 11
Magnificat 131, 136, 141
Milan 112–14, 118, 135
Nunc Dimittis 75
Penitence 63, 65, 73–4, 76–7, 82, 100–1, 102–3
Phos Hilaron 76, 82
Pliny 28, 42–3, 45
Prime 107f., 127, 130, 136, 137, 138, 140, 141, 148
Psalm-collects 117, 129, 142, 149, 152
Responsorial psalmody 83, 89, 101, 113–14, 117, 125–6, 131–2, 136–8, 140–1, 144–6
Rome 18, 34, 55, 61, 62, 69, 70, 115, 119, 120, 122, 134–9, 144, 145, 147, 148
Sabbath 3, 19, 21, 23, 40, 41, 68, 89
Shema' 1–3, 6, 11, 18, 19, 20, 27–8
Shemoneh 'Esreh 16, 17, 24, 29; see also *Tefillah*
Spain 115–23, 126f.
Station days 40–1, 55, 60, 62, 65, 66–8, 91–2, 122
Sunday 41, 42, 50, 62, 64, 66, 68, 71, 84–8, 92, 120, 130, 132, 134, 136, 137–8, 139, 142, 143, 145–6, 147, 148